# BLACK MAYORS, WHITE MAJORITIES

**JUSTICE AND
SOCIAL INQUIRY**

*Series Editors*

Jeremy I. Levitt

Matthew C. Whitaker

# BLACK MAYORS, WHITE MAJORITIES

## The Balancing Act of Racial Politics

RAVI K. PERRY

UNIVERSITY OF NEBRASKA PRESS | LINCOLN AND LONDON

Portions of the introduction and chapters 1, 5, 6, 7, 8, and 9 were previously published in Ravi K. Perry, "Kindred Political Rhetoric: Black Mayors, President Obama, and the Universalizing of Black Interests," *Journal of Urban Affairs* 33, no. 5 (2011): 567–90. Portions of this book originally appeared in Ravi K. Perry and Andrea Owens-Jones, "Balancing Act: Racial Empowerment and the Dual Expectations of Jack Ford in Toledo, Ohio," in *21st Century Urban Race Politics: Representing Minorities as Universal Interests*, ed. Ravi K. Perry (Bingley, UK: Emerald Group Publishing Limited, 2013); and Ravi K. Perry, "Black Mayors in Non-Majority Black (Medium-Sized) Cities: Universalizing the Interests of Blacks," *Ethnic Studies Review* 32, no. 1 (Summer 2009): 89–130. Used with permission.

Manufactured in the United States of America ∞

Library of Congress Cataloging-in-Publication Data

Perry, Ravi K.

Black mayors, white majorities: the balancing act of racial politics / Ravi K. Perry.

pages cm. — (Justice and social inquiry)

Includes bibliographical references and index.

ISBN 978-0-8032-4536-5 (pbk.: alk. paper)

1. African Americans—Politics and government. 2. African American mayors. 3. Municipal government—United States. 4. African Americans—Social conditions. 5. United States—Race relations—Political aspects. 6. United States—Politics and government. I. Title.

E185.615.P434 2014

323.1196'073—dc23          2013022400

Set in Lyon Text and Neutraface by Laura Wellington.
Designed by A. Shahan.

To my parents,
Drs. D. LaRouth Perry
and Robert L. Perry,
for their unconditional
love and support

To be an Afro-American, or an American black, is to be in the situation, intolerably exaggerated, of all those who have ever found themselves part of a civilization which they could in no wise honorably defend—which they were compelled, indeed, endlessly to attack and condemn—and who yet spoke out of the most passionate love, hoping to make the kingdom new, to make it honorable and worthy of life.

James Baldwin

# CONTENTS

## ILLUSTRATIONS

## TABLES

## FIGURES

The ideas expressed and researched in this book began as I was a high school student in Ohio. There, in Lucas County, I was actively involved in local and regional politics. A reliable volunteer for many candidates in my home county, I was infatuated with politics, so much so that the study of politics became my academic interest while I was an undergraduate at the University of Michigan. While at Michigan, my interest in wanting to know more about how the representation of black interests functioned in non-majority-black contexts blossomed under the direction of my recently deceased mentor, Professor Hanes Walton Jr. This research interest began as conversations in his office in Ann Arbor. His loss is still heavy and I expect it to always remain so, for this book and my career are a direct result of his encouragement.

This book offers a substantive critique of deracialization as applied to the black urban governing context in majority-white cities. Based in part on the normative argument that the election of black mayors in major cities *should* improve the quality of life for blacks in those cities, it explores how two such black mayors sought to advance black interests in their majority-white cities.

The "should" argument referenced above is based on the classic proposition that blacks expect so much from major-city black mayors.

Because blacks expect such a path, it warrants this book's claim that it is viable to examine how the election of black mayors impacts the material and non-material lives of blacks in those cities.

In so doing, though, the book provokes a question: why hasn't the increased political power of black mayors resulted in the vast improvement of blacks as a group? I am of the opinion that the question returns scholars of urban and black politics to the root of black political emergence in the twentieth century. For example, in reference to Carl Stokes's campaign for mayor of Cleveland in 1967, during the height of the civil rights movement, Stokes had to decide whether it was more important for the black community to elect black mayors to advance a just society or to win elections.[1] For Stokes a successful bid for election as Cleveland's first black mayor was more important than the continued use of civil rights tactics to improve the quality of life and potential outcomes for Cleveland's black residents. Stokes's stance, though, explains why this book is a great fit for the Justice and Social Inquiry series at the University of Nebraska. Stokes's reflections on the opportunity to bring Dr. Martin Luther King Jr. to Cleveland while he was running for mayor positioned two styles of black mobility against each other—old-school civil rights tactics of civil disobedience and electoral advances said to benefit the black community. Now, more than forty years later, we still don't know which method has produced the most for African Americans.

According to Leonard N. Moore, Stokes ran because "he was driven by three overlapping purposes: to improve the lives of the black poor, to give blacks a voice in municipal government, and to prove to the nation that an African American could govern."[2] Yet, as Stokes's reflections on his 1967 campaign decision indicate, his electoral strategy was deracialized. Conclusively the trend toward deracialization and urban regime theories has undoubtedly changed the motives, or it has at least emphasized the alleged limited options available to contemporary black mayors. J. Philip Thompson, however, is pointing in a different direction. He concludes that black mayors suffer from a "lack of substance."[3] In this blunt recognition, he makes a call for a renewed thinking about how politics and community might work together to improve the quality of life of blacks. In the interim I contend Manning Marable is correct in his assertion that the effects of deracialized campaign strategies are "psychological triumphs."[4]

The U.S. census indicates that blacks have not made considerable improvements since the advent of deracialized politics. Thus the election of deracialized black mayors does not mean much for blacks in general. Hosea Williams's statement that "All these black politicians—they're black until they're elected"[5] highlights the long-standing tension between the politics of electability and respectability in blacks' urban campaigns and the perceived expectation that elections should result in significant improvements for blacks. Accordingly, for many, as long as black mayors implement policies that benefit minorities but that do not threaten whites, they are supposedly "representing" black interests.

If black mayors are increasingly being elected because they employ deracialized strategies, does this suggest multiethnic governing coalitions are needed to implement the policies that benefit minority groups? There is a down side to deracialized coalition-building in both electoral and governing contexts. As evidenced in the evolution toward an increasing number of analyses that extol the benefits of deracialization as a means of winning elections with African American candidates, post-analyses that consider the substantive benefits for the black community given a hypothetical black politician's election are lacking in the political science literature. The predominant focus on campaigns and elections without a significant study of the effects of the campaigns and elections, particularly as they concern African Americans, not surprisingly, returns many to reconsider the benefits to African American communities given prior racialism in electoral and governing approaches. In other words, despite sensing that a more direct racial policy approach may not result in many elections for black candidates, many black voters may have increasingly become more sophisticated in their analyses of who is the "right" black candidate. This sophistication is evident, perhaps, in the decreasing numbers of eligible black voters choosing to vote in municipal elections in the post–civil rights era, the bounty of evidence that suggests deracialized black candidates, once elected, produce few substantive benefits for their black communities, and the electoral outcomes of black versus black contests that feature two styles of black leadership.

Ironically, then, the bifurcated goals of Stokes's 1967 campaign remain alive in the twenty-first century. The question still remains: is it more important to win elections or to complete a just sociopolitical agenda? Given this tension, for many the necessity of the return to movement-based, racially inclusive politics is imperative. In this book, the mayors studied suggest that a return to black political power, as understood by the black power activists of the 1960s, is perhaps blacks' best available option. Malcolm X summed up the approach eloquently in "The Ballot or the Bullet" speech at a Cleveland rally sponsored by the Congress for Racial Equality (CORE) in 1964: "The political philosophy of black nationalism means that the black man should control the politics and politicians in his own community more; the black man in the black community has to be reeducated into the science of politics so he will know what politics is supposed to bring him in return." According to Malcolm X, blacks needed to be reeducated about the purpose of the science of politics for their quality of life to improve in the United States. Presumably this reeducation does not allow much room for deracialization, urban regime theory, or any other theory or practical electoral and governing strategy where blacks are arguably circumscribed by white power interests. If we factor in "targeted universalism," a new governing approach by which black mayors can actively pursue black interests while maintaining reasonable white electoral and governing support, then they also get to avoid Williams's lamentation, all while they're able to seek the improvement of the socioeconomic conditions and quality of life of black residents—what some have characterized as the ability to "stay black." Thus in an increasingly diverse society, the effort to advance the interests of particular groups may involve a return to the past, as evidenced by Malcolm X's suggestion. Should we follow that path, the representation of black interests may be subject to increased scrutiny as voters measure one's "blackness" by the outcomes produced for their black constituencies, as opposed to one's self-professed black identity. As X's speech suggests, black voters might fare better by making voting preferences that account for pride in black identity and proven demonstrations of one's black consciousness as well—whether or not those black candidates are running for office in majority-black jurisdictions. This book explores how two mayors effectively used a new strategy to win election and govern while being inclusive of black interests in majority-white contexts. By strategically (and usually rhetorically) linking the needs of African Americans with the interests of whites, these mayors demonstrated that it was no longer political suicide to advocate for black interests. Like Olympic gymnasts successfully navigating the terrains of a balance beam, these mayors are strong examples for others who seek to advance the interests of minority populations even in political jurisdictions where those minority groups do not comprise a majority of the population. Seemingly, at least in some communities, deracialization has lost its balance.

This book was completed at Mississippi State University. Thanks are due to my colleagues in the Department of Political Science and Public Administration who provided the collegial and supportive environment necessary to complete this task. Throughout my various movements from undergraduate studies to graduate school and through two institutions, the support of my adviser, Marion Orr, has been invaluable. Marion has been and remains an inspiration and a really humble human being. A great adviser, he guides his students with a patterned simplicity that is warm and contagious. I can only hope, as I move through the profession, that I pick up some of his spirit.

Over the course of many years I have had the opportunity to interview dozens of stakeholders throughout Ohio. Without the giving of their time and offering of their trust to me, this project would not have been possible. Many interviewees, particularly both mayors for this project, welcomed me into their homes and indulged me greatly as I sought to describe their experiences as mayors of rust-belt cities in the Midwest.

Working with the University of Nebraska Press has been wonderful. Bridget Barry, Sabrina Ehmke Sergeant, Joeth Zucco, and Bojana Ristich have each been delightful stewards in bringing this book to fruition. Because of them, this process has been enjoyable and productive. Of course, without the invaluable support of series editors Jeremy I. Levitt and Matthew C. Whitaker, this book would not have been possible. The Justice and Social Inquiry series is a great fit for this project given the mayors' views on actively representing black interests even in their majority-white communities.

Finally, I want to thank my family. My husband, Paris F. Prince, was a continual firm and steady presence throughout every phase of this project. It is largely due to his patience that it is now finished. To my brother and sister, Bayé K. Perry and Kai M. Perry, I offer thanks for their support. My parents, D. LaRouth Perry and Robert L. Perry, have been my strongest supporters. In life they've been cheering for me loudly and proudly (literally) since day one! Their loving embrace has always inspired me to do better. For their unconditional love, it is to them that I dedicated this book.

# Introduction

## Theorizing the Representation of Urban Blacks in "White" Cities

---

We need to be universal in our goals but not in our process.
This is what fairness requires.

john a. powell, "Obama's Universal Approach Leaves Many Excluded"

---

As you read this, somewhere history is being made. Somewhere, right now, in the United States, an African American is considering running for mayor in a city wherein his or her constituents are mostly white. Somewhere else in the country, perhaps, another black politician—an elected mayor—is making a calculated decision about an important issue in his or her city and is weighing how the decision might impact different constituencies—that is, white and black voters. Those realities have been made possible by a host of elected black leadership—namely mayors—in prior decades. By most indications, forty years ago such statements would have been impossible to write, if not laughable in their audacity. However, because of many trailblazers and demographic shifts in population and political attitudes, it is not difficult to imagine those scenarios. The result: an ever-increasing number of blacks seeking elected office as mayors in majority white cities. This book is about two such mayors: Jack Ford of Toledo, Ohio, and Rhine McLin of Dayton, Ohio.

What makes the scenarios mentioned above so very interesting is the projected impact of black mayors. Pundits and scholars alike may call such an impact pandering, but it is also a question of representation, electability, governance, and—of course—one's legacy. It is also a complex question of how to define urban interests. In the national context many Americans are familiar with the concept of national interest. Presidents have regularly referred to the country's involvements as characterized by what is in the national interest of the country. Scholars have long used national polls to identify the interests of groups of Americans across a range of issues. In the state context Kerry L. Haynie became one of the first scholars to define "black" interests at the state level.[1] However, in the urban municipal context, those interests are much less easily ascertainable. Yet they are at least as important as state- or national-level definitions of interests.

Interests matter because the representation of our interests is of paramount importance in a representative democratic republic. Therein politicians are said to represent our interests on our behalf. However, if those interests are not easily discernible, such as in the urban context generally, how does representation function? Should those interests change as a result of demographic shifts in the electorate, how might representation be expected to develop?

I attempt to take up such questions and examine under what conditions black mayors of majority white cities can and do represent black interests. In other words, what do black mayors do for blacks if it is assumed that every eligible white voter supports their candidacy and they could win election without a single black vote? If we find that they have represented black interests, to what extent have they done so and at what political costs? Theoretically the questions presume that black mayors seek to represent black interests because blacks are a part of their constituency. Moreover, the questions are unique in that they ask if it is electorally possible and politically expedient to actively seek to represent black interests in majority white cities and still maintain critical white support.

Utilizing the sole term of Mayor Ford in Toledo (2002–2006) and the two terms of Mayor McLin in Dayton (2002–2010) and race and representation as my linchpins, I seek to shed light on the question of black representation in the municipal context. With these two cases I explore questions of political responsiveness, effectiveness, and accomplishment as governance issues. Long cited as one of the most favored methods in urban political research, case studies have been, and continue to be, the building blocks for social science generally and urban politics in particular.[2] As Gary King, Robert Keohane, and Sidney Verba observe, "Case studies are essential for description, and are, therefore, fundamental to social science. It is pointless to seek to explain what we have not described with a reasonable degree of precision."[3]

I begin to interrogate that precision with theory building concerning the normative expectation that black mayors Ford and McLin will be found to represent black interests even in the majority white cities of Toledo and Dayton.[4] Additionally, I have assumed that these black mayors should represent black interests because blacks are their constituents, too. Particularly given the long history of varied voter turnout in municipal elections, seeking to represent the interests of the minority black community (of which one is a member) may result in significant benefits electorally. Scholars have found this to be true in terms of state and national politics and have labeled such efforts as those of a politician's shared racial experience.[5]

*Beyond Deracialization: Toward Targeted Universalism*

The first and second decades of the twenty-first century have seen more and more of that shared racial experience wherein African Americans are increasingly being elected to political offices in communities where the majority of the constituents are not black.[6] During the same period, scholars have turned their attention to the way in which these elected officials represent their black constituents' interests—and how the concept of the "black politician" has begun to change.[7] Whereas in the past scholars tended to characterize black politicians' efforts to represent their black constituents' interests as either "deracialized" or "racialized"—that is, either as focusing on politics that transcend race or as making black issues central to their agenda—the changing demographic environment and the greater acceptance of African American politicians in high-profile positions of power have exhausted the utility of that polarization.[8] Increasingly they can point to examples of black politicians who no longer find explicit racial appeals appropriate ways of advancing their electoral ambitions.[9] They also increasingly find that a lack of attention to racial disparities among constituents does not effectively address why certain groups suffer disproportionately compared to others across a range of issues. As a result, I argue that rather than continuing to make efforts to represent black interests within the frames of racialized or deracialized politics, twenty-first-century African American mayors elected to offices in non-majority black cities are increasingly adopting the governance strategy of universalizing black interests as interests that matter for the good of the whole. To "universalize" black interests suggests that a mayor seeks to gain significant support from whites (or other non-blacks) for policies and programs that benefit black communities. Such support is garnered through strategic political rhetoric and policy/program proposals that emphasize or at least reference race and/or racial disparities, establishing how race matters. Being careful to not deny the specter of race but also not to alienate non-blacks, the mayor presents black interests as important to the city's long-term socioeconomic interests. The result: "universalizing the interests of blacks," though controversial, can allow black politicians to represent the interests of African Americans without alienating the majority of their constituents.

Some scholars have already labeled many such politicians as "postracial" or "deracialized" and thus adhere to the aforementioned exhausted bifurcation of deracialization and racialization.[10] However, I posit that universalizing the interests of blacks is not a "deracialized" approach. McCormick and Jones define deracialization as the "conducting [of] a campaign in a stylistic fashion that defuses the polarizing effects of race by avoiding explicit reference to race-specific issues."[11] While this definition is limited to electoral strategy, scholars have begun to apply it to a politician's governing efforts, and hence it need not be stretched far to be applied as well to governance strategies.[12] If this understanding is accepted, it becomes clear that many black politicians no longer "[avoid] explicit reference to race-specific issues."[13] Rather, in their attempts to represent black interests, they increasingly note racial disparities where appropriate and craft their rhetoric in a fashion that encourages non-blacks (i.e., whites) not to feel threatened.[14] McCormick and Jones also note that a deracialized approach "at the same time emphas[izes] those issues that are perceived as racial[ly] transcendent."[15] While the McCormick and Jones definition emphasizes the avoidance of race-specific issues and the advocacy of issues that transcend race, the underlying assumption of the definition is that black politicians who employ this approach do not discuss the topic of race. Rather, they strive to "enhance effectively the likelihood of white electoral support" so that they may capture or maintain public office.[16] They do so, presumably, by simply running away from race at nearly all costs. As we shall see, the main difference in the approach of many black politicians in the twenty-first century, such as Ford and McLin, is that many are making an effort not solely to win public office and gain the necessary white votes but also to represent black interests in the context of a majority-white constituency.

Some of the components of deracialization are undoubtedly present in the "universalizing black interests" approach, however. McCormick and Jones emphasize the need for black politicians to project a safe image to whites—what James Q. Wilson called a "non-threatening image"—in order to make white support more likely.[17] Yet the meaning of "nonthreatening image" has changed. Black politicians who in the twenty-first century make efforts to represent black interests and do not wish to lose the support of some whites often have the support of liberal whites.[18] Hence their precise goal is no longer so much projecting a nonthreatening image as it is representing black interests and convincing whites that black interests are not represented at the expense of white interests.

An array of elections of African American mayors in non-majority-black cities corroborates the trend toward the universalizing of black interests. In Ohio, Columbus, Toledo, Dayton, Cincinnati, Youngstown, and Cleveland have all elected black mayors in the twenty-first century. Outside of Ohio many major cities with a history of black mayors continued to elect them, such as Washington DC, Atlanta, and Baltimore. Other cities with a less-established history of electing black mayors have brought them to office as well, including Buffalo, New York; Tallahassee, Florida; Alexandria, Virginia; Sacramento, California; Columbia, South Carolina; Philadelphia, Mississippi; Jacksonville, Florida; and Mobile, Alabama. This trend suggests that whites have become increasingly willing to vote for black mayoral candidates when they feel that their interests are not threatened.[19] In other words, when African American mayors are perceived as pursuing the interests of the majority and not the interests of particular racial constituencies, whites are more likely to support them. But white perception is only one part of the story.

Noticeably white support for black mayors excludes mention of the interests of the mayors. As of this writing, scholars know little about whether or to what extent the black mayors who have garnered substantial white support have personally desired to represent the interests of the white majority once elected. To the extent that they have done so, we do not know if they have done so preferentially—in terms of their personal values—or out of electoral expediency. The answers to these questions matter because they address the role that shared racial experience plays when black mayors consider how (if) to represent the interests of African Americans in non-majority-black cities. In an attempt to address these and related questions mentioned above, I analyze how, if at all, the representation of black interests has been actively pursued by black mayors Ford and McLin via the introduction of policies and programs designed to improve the quality of life of black residents in Toledo and Dayton.[20]

A historical trend and a recent demographic shift frame the various research questions. First, as members of a racial minority that has long been socially, politically, and economically marginalized, blacks have experienced disproportionate disparities in housing, education, and income. As a result, black residents in urban settings view the election of a black mayor as an opportunity to see city government work in their interests to address these inequities. Consequently African Americans embrace the election of one of their own with high expectations, as was the case when the first wave of black mayors won office in the 1960s and 1970s. In his biography of Cleveland's Carl Stokes, the nation's first major-city black mayor, Leonard Moore observed, "Black Clevelanders expected [Stokes] to revitalize their neighborhoods, provide low-to-moderate income housing, end police brutality, create a plethora of social welfare programs, and devise endless economic opportunities."[21] In an examination of Richard Hatcher, the first black mayor of Gary, Indiana, James Lane found that African American expectations were similarly high, perhaps unrealistically so: "During Hatcher's first days in office, his staff was preoccupied with, among other things, constituent requests for jobs, interviews, guided tours of city hall, and answers to homework questions. One woman, for example, wanted to know whether the mayor could marry couples, another whether he could get an errant husband out of the house."[22] When Kenneth Gibson was elected the first black mayor of Newark, New Jersey, in 1970, the "expectations of supporters during Gibson's first term extended beyond the question of changing benefits to meet needs of new constituents. . . . Many blacks felt the election was a moral and ideological victory. Minorities expected changes in attitudes in the business community and in government." A key member of Gibson's 1970 transition team observed that "after the election of a black mayor some blacks seem to think there will be jobs for everyone. Others look for immediate improvement of services and conditions in their neighborhoods."[23]

The black community's high expectations of black mayors continued into the 1980s and early 1990s. New York City's David Dinkins, for example, "had to be concerned about responding to the desires of the various elements of his victorious coalition—a collection of groups with numerous demands that had accumulated during the many years they had been excluded from power in city hall."[24] According to one observer, "like other black mayors," Dinkins "had been voted into office burdened by an imposing set of expectations," especially from fellow African Americans.[25]

Across the country the election of black mayors raised the expectations of black voters, who viewed black mayors as modern-day messiahs who, once in office, would dramatically alter the black community's social and economic predicaments.[26] William E. Nelson observed the following about this first generation of black mayors:

> The demands placed on their shoulders were enormous. Their positions as the chief executives of cities created strong expectations that they would be able to use the resources of their offices to deliver an unprecedented array of social and economic benefits to their black constituents. These politicians were expected to produce jobs for black workers during a period of economic crisis in America. They were also expected to be skilled political brokers, balancing demands from the media, the fraternal order of police, real estate entrepreneurs, and other establishment groups, with the claims of emergent racial and ethnic groups for greater access to the policy-making process and more substantial benefits from that process. Changes in the urban benefit system produced by black mayors were expected to be permanent, not temporary.[27]

Similarly, Michael B. Preston observed that black voters looked upon black mayors "as the new leaders who would help blacks achieve political power in urban areas. . . . The belief, by most, was that political power would also open the door to more economic power, as well as increase the probability of social justice." Black mayors were "expected to seek redress for the wrongs that had been perpetuated on blacks for so long."[28] As Maynard Jackson, the first black mayor of Atlanta, Georgia, commented, "The level of expectations of black people when a black mayor is elected is so intensely emotional until it is almost exaggerated. It may be impossible for any human being to satisfy the level of expectations."[29] In short, as William E. Nelson and Philip Meranto concluded, "The election of a black man as mayor of a major American city builds up extraordinarily high expectations from his black constituents."[30]

The research questions are also framed by recent population trends. Demographic changes in many American cities are steadily reversing the population dynamics that brought about the election of this nation's first African American mayors. The 2000 and 2010 U.S. censuses indicate that major cities are losing black population while gaining Latinos and whites.[31] Washington DC, Chicago, Los Angeles, San Francisco, Seattle, New Orleans, Atlanta, and Newark are examples of cities with significant declines in black populations.[32] Washington DC, for example, the nation's first black-majority city, recently lost its long-held status as such.[33] Should this trend continue, ambitious black politicians will increasingly find themselves running for mayor in cities that are not comprised of a majority of African Americans. This trend is of paramount importance as major cities lose majority black status and yet remain expected to elect black mayors for the foreseeable future.[34] The research presented here will hopefully serve to guide blacks' expectations in terms of representation in cities that have recently transitioned to a non-majority-black status, such as Washington DC.

*Shared Racial Experience*

The primary expectation guiding my research is that Ford and McLin were involved in actively pursuing black interest issues. This expectation is founded in scholarship on black representation in other political contexts. In the congressional literature, several factors have been shown to influence members' personal policy interests.[35] Despite increased diversity in the black community, for example, black members of Congress share the experience of being members of a historically marginalized group, and blacks generally (black mayors included) have a shared memory of oppression.[36] That shared history of racialized experiences should incline black mayors to take a personal interest in actively pursuing policies and programs that are designed to improve the quality of life of their black constituents.

In addition, scholarship suggests that African American mayors might actively pursue black interests in non-majority-black cities because of their feeling of connectedness to other African Americans— a feeling termed "linked fate" by Michael Dawson.[37] The linked fate hypothesis is that social and economic factors influence whether or not black individuals have strong ties to African Americans as a group. Finding that some blacks use the group's interests as a proxy for their individual interests when making political choices, Dawson argues that individual blacks, including black mayors, associate their life chances with those of the group. Research has found that many blacks do so because of social, political, and economic differences between themselves and whites.[38]

Finally, the congressional literature provides a clue as to why black mayors should be expected to actively pursue black interests in non-majority-black cities. Katrina L. Gamble notes that many black congressional members carry a heavy burden, as they are often expected to represent not only their districts but also "black America."[39] Moreover, Richard F. Fenno finds that African American members of Congress tend to perceive their black constituency as extending beyond their geographical districts to include blacks nationwide—what some label "surrogate representation."[40] The same may be true of black mayors, especially those in the high-profile roles as the first black mayors of their cities. Hence the confluence of life experience, the feeling of connectedness to African Americans as a group, and a commitment to represent black interests even within patterns of "surrogate representation" will make black mayors, and particularly Ford and McLin, more likely to commit personally to representing black interests. Thereby it can reasonably be expected that they will make a more conscious effort to actively pursue policies and programs to improve the quality of life of the black residents of their cities.

As powerful as the argument of shared racial experience is, some congressional scholars have argued that "theories that focus on shared experience ignore individual differences and the multiple and cross-cutting identities among members of marginalized groups, locking group members into essentialized identities and fixed policy perspectives."[41] Also, some urban scholars argue that contemporary black mayors face more challenges than the black mayors first elected in major cities.[42] Hence even with shared experience and history, theory suggests that in general black mayors may not be willing or able to actively pursue black interests.

## The Study of Medium-Sized Cities

It is significant that this study examines only medium-sized U.S. cities. With the exception of a few scholars, urbanists have long ignored the public policy impact of black mayors in medium-sized cities, especially as it relates to their representation of black interests.[43] Yet according to 2011 data from the U.S. Census Bureau, most Americans live in medium-sized cities—that is, of the urban Americans who live in cities with a population of fifty thousand or higher, 60 percent of them live in cities with populations between one hundred thousand and five hundred thousand. Limiting studies of black mayoral governance to cities of five hundred thousand or more examines only 8 percent of the country's total population and 31 percent of the urban Americans who live in cities with a population of fifty thousand or higher. The lack of studies of black mayoral governance in cities with populations between one hundred thousand and three hundred thousand means that approximately 11 percent of the country's total population and 46 percent of the urban Americans who live in cities with a population of fifty thousand or higher is not being studied. Thus although my focus is on Toledo and Dayton, my findings will apply equally to cities like Tampa, New Orleans, Newark, Providence, Buffalo, and other similarly sized cities.

The scholarship that has focused on mayors of medium-sized cities, even if indirectly, has examined their leadership styles generally,[44] their impact on black social change over time,[45] or leadership in respect to a specific issue.[46] While such studies use great skill to explain the stylistic approaches, structural conditions, and single-issue responsiveness over time under which mayors of medium-sized cities win elections and govern, missing in terms of "white" cities is a detailed analysis of the mayors' responsiveness to the issues of blacks' quality of life.

Such a lack of research is increasingly significant as black mayors now govern cities that are the size of those in which most of the world's urban population resides. According to 2005 figures from the United Nations, "Almost half of humanity lives in cities," and

"Small cities, that is, those with a population of fewer than 500,000 people, were the place of residence of about fifty-one percent of all urban dwellers in the world in 2005. Thus, the majority of urban dwellers lived in fairly small urban settlements."[47] The 2006 UN's report projected that by 2030, 87 percent of residents of the United States would be urban dwellers, whereas nearly 50 percent of the population currently lived in small and medium-sized cities. The Brookings Institution and the National League of Cities found in 2002 that medium-sized cities grew faster in population than the largest cities during the 1990s and in general found that medium-sized U.S. cities were more white and less black, Hispanic, and Asian than larger cities, despite their having experienced significant growth in minority populations.[48] More recently, according to the UN State of the World's Cities 2010/2011 report, "The world's urban population now exceeds the world's rural population."[49] Therefore, the actions of mayors who govern small- and middle-sized cities arguably have relevance to a larger number of people than studies limited to larger cities.

*Impact of White Perceptions of Black Mayoral Governance*

Political scientist Zoltan Hajnal writes in his study of white attitudes toward black political leadership that "despite the hopes of the civil rights movement, researchers have found that the election of African Americans to office has not greatly improved the well-being of the black community."[50] As a solution, Hajnal suggests that scholars redirect their research efforts from a focus on the impact—both substantive and symbolic—that black mayors have had on black residents to focus on the impact that they have had on changing the attitudes and preferences of whites toward African Americans. Hajnal notes that scholars have ignored the role of the white community in studies of the gains associated with black office holding. He finds that attention to white reactions under black mayoral leadership yields important conclusions not previously known about the effects of such leadership on whites. A key finding of Hajnal's research is the process by which whites who reside in cities under the leadership of black mayors change previously held beliefs and low expectations. Hajnal posits, "When blacks have the power (or are perceived as having the power) to inflict harm on the white community and they choose not to do so, many whites are forced to re-evaluate their assumptions."[51] He suggests that once blacks secure powerful positions, such as the mayor's office in non-majority-black cities, whites "fear that a black leader will favor the black community over the white community [and] they expect a black leader to redistribute income, encourage integration, and generally channel resources toward the black community."[52] When black mayors do not advocate such positions, whites slowly gravitate toward them and begin to support their efforts. Hajnal does not examine whether the black mayors he studied *wanted* to seek the policies and programs in the interests of blacks that Hajnal claims whites feared.[53]

While Hajnal's unit of analysis is the white community's reactions to black mayoral leadership in primarily non-majority-black cities, I focus on the black mayor and his/her policy actions and program development policies over time. Hajnal suggests that black leadership is relevant in the twenty-first century because black mayors have been shown to have a positive impact on communities of white Americans. My study will show that black leadership is also relevant because what black mayors actively pursue in terms of policy and program development in the black community may also comply with the interests of the white majority in their municipalities. As national polling data indicate, whites and blacks largely share similar concerns. A survey conducted by the Joint Center National Opinion Poll in September and October 2008 found that 62 percent of blacks cited the economy as the single most important national problem, whereas 55 percent of Americans generally named the economy as "extremely important" in an October 2008 Gallup Poll.[54] To the extent that the shared concerns of whites and blacks can be applied to the urban context, the study of black mayors in the non-majority-black context may indicate that even in cases where policies of direct benefit to blacks are proposed or implemented, they often pose no threat to whites, as the mayors are careful to represent whites with comparable resources and as whites and blacks generally have similar concerns.[55] Additionally, respective to McLin and Ford, in chapter 7, I detail white and black attitudes concerning the representation of black interests in Toledo and Dayton.

*Toward Universal Black Interests: The Human Relations Approach*

This study encourages readers to think beyond the black-white dyad and to instead envision the development of policies that can both serve the constituencies with the greatest needs (including but not limited to black communities) and simultaneously serve the white majority. Adopting what Cornel West suggests is a "human relations approach" to solving the pervasive problems that plague blacks in many of America's cities is important for mayors who wish to implement policies and programs designed to improve the quality of life of black residents. Such an approach is best understood as a form of governance that appeals directly to people's common humanity.

West asks, "How do we capture a new spirit and vision to meet the challenges of the post-industrial city, post-modern culture, and post-party politics?"[56] He prescribes "admit[ting] that the most valuable sources for help, hope, and power consist of ourselves and our common history. . . . We must focus our attention on the public square— the common good . . . generate new leadership . . . a visionary leadership . . . grounded in grassroots organizing that highlights our democratic accountability."[57] In respect to addressing black issues, West attempts to cast aside the ideological divide that frames black issues from others. He observes that for liberals, blacks "are to be 'included' and 'integrated' into 'our' society and culture, while for conservatives they are to be 'well behaved' and 'worthy of acceptance' by 'our' way of life."[58] Finding such a situation inadequate, West concludes that neither group understands that "the presence and predicaments of black people are neither additions to nor defections from American life, but rather [are] constitutive elements of that life."[59] Hence, for West, a new framework is needed that views blacks and their presence in American life as American. He maintains that such a framework should "begin with a frank acknowledgment of the basic humanness and Americanness of each of us."[60]

Donald Cunnigen has similarly called for a full integration of black Americans' social and economic problems into the patchwork of American society: "The failure of America, black and white, to recognize its commonality regarding racial matters lies at the heart of the problem. Whites should not be left off the hook in dealing with societal conditions that will eventually impact their lives. Not surprisingly, many of the problems faced by the black community, such as poor performance of young black males, relocation/outsourcing of jobs overseas, and the feminization of poverty, have become social issues within the white community."[61]

While West's and Cunnigen's observations, which I refer to as the "human relations approach," are philosophical and conceptual in nature, they can be applied to black mayoral representation of black interests in non-majority-black cities. This application generates the hypothesis that in their efforts to represent blacks by universalizing their interests in the non-majority-black context, black mayors may find success by appealing to the shared human condition. Such an appeal begins with successful rhetoric that convinces whites that the programs and policies proposed will advance their interests as well. This approach may allow mayors to actively pursue black interests without threatening their majority-white constituency or making whites feel that their interests are taking a back seat. If embraced by mayors, the human relations approach could have a direct racial benefit without raising the specter of preferential treatment.

The human relations approach stands in contrast to other suggested means of helping the disadvantaged. William Julius Wilson, for example, argues that "an emphasis on coalition politics that features progressive, race-neutral policies" is the best way to address pervasive problems facing blacks and other disadvantaged groups.[62] This method relies, arguably, on a trickle-down effect, an indirect process of distributing resources. The human relations approach, on the other hand, has the potential to improve the quality of life of black

Americans in the twenty-first century. Many black mayors in the modern era govern in non-majority-black contexts that have favorable race relations in comparison to the cities governed by the nation's first black mayors. With a new generation of black mayors came a change in perspective regarding how to garner support for policy and program development in the interests of blacks.[63] If we find that black mayors are adopting the human relations perspective, this may suggest what Hajnal hopes for: that whites will support policies that work to improve the quality of life of blacks without harboring the fear that their well-being will suffer as a result.

# BLACK MAYORS, WHITE MAJORITIES

# CHAPTER 1

# A Way Out of No Way

## Reconsidering the Hollow Prize Thesis

We are troubled on every side, yet not distressed;
we are perplexed, but not in despair.

2 Corinthians 4:8

Black mayors were a new American phenomenon in the late 1960s. By the 1970s and 1980s political scientists began examining the impact of black mayors. Did black mayors live up to the black community's expectations? Were black mayors successful in delivering on their campaign promises? H. Paul Friesema was one of the early commentators to caution about the high level of black expectations, warning that black mayors were inheriting what he labeled a "hollow prize."[1] Friesema argued that African Americans were gaining control of cities that businesses and white middle-class residents were leaving, depleting the cities' tax bases and providing inadequate resources to address the social and economic needs of the black community.

One of the earliest empirical studies to test the hollow prize thesis was conducted by Edmond Keller.[2] Keller examined whether there was a discernible difference in the policy preferences and positions on municipal expenditures between white and black mayors in six cities. He found that African American mayors were more likely to support social welfare policies than white mayors. According to Keller, "Black mayors, because of the constituencies they serve, would like to make welfare-type policies their central concern; but they are often constrained from doing this by structural and human factors."[3]

Albert K. Karnig and Susan Welch discovered modest shifts in spending policy preferences when a city had a black mayor. They found, for example, that "cities with Black mayors made greater gains in educational spending and in the social welfare areas."[4] In his study of forty-three cities, Peter K. Eisinger observed, "The presence of a black mayor has a modest incremental effect on levels of black employment and on affirmative action effort, enabling us ultimately to conclude that a small but discernible portion of black employment is a product of black political authority."[5] In a subsequent study Eisinger noted that the capture of city hall by blacks could have important and positive economic consequences for the black community.[6] In their classic study of ten California cities, R. P. Browning, D. R. Marshall, and D. H. Tabb found that black political incorporation, especially black control of the mayor's office, was "associated with important changes in urban policy—the creation of police review boards, the appointments of more minorities to commissions, the increasing use of minority contractors, and a general increase in the number of programs oriented to minorities. . . . Cities with strong minority incorporation were much more likely to be responsive to minority interests."[7] In their political incorporation model Browning, Marshall, and Tabb gave extra weight to cities where an African American occupied the mayor's office. From their perspective leadership from black mayors played a stronger and more important role than efforts of African American city council members.

Grace Hall Saltzstein found that a mayor's race had a clear effect on the types of policies implemented.[8] More recently Robert A. Brown found that the presence of a black mayor in many financially strapped cities "had a substantive impact upon increased spending for housing and community development."[9] He also found a positive impact upon an increase in health spending. In the final analysis, he notes, "Black mayors had a significant influence upon increasing city government spending for social programs."[10] In general, then, the research seems to conclude that the election of a black mayor has a positive impact on the design and/or promotion of city policies that work to change the quality of life of African American residents.

In addition to research on black mayors' impact on policy, scholars have recognized their symbolic, or psychological, impact. Lawrence Bobo and Franklin D. Gilliam Jr., for example, found that having a black mayor increased the political incorporation and participation of black constituents, leading to the greater political knowledge and political empowerment of black voters.[11] Bobo and Gilliam's conclusions suggest that black residents who are descriptively represented at the mayor's office are more active participants in local politics. More recently Melissa J. Marschall and Anirudh V. S. Ruhil found that blacks reported higher levels of satisfaction with their neighborhood conditions, police services, and public schools when blacks in city government represented them, including in the mayor's office.[12] Such research confirms the work of scholars who found that having blacks in high leadership positions at the municipal level led to higher levels of political trust among blacks and, at times, participation, as well as feelings of empowerment.[13]

Considerable literature points to the limitations black mayors face in shaping urban public policy, however. Much of this literature is in line with the hollow prize thesis. Keller found that black mayors spent more on welfare-related items than white mayors, but institutional structures limited their actions on policies of relevance to blacks and their efforts to make such policies permanent.[14] Adolph Reed Jr. has pointed to the "structural and ideological constraints" that considerably hinder the extent to which black mayors can respond to the needs and concerns of their black constituents, especially the black poor.[15] Carl Stokes, the nation's first major-city African American mayor, discovered such limitations. After two terms in office, Stokes concluded that being a black mayor held only the "promises of power."[16] He found, for example, that as mayor he had little control over the city's bureaucracy. As Bette Woody concluded, African American mayors "quickly discover [they have] little or no power over the bureaucracy and can meet few demands of [their] supporters . . . [due to] problems developing good intergovernmental relations with the state and federal bureaucracy [and to] limits [that] are structural and institutional and . . . embedded in local charters."[17]

Preston found that black mayors in large and medium-sized cities were without the power necessary to bring about significant changes to the quality of life of their residents, especially black residents.[18] Describing the wave of black mayors elected in the 1970s, Preston lamented, "The new black mayors have limited powers." Black mayors, according to Preston, became "facilitators or housekeepers."[19] Nelson similarly noted the lack of institutional power for black mayors.[20] Citing a study by the Joint Center for Political Studies, Nelson wrote that most of the twenty-three cities with black mayors under review did not give the mayor statutory power: "Many black mayors are denied substantial control over the policy-making process of city government by city charters." Nelson discovered that "crucial powers of budget control and appointment were assigned either to city councils or to city managers."[21]

Yet even in Chicago, Illinois, when a black mayor had budgetary and appointment authority, Harold Washington, elected in 1983 as the city's first black mayor, was frequently met with resistance to his proposals from the city council. As Dennis R. Judd and Todd Swanstrom recorded, "Washington was hampered throughout most of his first term by the so-called council wars. Led by Edward Vrodlyak, a longtime machine Democrat, white machine politicians, who held a majority on the city council, did everything possible to thwart Washington's agenda."[22] J. Philip Thompson argues that similar resistance from city councils to a black mayor's agenda was found in New York, Cleveland, and Philadelphia.[23] In response the African American mayors of these cities sought to restructure city councils by influencing future council elections, but to little avail. The constraints on black mayors' power, then, are not limited to institutional structures. Intragovernmental resistance also constrains them; structural limitations and race work together to prevent the enactment of legislation, particularly in contexts in which white council members are not ideologically in sync with a black mayor.

Most scholars seem to agree with Reed, who finds that "these constraints stem from three main sources: 1) the city's changing economic base and functions, 2) fiscal and revenue limitations, and

3) competition and conflict—both latent and overt—among the [black mayor's] constituencies."[24] Some scholars have gone so far as to argue that "minority mayors do not just inherit distressed cities, they *cause* them, simply by being elected, not through any policies they pursue."[25]

In general previous research leaves no clear conclusion as to the efficacy of black mayoral "power" and a black mayor's ability to use the mayor's office to the benefit of the black population. Some scholars find that institutional and political conflict constraints are in line with the hollow prize thesis, concluding that there are limitations of black mayors to pursue black interests. Yet others conclude that black mayors may confront multiple limitations but that many still have been successful in their efforts to positively impact the quality of life of their black residents.

*The (Not So) Hollow Prize*

Scholarship on the governing of black mayors and their black communities varies in content and approach. While many contributions focus on single issues like education or housing development, others recognize the structural limitations black mayors face.[26] Meanwhile, urban scholars have attempted to ferret out conditions that are more likely to lead to mayors having an impact on local policy.[27]

The findings of these scholars indicate that several black mayors have been able to make substantive changes for African American residents within the formal constraints of the mayor's office. Harold Washington's tenure in Chicago is a vivid example. Washington is generally recognized as having put in place policies that, had he not died unexpectedly, could have helped blacks in Chicago. Though Washington enjoyed mayoral jurisdiction to create social welfare programming and a full-time salary as mayor, in many efforts he lacked support from the Chicago City Council. Washington also inherited a city without a financial surplus. Nevertheless, as Judd and Swanstrom note of his first term, Washington was able to "create a more open and participatory atmosphere in city government" by including numerous agencies and community organizations in his office's consultations about social policy, housing, and economic development.[28] Many of these groups were predominantly African American in composition. Hence, while the city council and other political groups lobbied against his efforts, Washington effectively garnered the support of other organizations to assist his policy development and implementation. This political maneuvering was effective for the socioeconomic progress of the black community particularly. As Robert Mier and Kari J. Moe note, a critical feature of Washington's plan for economic development involved minority participation.[29] As a result, the number of minority firms receiving city contracts increased from nine to sixty in a three-year period under Washington. His brief tenure illustrates that one effective avenue for mayors to get beyond the financial and political constraints of their city or office is to establish relationships with active groups who might assist in the mayor's implementation of some goals.

Mack H. Jones observed a similar network of support for Maynard Jackson in Atlanta after his administration's creation of an office of contract compliance.[30] For the first time in the city's history, a city department was established with the responsibility for reviewing all contracts entered into by the city and all purchases made by the city to ensure minority participation. The result of this policy change was that minority participation in city contract work rose from 2 percent soon after Jackson took office to 13 percent near the end of his first term. Noticeably Jackson faced opposition, especially from Atlanta's white business elite. Jones notes, however, that Jackson rebuffed some criticism and attempts at stalling the contract compliance project and others like it, in large part because of active groups that assisted his efforts. Jackson's success in reordering some of Atlanta's municipal priorities to the benefit of the black community was a result largely of ideologically congruent active group participation. As Jones notes, "The key to effective community empowerment is the presence of a well-organized and highly disciplined organization which not only works to help elect candidates sympathetic to its interests, but also develops a plan for action . . . to convert agenda items into policy."[31] According to Jones, mayoral constraints and limitations make it difficult for black mayors to reorder existing priorities so that significant efforts to increase black political empowerment in Atlanta in the late 1960s and mid-1970s were limited to "a more equitable share for the black community within existing priorities."[32]

Nelson writes about Carl Stokes's ability to drum up funds for the construction of 5,496 low-to-moderate-income housing units in Cleveland by the end of his second term, despite the resistance of the city council.[33] Even in the face of threats, Stokes "assisted black businesses by initiating a policy that encouraged competitive bidding by black firms for city contracts." Nelson credits Stokes's "activist-entrepreneur style of leadership."[34] Karnig and Welch similarly note that "black mayoral representation does result in some changes in the level of municipal expenditures," even in contexts of resistance to black mayoral leadership.[35] In short, many scholars have concluded that there is room for a black mayor, even in a non-majority-black city facing considerable financial and political opposition, to actively pursue policies that are designed to improve the lives of black residents. Somehow black mayors "make a way out of no way" and are capable of introducing substantive change for blacks.

As noted, to create more favorable conditions to implement such policies, black mayors benefit from soliciting the support of active groups that share their administration's goals. Supportive groups may be the key determinants of a black mayor's success in this regard. Moreover, a black mayor may take an unconventional approach in pursuing policies for blacks in order to avoid potential backlash. For example, black mayors might seek out black community-based organizations and neighborhood associations or groups to illuminate black interests and assist in the governance of the city.[36] In contrast, the urban politics literature has long focused on conventional channels of political influence.[37] Browning, Marshall, and Tabb found that government effectively represents minorities when blacks form active electoral coalitions, win elected office, and comprise a significant part of a dominant, liberal governing coalition. They concluded that when blacks were members of the dominant coalition, their cities were more likely to create civilian review boards of the police, increase black presence on boards and commissions and in municipal employment, and expand the number of city contracts awarded to blacks.[38] Building on this research, other scholars have found that the presence of black elected representatives resulted in an increase of black personnel in the public sector and had an impact on the effectiveness of fire and police services and road and park conditions in black communities.[39]

Hence, the likelihood that a city's government will be responsive to black interests appears to be highest with blacks in key leadership roles, such as in the mayor's office or on the city council. Often without the power of those positions the degree to which blacks may expect government to effectively respond to their interests is slim.

### The Shared Racial Experience Variable

In addition to the powers of the office of the mayor, the assumption of shared racial experience affects a black mayor's responsiveness toward his or her black constituents and helps explain why the representation of black interests matters. However, scholars' views conflict regarding the role a black politician has on the introduction and implementation of black-interest programs and policies. The most recent scholarship clearly finds that African American congressional representatives more actively represent black interests than do white members of Congress.

A strong theoretical and empirical body of literature describes how the representation of black interests differs from other kinds of representation because of "descriptive" characteristics, such as shared racial experience. A number of scholars have investigated to what degree politicians are responsive to their constituents. By detailing how shared racial experience defines a strong connection between a black politician and his or her constituents, congressional scholarship literature helps to explain why we might expect the interests of blacks to be represented by a black mayor in a non-majority-black city. Scholarship on political representation suggests that black politicians more often actively pursue the interests of blacks than do white politicians. The debate frames the argument for why I expect that a black mayor would pursue black interests when black constituents are the minority.

## The Debate over the Representation of Black Interests

Scholars disagree concerning what factors contribute to the representation of black interests. For example, Carol M. Swain has posited, like Hanna Pitkin, that there is a distinction between "substantive" and "descriptive" representation and that black and white Democratic members of Congress at the very least equally represent African Americans.[40] Hence for Swain, who examined black representatives in a variety of different districts, including majority-white districts, descriptive representation has no place: "Black interests on Capitol Hill, at least measured by the policy congruence between the representative and his or her Black populations, are better looked after by the Democratic congressional party. . . . It suggests that Black interests will certainly be represented in Congress, even if the number of Black faces remain[s] low."[41] What surfaces in Swain's argument is the significance of party membership, platform, and ideas—not the race of individual representatives. In this view substantive representation supplants descriptive representation, and black constituents rarely gain more from electing a black representative, provided the non-black representative belongs to the Democratic Party. What the "certain" representation of black interests requires is an increased number of representatives from the Democratic Party. Consequently Swain thinks blacks and whites should form biracial coalitions to maximize the representation of one another's interests. Swain's findings and recommendations are limited, however, to a comparable measurement of white Democratic members of the One Hundredth Congress.

Katherine Tate criticizes Swain for equating partisanship to black interests, noting that "descriptive representation turns out to be very important to Blacks, as Blacks were generally approving of their legislator when that representative was Black."[42] Yet Swain argues that aggressive pushes for descriptive representation for blacks in Congress can be damaging: "The assumption that only Blacks can represent Black interests puts African Americans who want to maximize the descriptive and substantive representation of Blacks in Congress in an untenable position. . . . It operates to hurt Black politicians who need White support—those Black politicians who seek to emphasize racial commonalities, those who seek to represent Whites as well as Blacks."[43] Swain does not suggest that white representatives can unequivocally represent blacks: "Although a White representative can 'think, act, and talk Black,' he or she can never *be* Black. White representation of Blacks will never replace Black representation."[44] Nevertheless, Swain's overall conclusion is that white Democratic representation in Congress is equal to or better for blacks than descriptive black representation.

Tate, among others, finds this prioritization of party over racial group membership in the representation of black interests to be troubling. She argues that black representation is not only best achieved through black members of Congress because black representatives share a particular interpretation of history with their black constituents, but also that all groups, including whites, place a strong value on descriptive representation. This is a consideration that both Pitkin and Swain ignore. For them, it appears, descriptive representation is not only pejorative but is also limited to minority group experience.[45] Tate, on the other hand, is adamant that "all Americans place a strong value on [descriptive representation,] as it is a component of political representation continuously stressed by members of those elected to the U.S. Congress."[46] Both Tate and David Runciman concur that descriptive representation is endemic in the institution of political representation.[47] Challenging Swain's conclusion that party trumps racial identification, Tate asserts, "Black Democrats are strikingly more liberal or less conservative than White Democrats."[48] This finding contrasts with Swain's finding that white Democratic Party members of Congress represent black interests as well as black members do.[49]

*The Black Representation Variable in Local Politics*

Given the unique nature of city cultures, every city unveils its own challenges to a mayor's active pursuit of policies and programs.[50] Some cities' histories may require that mayors consult union leaders prior to any major policy development that affects certain local neighborhood communities. In other cities the mayor may find himself or herself more likely to pursue policies that have party endorsement. V. O. Key has argued that a two-party competitive politics environment is better suited to guarantee responsiveness than is one-party dominance.[51] In other words, when the electorate is given "political options," elected officials within a two-party system are more likely to be responsive to their supporters' concerns. In addition, district elections may influence the quality of representation on city councils and commissions because these elections have been found to provide a closer connection between an officeholder and the constituents than at-large elections.[52]

As noted, community-based organizations may be effective supporters of black elected officials. Barbara Ferman argues that neighborhood and community groups play key roles as channeling agents to achieve responsiveness for or from government leaders.[53] By lobbying for their interests, they make public officials better informed about and more responsive to their concerns. While some note the limitations of such groups' effectiveness,[54] the combined presence of a strong and mobilized black community and shared racial experience between a black mayor and his or her black constituents tends to produce greater levels of responsiveness to black interests. Still other scholars have found that traditionally excluded groups use neighborhood organizations to gain attention, service, and access to government and that organizational resources empower racial and ethnic minorities.[55]

*The Way Out of No Way: Targeted Universalistic Governance*

Rhine McLin and Jack Ford sought to represent black interests via a leadership style and governance choice to (unknowingly) utilize John A. Powell's concept of targeted universalism.[56] The concept is a political strategy and governing approach that recognizes the need for a universal platform that is simultaneously responsive to the needs of the particular. By extension, then, targeted universalism is a rhetorical strategy and also a public policy development strategy wherein policy output is determined in part by how a program effectively can be described as benefitting all citizens yet has a targeted focus toward the problems of specific groups.

As explained in the introduction, I reframe Powell's concept as a "common humanity, human relations" approach. I do so because Powell's concept is based in part on the scholarship of others who were also concerned with questions of how best to implement social welfare and urban public policy initiatives. Most recently scholars have debated the question of how to represent the disparate "other" in terms of initiatives' universal or targeted impact.[57] William Julius Wilson and Theda Skocpol are often cited as supporting a universalistic approach to public policy implementation.[58] For example, Wilson describes how targeted programs such as Aid to Families with Dependent Children, introduced by President Franklin D. Roosevelt under the New Deal, were successful in gaining political support only because they were perceived to provide "a modicum of security for all."[59] President Lyndon Johnson's targeted War on Poverty programs, on the other hand, gained little political support because "this system amounted to taxation to pay for programs that were perceived to benefit mostly minorities, programs that excluded taxpayers perceived to be mostly white."[60] Thus in rejecting race-specific policies and programs with a targeted focus, Wilson has argued for universal, economic-reform-based programs "to improve the life chances of groups such as the ghetto underclass by emphasizing programs in which the more advantaged groups of all races can positively relate.[61] Economically based and universally applied social programs, Wilson argues, will address racially disparate problems in inner-city communities and the "substantive inequality" that would remain if the policy focus were limited to race-specific policies and means-tested goals and objectives.[62] Consequently universalistic policies and programs can have targeted benefits for African Americans in the urban context.[63]

Skocpol has agreed with Wilson that social welfare and urban public policy programs require universalistic benefits.[64] Skocpol, who champions the universalist approach toward social welfare and urban public policy programs that may benefit particular constituencies such as blacks, argues that policymakers' efforts should be guided by fundamental values and moral obligations that are alleged to be monolithically understood or accepted.[65]

Not all scholars agree with Skocpol and Wilson.[66] For example, Robert Greenstein argues that Skocpol makes incongruent comparisons: "[Skocpol] overstates the relative political strength of universal programs because she compares universal programs providing entitlements to targeted programs that are not entitlements and must have their funding levels determined in the appropriations cycle each year."[67]

As a solution, Greenstein argues for a combination of universal and targeted approaches. He cites an unpublished paper by Isabel V. Sawhill that found "if there is one lesson that we have learned from all the evaluations and research that has been conducted since the War on Poverty began, it is that [service] programs that provided limited benefits to many people, although politically popular, are not effective in responding to the problems of the most seriously disadvantaged."[68] Douglas S. Massey and Mitchell L. Eggers have also found that social conditions vary significantly among ethnic groups and across regions.[69] Hence social programs should perhaps be targeted to certain ethnic groups or within certain regions to achieve the best possible outcome.

I share many of the universalist criticisms of scholars such as Greenstein, Roger Wilkins, and Massey. The findings support the targeted thesis based on the fact that blacks and whites in the cities examined reported that black interests were more actively pursued with black mayors than under their white predecessors. By extension, it is striking how similar proponents of universalism appear to be to communitarian theorists. Communitarians often view the public realm as unified and homogenous, where collective interests and "equal citizenship" are normative values. It follows, then, that by embracing the commonality of citizens, all persons' interests and problems are addressed in civic life. Similarly proponents of universalist-based public policy approaches to racially disparate and urban problems suggest that by appealing to the universal, the needs of the particular are served.[70]

As theorist Iris Marion Young has indicated, however, "the universal citizen is also white and bourgeois."[71] Thus for Young, who argues against Rousseau and other early political philosophers—whose views embodied "the universal point of view of the collective interests and equal citizenship" yet denied citizenship to women—the universal or impartial ideal is insufficient. In rejecting what she calls the universality of the ideal of impartiality, Young distinguishes between two kinds of universality: "Universality in the sense of the participation and inclusion of everyone in moral and social life does not imply universality in the sense of the adoption of a general point of view that leaves behind particular affiliations, feelings, commitments, and desires. . . . Universality as generality has often operated precisely to inhibit universal inclusion and participation."[72] As a result, for Young approaches to civic life that construct the universal as general and subsume the differences embodied in the particular experiences of those who are not "white and bourgeois" inherently fail to adequately address the interests of those who are different.

Young finds that the communitarian approach excludes the value of citizenship for those who are socially different from the norm. She finds that "this ideal expresses a desire for the fusion of subjects with one another, which in practice operates to exclude those with whom the group does not identify. The ideal of community denies and represses social difference."[73] Correspondingly proponents of universal programs to address the interests of particular constituencies presume that the urban problems of blacks can be addressed by crafting economic policies to meet the needs of all low-income citizens, including blacks. However, as Young suggests, if we presume the universal approach to be successful in addressing low-income black problems in the urban context because it addresses low-income economic limitations for all citizens, then it would follow that other black "problems" experienced by those who are not low-income would not be addressed. Hence by suggesting that urban black problems can be fixed by appealing to macroeconomic restructuring, one in effect denies the potential problem of racially disparate issues that affect blacks who are not low-income.[74]

Young notes, "Appeals to community are usually antiurban."[75] Her solution to the many urban problems is regionally based governmental units and public policy and service delivery initiatives.[76] Both Ford and McLin championed a regionally based network of shared responsibility and investment. While Young's alternative to the communitarian universal approach is important, most significant is the theoretical comparison her research affords; it can be applied to the targeted versus universal social policy debate.

Similar to Greenstein's proposal to combine the targeted and universal approaches in an effort to substantively address social welfare policies, Powell has argued that universal laws and policies do not effectively address the needs of black and urban communities. He thus argues for targeted universalism in race politics, a strategy in which arguments are made in a way that is racially inclusive rather than polarizing. It is this rhetorical strategy that Ford and McLin utilized in their State of the City speeches and related addresses (see chapter 8). Powell's notion of targeted universalism is similar to Skocpol's notion of "targeting within universalism," wherein extra benefits are directed to low-income groups within the context of a universal policy design.[77] As an example of targeting within universalism, Skocpol cites the hypothetical development of a family security program as an extension of preexisting social security programs for the elderly.[78]

Powell's targeted universalism has a different focus and describes why universal, race-neutral policies are ineffective in race politics:

Policies that are designed to be universal too often fail to acknowledge that different people are situated differently. For racially marginalized populations, particularly those who live in concentrated-poverty neighborhoods, there are multiple reinforcing constraints. For any given issue—whether it is employment rates, housing, incarceration, or health care—the challenge is to appreciate how these issues interact and accumulate over time, with place as the linchpin holding these arrangements together. Universal policies that are nominally race-neutral and that focus on specific issues such as school reform will rarely be effective because of the cumulative cascade of issues that encompass these neighborhoods.[79]

Thus Powell argues for the necessity of a policy and programmatic approach that acknowledges that any social problems affect more than just blacks yet still require targeted implementation.

In addition, proposed remedies, such as affirmative action, should examine a broader array of factors than race alone.[80] Powell's "targeted universalism" is a strategy that achieves what racialized politics attempted in the 1960s and 1970s with, for example, programs focused on urban renewal. In a new era in which scholars at least question how a preference for "diversity" in the job sector may negatively impact blacks,[81] however, Powell recognizes that racialized efforts are ineffective and that universal interests deny the specter of race:

> What is required is a strategy of "targeted universalism." This approach recognizes that the needs of marginalized groups must be addressed in a coordinated and effective manner. To improve opportunities and living conditions for all residents in a region, we need policies to proactively connect people to jobs, stable housing, and good schools. Targeted universalism recognizes that life is lived in a web of opportunity. Only if we address all of the mutually reinforcing constraints on opportunity can we expect real progress in any one factor. My research suggests targeted efforts—ones that target both racial and spatial arrangements—to break this cycle of the racial dimension of the geography of opportunity . . . [can be effective]. While these practices may be less dependent on deliberate racialized policies today than earlier in America's history, only deliberate policy interventions that are sensitive to the structural dynamics of opportunity are likely to be effective in ending this cycle of opportunity segregation.[82]

Powell cites former Los Angeles mayor Antonio Villaraigosa and former Chicago mayor Harold Washington as examples of public officials who have actively utilized the targeted universalism approach successfully. Both of these men "built broad-based multi-racial, multi-class coalitions and succeeded by keeping both race and class issues in focus. . . . There has never been—at least in 20th Century America—a progressive political movement built solely on class. To inoculate such efforts from divisive race-baiting, there must be discourse to inspire whites to link their fates to nonwhites." The concept of targeted universalism is thus meant to establish a discourse and to develop related actions and programs that inspire "Whites to link their fates to non-Whites."[83]

What Powell considers targeted universalism I characterize as Jack Ford's and Rhine McLin's efforts to universalize the interests of blacks. In these attempts the mayors garnered white support for seemingly racialized initiatives. While their reelections may have been threatened, as Joseph P. McCormick and Charles E. Jones have noted, at the very least they initiated a discourse on racial equal opportunity that potentially could affect the city culture for years to come.[84]

As proponents of targeted universalism have argued, though, while an opportunity for positive discourse may develop out of a targeted universalistic approach, the approach has limitations. As Young has indicated, notions of what is universal are understood insofar as they stand in contrast to background assumptions that are particular or non-universal. When it comes to universal public policies and how best to implement them, however, often such policies, even if targeted under the framework of universalism, tend to be perceived as racially polarizing. President Johnson's aforementioned War on Poverty programs are one example: though these programs were promoted in universal language, many white citizens felt that their tax dollars were being spent to benefit black people. Some scholars have noted, moreover, that Aid to Families with Dependent Children, a universal program, came to be perceived as predominantly for the black urban poor.[85] Even though blacks were disproportionately excluded from the program when it was first established, demographic changes and changes in the development of media led many Americans to believe poor blacks were the dominant group affected by poverty. Thus according to some scholars, most universal programs are de facto targeted or particular, either because of how they are perceived or in terms of how their benefits are implemented.[86] In the final analysis, it appears that particularly at the implementation stage, targeted universalism can become racialized.

A second limitation with the targeted universalism approach concerns how to measure what it is that proponents of the approach are in fact attempting to accomplish. There is no way to answer the question directly, as some may utilize the approach, as Ford and McLin arguably have, to achieve racial justice or fairness, while others may focus less on the "targeted" dimension of the concept and more on the "universal" dimension and seek to accomplish racial or color blindness.[87] This possibility, as Powell has noted, leads to a problem because while theoretically these two versions of the concept could "work in tandem, in practice they are often in conflict."[88] Universalism is not the same as targeted universalism—and it's easy to confuse them.

Moreover, Dona and Charles Hamilton examined a variety of targeted universal programs, particularly those in the civil rights era, and found that none promoted racial justice, in part because of salient racial resentment.[89] Finally, Powell argued that the framing of the particular within the confines of the universal created a legal and policy limitation, as those who were either aggressively pro-racialization or pro-deracialization occupied better positions in terms of argument strength, given that they did not suffer from the weakness of trying to occupy both ends of the spectrum simultaneously.[90] Consequently according to some scholars, the implementation of targeted universal policies and programs rather than universal programs and race-specific programs is not a perfect solution.

As emphasized in the introduction, though, the practice of universalizing the interests of blacks is not the same as deracialization, and as a result, it is conceivably a better option, even if its targeted focus is not perfect. The targeted universalist approach is different, as the process includes black elected officials that consider the interests of black constituents, develop particularized policy actions and programs, and popularize them by rhetorically advocating for these interests in a way that does not deemphasize race or alienate all whites. The context in which this process functioned in the case studies that we will consider was one in which the mayors emphasized citizens' common humanity. Hence, in addition to noting the significance of race while supporting certain policies and programs, the mayors carefully tapped into the common humanity of city residents through strategic rhetorical framing. As a result, the mayors received support for their causes in neighborhoods and groups not their own, as when Ford received initial assistance from the Associated General Contractors of Northwest Ohio to support his Capacity Building program or when McLin received the support of the business community, as recognized by an anonymous business leader and by the president and CEO of the Dayton Area Chamber of Commerce (see chapters 5 and 6). Their approach is a good example of how to maintain some white electoral and governing support in a non-majority-black city while at the same time advocating for black interests. Their willingness to do so and their ability to do so suggests the hollow prize thesis also has a limited application to twenty-first-century black mayors.

# CHAPTER 2

# The Model of Ohio

Political History and Demographic
Change in a Rust-Belt State

---

Every group, when it reaches a certain population percentage, automatically
takes over.... They don't apologize ... they just move in and take over.

Harold Washington

---

Ohio politics has generated significant interest from scholars seeking to observe political behavior throughout the nineteenth and early twentieth centuries.[1] The early twenty-first century also brought
reasonable scholarly attention to the state's politics because of both
historically significant and contemporarily relevant issues.[2] In addition, the Midwest rust-belt cities of Dayton and Toledo are significant
as their histories explain the context in which Ford and McLin developed their political profiles. I chose to focus on Dayton and Toledo
also because of the limited scholarly and contemporary research on
those cities, particularly concerning the variable of race in such medium-sized, majority white cities.[3] Dayton, in southwest Ohio, with
a 2010 population of 141,527, is 43 percent African American, and
Toledo, in northwest Ohio, with a 2010 population of 287,208, is 27
percent African American. The cities are comparable in population
to many cities in which Americans live. Finally, the cases of Dayton
and Toledo represent a number of Ohio cities in which black mayors
were elected in the early twenty-first century. As table 1 indicates,
every major city in Ohio (except Akron) elected a black mayor at the
turn of the twenty-first century, beginning with Michael Coleman in
Columbus in 1999.[4]

**TABLE 1. Twenty-first-century black mayors in Ohio**

| MAYOR | TERM(S) | CITY | NOTES |
|---|---|---|---|
| Michael Coleman | 1999–present | Columbus | City's first black mayor of Ohio's largest city |
| Jack Ford | 2002–2006 | Toledo | City's first black mayor |
| Rhine McLin | 2002–2010 | Dayton | City's first female mayor |
| Mark Mallory | 2006–2013 | Cincinnati | City's first popularly elected black mayor |
| Frank Jackson | 2006–present | Cleveland | City's third black mayor |
| Jay Williams | 2006–2011 | Youngstown | City's first black mayor |
| Michael Bell | 2010–present | Toledo | City's second black mayor |

Of course Ohio is famous because it was in Cleveland that the nation's first major-city black mayor, Carl Stokes, was elected in 1967. However, in 1966, one year before Stokes's election, the Springfield City Commission appointed Robert C. Henry mayor. (Jack Ford's hometown is Springfield.) Moreover, Isaiah Tuppins, the first black man to win a medical degree in Ohio, won election as Rendville's mayor in 1888, becoming the first African American man to serve as mayor of any community in Ohio.

Ohio's unusual past and recent history of electing and appointing black mayors in majority-white cities is but one example of regions in demographic transition—the result of which for Ohio has been the fairly consistent election of black mayors throughout the state. Beginning with Michael White's tenure as the second black mayor of Cleveland in 1990–2002, the state has had at least one elected black mayor consistently since 1990. Each of those mayors has governed cities that are majority white. This fact is critical because their efforts to represent black interests in a majority-white context may help explain what black mayors in racially transitioning cities may be able to do in terms of black interests. As noted in the introduction, with cities like Washington DC, Atlanta, and Newark losing significant black population, the efforts of black mayors in "white cities" may guide scholarly expectations of what future mayors of formerly black-majority cities may be able to do to maintain significant black and white support (and therefore the mayor's office).

Ohio's political history at first glance seems ripe for watershed elections of many black political leaders. For example, Ohio is one of twenty-five states where the governor and lieutenant governor are elected on the same ticket, ensuring that they come from the same political party. It is significant that Jennette Bradley, a Republican, was the first African American to be elected lieutenant governor, along with incumbent Bob Taft. Bradley was also the first black woman ever elected as lieutenant governor in the history of the United States.

As a "free" state, Ohio has long been a refuge for African Americans and has a rich Underground Railroad history, resulting in educational and political opportunities for blacks in the state. For example, in 1856 the Methodist Episcopal Church established Wilberforce University (near Xenia), the first private black college in the United States. And in 1863, two years before President Lincoln's Emancipation Proclamation was signed, the African Methodist Episcopal Church, the oldest black denomination in the country, took ownership of Wilberforce. Some years later, in 1880, George Washington Williams became the first African American elected to the Ohio legislature, notably after the period of Reconstruction, which resulted in significant African American political achievements in the southern United States. On the other hand, the president who ordered the end of the post–Civil War federal protection of blacks in the South was an Ohioan, Rutherford B. Hayes. The Hayes-Tilden Compromise resulted in Hayes's election as president and the withdrawal of federal troops from some Southern states. As a result of the compromise Southern blacks were no longer protected in the exercise of their constitutional rights—Southern localities did not protect blacks after the removal of federal protection—resulting in the rise of black codes, "Jim Crow," and second-class citizenship. Indeed much Southern local law enforcement aided in the discrimination of blacks throughout the nineteenth and much of the twentieth centuries.

Clearly not everyone, then or now, celebrates the historic relationship between whites and blacks in Ohio, and conflict between whites and blacks continues to this day. As a result of the state not enforcing several provisions of earlier civil rights laws to help eliminate racial discrimination in Ohio, the Ohio General Assembly created the Ohio Civil Rights Commission in 1959.

The legislation that created the Ohio Civil Rights Commission was the Ohio Civil Rights Act of 1959. As a result of the legislation, Ohio, the seventeenth state to join the Union (in 1803), a century and a half later became the sixteenth state to enact fair employment practices legislation to prohibit unlawful racial discrimination. Signed into law by Governor Michael V. DiSalle (a former Toledo mayor) on July 29, 1959 (during his first six months in office and in the same month that he signed another noteworthy bill establishing Ohio's famous motto, "With God All Things Are Possible"), the act reinforced many of the provisions of the Ohio Public Accommodations Law of 1884, which had not been enforced.[5] The passing of the act indicates two key points: (1) Ohio, along with a few other states, led the nation in equal employment opportunity legislation, establishing strong provisions well before Congress enacted the Civil Rights Act of 1964, and (2) Ohio's relative urgency was needed as a result of several reported incidents of discrimination and lack of enforcement of the 1884 law.

The paradox of Ohio leading the nation in racial progress yet also doing so in part out of necessity is best represented in the cases of Rhine McLin as the first female mayor of Dayton and the loss of her bid for a third term and Jack Ford's tenure as the first black mayor in Toledo and his reelection campaign in 2005, where members of the National Socialist Movement (self-proclaimed neo-Nazis) descended on the north side of the city to march, claiming alleged harassment of whites in the neighborhood. Ford's handling of this episode, which garnered significant national attention because it resulted in neighborhood looting, many small riots, and local outrage, overshadowed his historic mayoralty and reelection effort. McLin's third election bid in 2010 also exemplifies the complicated history of Ohio's experience on race.

*Changing Demographics: Implications for Black Mayoral Politics*

For many Robert A. Dahl's pluralist theory of ethnic succession in *Who Governs* helps to explain the rise in political power of blacks in

American cities. Wilbur Rich supports Dahl's argument, as do Neil Kraus and Todd Swanstrom.[6] However, Reuel R. Rogers disagrees, noting that the theory is more of an "appendage" for blacks in New Haven (the subject of Dahl's study) as the incorporation of blacks in that city (and other cities) did not happen at all or nearly at the same pace or with similar effect (or benefit) as the incorporation models for white ethnics.[7] For Rogers the model is also not the "best fit" for blacks in urban cities as it ignores the necessary strife of the civil rights movement, which most scholars agree paved the way for blacks such as Carl Stokes to run for mayor in Cleveland in 1967 and others after him. Despite disagreement, the theory that demographic change—as amplified through population movements or evidenced through the census—tends to result in greater political incorporation for minorities remains a powerful indicator of electoral success for African Americans in American cities.

Demographic changes in the U.S. population in the last two decades have eroded or are potentially eroding a key variable in the election of black mayors: a black majority in the population of a city. With cities losing black population while gaining whites and Latinos, the conditions under which black candidates run for mayor in many cities are quite different from those of the first elected black mayors. Since 2000 the black population of Washington DC has decreased by more than 6 percent, while its white population has risen more than 14 percent. The district is now no longer majority black.[8]

Atlanta, Georgia, also has experienced a loss of black population. Since 1990 the white population has increased over 6 percent, totaling 40 percent of the population in 2006, while the black population decreased nearly 12 percent, totaling 55 percent. It remained steady at 55 percent through 2010, and the white population continued to grow. Between 1990 and 2010 the Latino population also increased to nearly 6 percent. According to former Atlanta mayor Shirley Franklin, the black population has shifted from a majority of 70 percent in 1980 to less than 60 percent post-2000.[9] These trends, if they continue, suggest that ambitious black candidates for mayor may have to form electoral coalitions comprised of increasing numbers of whites and Latinos in areas where blacks have dominated for decades.

The decline in black population across many cities such as Washington DC, Atlanta, and New Orleans is not the entire story, however. In some cities a change in the black population correlated with fluctuations in the white population—for example, in some cities the black population decreased as many younger whites moved away from suburbs to cities.[10] Other cities lost both white and black population. In either event the compelling story is the fluctuation of white and black populations in many cities, coupled with an increase in the Latino population (though only marginal in some cities). What matters for black representation, though, is the loss of African American population as a share of total population in many cities. This is the case regardless of whether the black population actually declines, but it is particularly problematic when it does.

Some scholars cite blacks' exit to the suburbs as the reason for the numeric decline in the black population of cities.[11] Blacks in Washington DC, for example, are said to be moving into Prince George's County, Maryland, while blacks in Atlanta are said to be moving into suburbs like Stone Mountain and Decatur. According to the U.S. Census Bureau and survey reports, Newark, New Jersey, had a black population of near 60 percent in 1990, yet in 2010 it was 52 percent. Rising crime and the black middle-class exodus from the city limits are cited as possible reasons for the decline. New Orleans is another example. The decline of its black population can be attributed in part to 2005's Hurricane Katrina. A survey commissioned by several state agencies and reported in the *New York Times* indicates that the city had a black population of 67 percent before Katrina while the population in 2008 was approximately 46 percent.[12] It has since increased to just below 60 percent as blacks began to slowly moved back to the city post-Katrina, but the loss in black population partially explained the election of the city's first white mayor in decades in 2010.[13] While the reasons for the decline in black populations across many cities vary, the fact of the decline remains.

Given the changing demographics in many cities, black mayors may be elected less often as majority-black cities disappear. Thus one reason why it is important to study two medium-sized non-majority-black cities and their black mayors' efforts to address black interests is that doing so can contribute to scholars' understanding of the implications of the national trends. Given the entrenched history of black politics in many cities nationwide, we can expect their black mayors to continue to actively pursue black interests even as these cities shift to be non-majority black.

At issue is how, if at all, the representation of black interests is changing. The demographic trends indicate that researchers may no longer be able to count solely on descriptive characteristics as a proxy for a black politician's promotion of black interests. With many cities changing from black-majority to black-minority populations, black mayors will find it increasingly difficult to promote black interests to the exclusion of white and Latino interests. Given the increasing diversity of America's population, the skill of advancing one group's interests becomes more complex, especially when it involves allocating resources in a way that advantages one group over others.

### "Waves" of Black Mayors in "White" Cities

The nation's first black major-city mayors were elected in non-majority-black cities. At the time of Carl Stokes's election in Cleveland in 1967, the city was majority Caucasian, as was the case when Tom Bradley was elected mayor in Los Angeles in 1973, Harold Washington in Chicago, Wellington Webb in Denver, Norman Rice in Seattle, Lee Brown in Houston, and Willie Brown in San Francisco. Thus, it is fair to ask how my research differs from the literature investigating the first-wave black mayors and their efforts to address constituent interests. The answer is threefold. First, as we have seen, Dayton and Toledo are medium-sized cities where scholars have understudied black mayors' active pursuit of black interests. This omission is significant, as city size and culture affect the role of government and leadership development. Bowers and Rich find the following about medium-sized cities:

Although their small scale affects the resources available to middle-sized cities to promote their sustainability, their size also presents opportunity for quality mayoral leadership absent in big cities. Given medium-sized cities' smaller and more geographically compact populations, their mayors possess the opportunity for a sustained relationship between their communities and themselves that is more intimate than that ever experienced by a president, governors of all but the smallest and more sparsely populated states, or big-city mayors. This close proximity to the inhabitants of their cities creates for these mayors, opportunities to aggressively engage in leadership.[14]

The geographic and constituent composition of medium-sized cities differs from that of larger cities. Thus the potential for substantive change in urban policies and programs that work to benefit black residents is plausible, and likely probable, in the context of medium-sized cities with black mayors.

Second, the twenty-first century has created macroeconomic challenges for black mayors that the first wave of black mayors did not experience. Nelson argues: "The success of Black mayoral regimes in the twenty-first century will depend, in great measure, on the ability of Black mayors to recognize, and effectively respond to, changes in the economic environments of state and federal governments. The fiscal problems that confront Black mayors today are far different from those faced by the first wave of Black mayors in the 1960s and 1970s."[15] While some challenges are unique to the century, others, like high expectations to work on behalf of the less privileged, remain, as Nelson points out: "Black mayors are expected to be agents of change who possess the power and authority to radically alter both the structure and distributional impact of urban decision-making. . . . Standing at the center of the local governing process, Black mayors must be frontline fighters in the efforts to litigate the negative impact of devolution in the federal system on the social and economic status of the poor and minorities in cities."[16]

High expectations have remained constant over time. The high expectations that accompanied the election of black mayors in major U.S. cities in the 1960s, 1970s, 1980s, and early 1990s, according to Nelson, represented "the extension of the black civil rights movement in the South into the dynamic terrain of city politics."[17] Hence the first wave of black mayors in non-majority-black cities campaigned in a racially divisive context. The expectations black citizens had for their black mayors were partly the result of the electoral style embraced by black mayoral candidates, who articulated campaign positions purposely designed to mobilize black voters.[18] Nelson explains: "The first wave of Black mayors came into office in an environment of widespread and deep-seated racial polarization and conflict. Political mobilization in the Black community was fueled by bruising conflicts over open housing and public education policies in cities."[19] The first wave of black mayors was elected under racially volatile conditions, and these mayors were expected to serve black constituencies.

It is because of the racial climate in which many of the first-wave black mayors were elected that any efforts they made on behalf of their black residents must be analyzed with caution.[20] As Thompson explains in his analysis of the electoral victory and reelection loss of New York City's first black mayor, David Dinkins, the appeal to efforts in the black communities must be made cautiously. The elections of the first black mayors were viewed as watershed events and therefore as opportunities to make an immediate, substantive impact on the black community. Winning office in part due to strong black support, these mayors felt enormous pressure to make substantive socioeconomic changes in the black community, and they pursued policies and programs to realize these goals. Yet many were unsuccessful, especially in efforts to assist the black poor.[21] Consequently Ford's and McLin's terms in Ohio were significant in that the responsibilities and expectations associated with a black mayor's election were heightened or at least remained constant in comparison to the 1960s and 1970s, even though modern-era mayors were facing challenges specific to the twenty-first century and were governing in a more favorable racial climate.

In the twenty-first century black mayors did not experience campaigns as racially divisive as those of the first wave of black mayors. In fact the shift in racial understanding in the American political landscape in the twenty-first century is, as one scholar suggests, a "social transformation."[22] The prolonged history of racial discrimination and prejudice remains in the minds of some Americans, of course, leading Cunnigen to conclude: "The role of black leadership [in the twenty-first century] should begin with the acknowledgement of its limitations. The limitations include the leadership's inability to solve every conceivable problem facing the [black] community. It should recognize that the black community's problems are American problems that require an American solution."[23] For Cunnigen the problems in the black community in the modern era are problems that affect others as well. It follows, then, that others should be involved in solving them.

In the modern era, given the new challenges facing black mayors, they, like all public officials, have a responsibility to work on behalf of all of their constituents. This is not to suggest, however, that specific goals and policies cannot be directed toward a particular constituency. Many mayors direct policy benefits toward specific groups in the form of libraries, pools, schools, and park development. Many mayors also address the needs of blacks by tending to problems in black neighborhoods. One major contribution of the chapters that follow will be to examine how actively Ford and McLin pursued these types of efforts on behalf of blacks.

### Black Mayors, Black Interests, and Medium-Sized Cities

Bowers and Rich argue that governing medium-sized cities presents unique challenges and opportunities for all mayors.[24] The study of black mayors of medium-sized cities is no different. As table 2 indicates, of the numerous black mayors in office during the twenty-first century, many governed medium-sized cities.

Of those listed in table 2, more than half (thirteen) are/were mayors of non-majority-black cities, with another six governing cities that were close to losing their majority-black status. Our understand-

**YBP Library Services**

PERRY, RAVI K.

BLACK MAYORS, WHITE MAJORITIES: THE BALANCING ACT
OF RACIAL POLITICS.

                                    Paper    323 P.
LINCOLN: UNIV OF NEBRASKA PRESS, 2013
SER: JUSTICE AND SOCIAL INQUIRY.


AUTH: MISSISSIPPI STATE UNIVERSITY.


LCCN 2013-22400
  **ISBN** 080324536X      **Library PO#**  FIRM ORDERS
                                    **List**      40.00   USD
  8395 NATIONAL UNIVERSITY LIBRAR         **Disc**       5.0%
  **App. Date**   1/07/15   COLS          8214-08 **Net**      38.00   USD


SUBJ: 1. AFRICAN AMERICANS--POL. & GOVT. 2.
AFRICAN AMERICAN MAYORS.

CLASS E185.615       DEWEY# 323.1196073   LEVEL ADV-AC

---

**YBP Library Services**

PERRY, RAVI K.

BLACK MAYORS, WHITE MAJORITIES: THE BALANCING ACT
OF RACIAL POLITICS.

                                    Paper    323 P.
LINCOLN: UNIV OF NEBRASKA PRESS, 2013
SER: JUSTICE AND SOCIAL INQUIRY.


AUTH: MISSISSIPPI STATE UNIVERSITY.


  LCCN 2013-22400
  **ISBN** 080324536X      **Library PO#**  FIRM ORDERS
                                    **List**      40.00   USD
  8395 NATIONAL UNIVERSITY LIBRAR         **Disc**       5.0%
  **App. Date**   1/07/15   COLS          8214-08 **Net**      38.00   USD


SUBJ: 1. AFRICAN AMERICANS--POL. & GOVT. 2.
AFRICAN AMERICAN MAYORS.

CLASS E185.615       DEWEY# 323.1196073   LEVEL ADV-AC

TABLE 2. Black mayors in medium-sized cities, 2000–2012

| MAYOR | CITY | 2010 POPULATION | PERCENT BLACK |
|---|---|---|---|
| Michael Bell, 2010– | Toledo OH | 287,208 | 27.2 |
| William A. Bell Sr., 2010– | Birmingham AL | 229,493 | 73.4 |
| William V. Bell, 2001– | Durham NC | 228,330 | 40.9 |
| Stephen K. Benjamin, 2010– | Columbia SC | 129,272 | 42.2 |
| Corey A. Booker, 2006– | Newark NJ | 277,140 | 52.3 |
| Carl Brewer, 2007– | Wichita KS | 382,368 | 11.4 |
| Byron W. Brown, 2005– | Buffalo NY | 261,310 | 38.5 |
| James T. Butts, Jr., 2011– | Inglewood CA | 109,673 | 43.9 |
| Ron Dellums, 2007–2011 | Oakland CA | 390,724 | 28 |
| William D. Euille, 2003– | Alexandria VA | 139,966 | 21.7 |
| Jack Ford, 2002–2006 | Toledo OH | 287,208 | 27.1 |
| Shirley Gibson, 2003–2012 | Miami Gardens FL | 107,167 | 76.3 |
| Cedrick B. Glover, 2006– | Shreveport LA | 199,311 | 54.6 |
| Henry W. Hearns, 2006–2008 | Lancaster CA | 156,633 | 20.4 |
| Melvin "Kip" Holden, 2005– | Baton Rouge LA | 227,818 | 54.5 |
| Edna Jackson, 2012– | Savannah GA | 136,286 | 55.4 |
| Frank Jackson, 2006– | Cleveland OH | 396,815 | 53.3 |
| Harvey Johnson Jr., 2009– | Jackson MS | 173,514 | 79.3 |
| Kevin Johnson, 2008– | Sacramento CA | 466,488 | 14.6 |
| Yvonne Johnson, 2007–2009 | Greensboro NC | 269,666 | 40.6 |
| Dwight C. Jones, 2009– | Richmond VA | 204,214 | 50.6 |
| Ronald Jones, 2007– | Garland TX | 226,876 | 14.5 |
| Samuel L. Jones, 2005– | Mobile AL | 195,111 | 50.5 |
| Mark L. Mallory, 2005–2013 | Cincinnati OH | 296,943 | 44.8 |
| John Marks, 2003– | Tallahassee FL | 181,376 | 34.9 |
| Rhine McLin, 2002–2010 | Dayton OH | 141,527 | 42.8 |
| C. Ray Nagin, 2002–2010 | New Orleans LA | 343,829 | 60.1 |
| Kasim Reed, 2010– | Atlanta GA | 420,003 | 54 |

*Sources:* U.S. Census Bureau figures, 2010; Joint Center for Political and Economic Studies, "Black Elected Officials Roster" (Washington DC, 2012).

ing of how black mayors have actively pursued policies designed to improve the quality of life of blacks in medium-sized, non-majority-black cities is limited, however. As noted, the existing scholarship often confines critical analyses of black mayors' efforts on behalf of black interests to particular issues. James R. Bowers and Paul C. Baker, for example, examine the efforts of William A. Johnson Jr., the first black mayor of Rochester, New York, (1994–2006), in respect to educational reform.[25] Huey L. Perry examines the efforts by Mayor Richard Arrington Jr., the first black mayor of Birmingham, Alabama, (1979–1999), in respect to crime and public safety.[26] Keenan D. Grenell and Gerald T. Gabris examine the efforts by Mayor Charles Box, the first black mayor of Rockford, Illinois,(1989–2001), related to economic development.[27]

Although limited in scope, the issue-specific approach to analyzing medium-sized city mayors' governance makes a significant contribution to our understanding of medium-sized cities in that it demonstrates that "when mayors of middle-sized cities exercise strong and vigorous leadership, they and their cities are better able to weather and mitigate the negative forces threatening their sustainability than are mayors who lead less energetically."[28] In chapters 5 and 6 I examine the impact that the black mayors of Toledo and Dayton have had (or have not had) on their black residents' general quality of life in respect to specific issues.

*Writing History: Toledo's and Dayton's Path to Black Mayors*

As they campaigned for mayor and the elections in November 2001, Jack Ford and Rhine McLin prepared to govern rust-belt Ohio cities with noteworthy demographics of their own. As table 3 indicates, while Toledo had a significantly larger population than Dayton, Dayton's African American population was substantially higher than Toledo's. In addition, Dayton had a much larger population of individuals and families living below the poverty level, suggesting that its black community had far fewer members of the middle class, despite having elected more black mayors than Toledo.

Of additional note is that Toledo had a higher median family income and higher educational obtainment, suggesting likely larger political contributions, a more liberal voting base, a higher number of persons seeking elected office, and more informed voter participation, among other variables. As subsequent chapters explore, Ford's and McLin's different paths to mayor and their different levels of success may in part be explained by the comparative economic disadvantages between Toledo and Dayton.

**TABLE 3. Dayton and Toledo: Selected U.S. census demographics, 2000**

| CITY | TOTAL POPULATION | BLACK | WHITE | MEDIAN AGE (YEARS) | PEOPLE OVER AGE 18 | AVERAGE NUMBER IN HOUSEHOLD SIZE | AVERAGE NUMBER IN FAMILY SIZE | PEOPLE WITH GRADUATE DEGREES |
|---|---|---|---|---|---|---|---|---|
| Dayton | 166,179 | 71,668 (43.1%) | 88,676 (53.4%) | 32.4 | 124,447 (74.9%) | 2.30 | 3.04 | 4,899 (4.9%) |
| Toledo | 313,619 | 73,854 (23.5%) | 220,261 (70.2%) | 33.2 | 231,488 (73.8%) | 2.38 | 3.04 | 10,597 (5.4%) |

| CITY | PEOPLE WITH BACHELOR'S DEGREES | PEOPLE WITH HIGH SCHOOL DIPLOMAS | UNEMPLOYED (NUMBER AND PERCENT) | FAMILIES BELOW POVERTY LEVEL | INDIVIDUALS BELOW POVERTY LEVEL | FAMILIES WITH FEMALE HOUSEHOLDER BELOW POVERTY LEVEL | MEDIAN ANNUAL FAMILY INCOME | MEDIAN ANNUAL RETIREMENT INCOME | MEDIAN ANNUAL HOUSEHOLD INCOME |
|---|---|---|---|---|---|---|---|---|---|
| Dayton | 9,578 (9.5%) | 32,110 (31.9%) | 7,090 (5.5%) | 18.2 | 23.0 | 4,809 (36.3%) | $34,978 | $20,578 | $27,423 |
| Toledo | 22,494 (11.4%) | 66,377 (33.7%) | 11,741 (4.9%) | 14.2% | 17.9% | 7,506 (35.6%) | $41,175 | $16,175 | $32,546 |

Source: U.S. Census Bureau, U.S. Census, 2000.

In chapters 3 and 4, I detail the racial, political, electoral, and governing climates of Toledo and Dayton. Here, I explore how those cities were "prepared" to elect black mayors by examining the cities' respective histories with black leadership, residency, and organizational development.

As table 3 indicates, candidates Ford and McLin ran for office in cities with limited economic vitality. The data in appendix A—which give percentages for people living below the poverty line, the college educated, and the votes received by McLin and Ford in the 2001 elections (among other statistics)—confirm the implications of the demographics noted above. In both cities, the higher the black population, poverty level, and unemployment rate, the larger the percentage of the vote the two candidates received. Conversely, the lower the percentage of college educated persons, the better Ford and McLin did in the elections. These data suggest how integral the black community vote was to their victories and in part explain their rise to power.

### Toledo's Black Community Development

Despite their small population, blacks have been an active citizenry in the Toledo area for many decades. In addition, progressive white Democratic leaders and the Progressive Era often aided the cause of civil rights and equal opportunity in Toledo throughout the twentieth century.

One of the earliest leaders assisting in the black community's striving for rights and access was Brand Whitlock. Whitlock, a minister to Belgium under President Woodrow Wilson, was a Progressive reformer and served as mayor of Toledo for four terms between 1905 and 1911. An author of eighteen books and an attorney, Whitlock is credited with extending the Progressive reforms of his predecessor, Samuel "Golden Rule" Jones. Notably Whitlock "attended and participated" in the National Conference of Concerned Citizens, a New York City multiracial conference on race relations organized by sociologist W. E. B. DuBois.[29] From this conference the National Negro Committee was organized in 1909. The committee was the precursor to the National Association for the Advancement of Colored People (NAACP). Whitlock's participation in and support of the organization in its infancy helped Toledo establish the third unit of the NAACP on February 2, 1915, and it still carries the distinction of being the third-oldest active unit in the national organization.

African American leaders within the NAACP in Toledo and several black churches in the area remained active in the social and political affairs of the city after the establishment of the NAACP chapter, with the support of several white mayors, including Whitlock, John Potter, Michael DiSalle, and others. While blacks in most other locales in the north and south were fighting civic leaders' racist policies and rhetoric, many white civic leaders in Toledo had long been supportive. However, such support came at a cost. Throughout its early days, the NAACP chapter in Toledo was often busy fighting off attempts by the Ku Klux Klan to march and rally on city streets. Moreover, in 1968, as the state of Ohio passed a fair housing ordinance, Toledo followed with an ordinance of its own under John Potter. Potter lost a bid for reelection after aggressively advocating for the ordinance.

Through the push and pull of Toledo's race relations between blacks and whites during the mid-twentieth century, blacks began to run for and successfully win local political offices and contribute greatly to the nation's business and music industry. Among Toledo's talented African Americans are the following: jazz pianist Art Tatum; artist and sculptor LeMaxie Glover; attorney J. B. Simmons, the first African American to serve on the Toledo City Council; and Ella P. Stewart, the first African American female to graduate from the University of Philadelphia as a pharmacist and who opened the first pharmacy owned and operated by an African American in Toledo. Casey C. Jones served as an Ohio state legislator from November 1969 to November 1995, representing Toledo's urban neighborhoods for over twenty years. The impact of Toledo's black community on the region is evident today. Even though the city's black population remains at less than 30 percent of the total, the black community has established (with congressional, state, and local support) active repositories of its history, including the Toledo-Lucas County Public Library's Art

Tatum African American Resource Center (established in 1989) and the African American Legacy Project, a nonprofit organization established in 2004 with significant support from then mayor Jack Ford. Other prominent black institutions that developed in the twentieth century in Toledo include the Northwest Ohio Black Media Association; two black newspapers (*Sojourner's Truth* and the *Toledo Journal*); the Frederick Douglass Community Center; the Northwest Ohio Black Chamber of Commerce (renamed the African American Bureau of Commerce); and numerous local units of national black fraternal or sororal organizations, including the Negro Women's Business and Professional Club, the Greater Toledo Urban League, and others. The strong organizational foundation within the black community in Toledo and its history with supportive whites led to significant black leadership achievements in the late twentieth century, including the election of Jack Ford as the first black city council president, the appointment of Crystal Ellis as the first black superintendent of the Toledo public schools, and the appointment of Michael P. Bell as the city's fire chief. These earlier and sustained examples of black leadership helped Ford's rise from city councilman to council president to state representative (replacing Jones) to mayor and (after mayor) to member of the Toledo school board and a 2013 candidate for city council. Such a history of power and influence and black relationships with key white constituencies made Ford's political rise possible and his governing strategy initially successful.[30]

*Dayton's Black Community Development*

Black community leadership and the McLin family name in Dayton are nearly synonymous. Beginning with the patriarch, "Mac" McLin, whose 1930s civil rights protests and political campaigns for office just an hour's drive north of the South resulted in house bombings and disparaging commentaries about his efforts, the McLin family has been active in Dayton politics, West Dayton, and the black community for generations. Mac's son, C. J., would become one of the most prolific state legislators in the nation as he represented the Dayton area in the Ohio State Legislature for decades in the mid-twen-

1. In her first bid for mayor in 2001, Rhine McLin's campaign literature captured her family's history in Dayton politics. Courtesy of Rhine McLin.

tieth century. C. J. McLin wrote and co-sponsored several bills of local, regional, and national importance to African Americans, including legislation encouraging the state of Ohio to divest from South Africa during the apartheid era and, notably, the state's affirmative action bill 584, which allowed the state to award 5 percent of state construction projects and 15 percent of state contracts for goods and services to minority applicants, making it one of the strongest such bills nationwide. C. J. McLin's family business included a highly successful funeral home in the Dayton region. In his shadow Rhine McLin, the eldest of his children, would face her own efforts to seek public office after helping her father run the funeral home. As C. J. described in his autobiography, "The most common perception of me is the champion of Black causes, and rightfully so. I have been wholeheartedly in the corner of my people because we are so far behind the rest of the nation. But, I have also championed the causes of many White people, women, other minorities, or whoever was on the side of what was right."[31]

Dayton's black community has often been larger than Toledo's, and Dayton has often been half the size of Toledo in overall population. With a population nearing 50 percent of the city's total, the black community in Dayton has long had a strong influence on area politics and community affairs. For example, Rhine was not the city's first black mayor but the third. One of her predecessors, James H. McGee, served as mayor (and a member of the Dayton City Commission) from 1970 to 1982, making him Dayton's longest-serving mayor. The other predecessor, Richard Clay Dixon, served from 1987 to 1994, losing a close election to Rhine's immediate predecessor, Mike Turner.

In addition to black mayoral leadership in Dayton since 1970, blacks have held integral positions in many other areas of civic, social, and political life. For example, Dayton's first black fire chief, Herb Redden, was appointed in 2008 by the city commission that Mayor McLin chaired. Like Toledo, Dayton has long had an active unit of the NAACP and other venerable organizations significant to black community advancement. One of these was the Dayton Urban

League, which suspended operations in 2010 due to a lack of funding.[32] It is not expected that Dayton will again have an affiliate of the Urban League. Despite its loss, other important and still active organizations remain. They include (among others) Parity, Inc. (which runs its own annual Black Leadership Development program for area residents); the Greater Dayton Minority Business Assistance Center; and the Greater Dayton African American Chamber of Commerce. Moreover, as a result of the city's proximity to two of the historically black universities in the north—Wilberforce University and Central State University—it has often had a large number of black intellectual leaders. Dayton's own Wright State University and University of Dayton, along with Sinclair Community College, have also educated a significant number of key African American leaders who have contributed greatly to Dayton's African American leadership development over the years. Such organizations and leaders in West Dayton's black religious community have helped Dayton maintain a key role in the advancement of black interests, particularly as share of the black's population has continued to rise.

This prolific cadre of black leaders and social service agencies has facilitated black leadership in Dayton's political and social arena. For example, in 1983 Lt. Col. Tyree Broomfield became the Dayton police department's first African American chief, nearly thirty years before Toledo promoted its first black police chief in 2011.

While the above discussion is not nearly the entire story of Dayton's and Toledo's black community development in the twentieth century, it details the strength of black leadership, which in most cases preceded the cities' election of the first female black mayor and first black mayor.

# CHAPTER 3

# An Ebb and Flow System

## Fluctuations in Black Political Advancement in Toledo

---

There's racism. . . . There is still a large percentage of this country as [there] is here in Toledo that is racist. They stereotype African American males by their manner of dress, by the clothes that they wear, and by the color of their skin.

Michael Navarre, former Toledo police chief

---

Described by native Toledoan and author P. J. O'Rourke as a city "in the middle of nowhere," Toledo is not often the focus of significant research or scholarship.[1] Toledo has a rich history, however. Nestled in Lucas County in the northwest corner of Ohio, a few miles south of what is now the Michigan border, Toledo developed as a result of a "war" known as the Toledo War or the Ohio-Michigan War. Early settlers fought without bloodshed in 1835–36 over which state had rights to the area. The genesis of the conflict was in the Northwest Ordinance of 1787, which set the southern boundary of Michigan Territory at a line drawn from the southern tip of Lake Michigan eastward to where it met Lake Erie. Later surveys determined that the southern tip of Lake Michigan was further north than previously thought.[2] Between 1787 and 1834 three different surveys were conducted, each resulting in different lines. The various surveys effectively created an area of approximately 450 square miles of disputed land between the territory of Michigan and the state of Ohio—what became known as the Toledo Strip.[3]

In 1812 Congress, hoping to end the dispute, authorized a survey of the boundary. The War of 1812 prevented the survey from taking place, however. Two additional surveys were conducted in subsequent decades by Ohio and Michigan. In 1833 the U.S. Senate sided with Ohio, but the House of Representatives refused to endorse the Senate's view. The governor of the Michigan Territory, Stevens Mason, proposed the formation of a commission to negotiate a solution, but governor Robert Lucas of Ohio refused to cooperate, and in 1835 the Ohio legislature formed Lucas County out of the disputed territory.[4]

In response Governor Mason dispatched his territory's militia to the disputed land. Governor Lucas responded in kind, sending Ohio's militia. Mason asked President Andrew Jackson to intervene; Jackson sent two representatives to negotiate a peaceful resolution to the conflict. The federal government's representatives suggested that Ohio and Michigan jointly govern the territory until Congress could decide the issue. Mason refused, intensifying the potential for bloodshed. As a result, President Jackson removed Mason as governor of the Michigan Territory, replacing him with John Horner.[5] Horner worked with Lucas to reach a conclusion. On June 15, 1836, President Jackson ratified an agreement between the two governors. Under the agreement Ohio would receive the disputed area, and the Michigan Territory would become a state and would receive nine thousand square miles of the Upper Peninsula. The state of Michigan's first convention of assent in Ann Arbor on September 26, 1936, refused to comply with the act of June 15, however. Michigan finally conceded on December 14, 1836, at its second convention of assent and was formally admitted into the Union as the twenty-sixth state on January 26, 1837.[6] The compromise gave the Toledo Strip to Ohio, allowing Toledo to be incorporated as a city within the state of Ohio on January 7, 1837.[7]

### Toledo's Political Culture

Toledo is part of a state with a varied political culture. Daniel Elazar describes the political culture of the state of Ohio in general terms as individualistic.[8] This designation suggests that the state's residents prefer that government involvement in residents' private activities, and particularly their economic affairs, be limited; they understand government to be solely for the purpose of serving the demands of the people. In considering the political culture of the Toledo area, however, Elazar notes that it is close to that of Michigan—a "moralistic" state in Elazar's typology—and has strong traces of a moralistic culture. A moralistic political culture emphasizes the good of society and measures good government in terms of the degree to which it promotes the public good. While the individualistic nature of the state is present in Toledo, then, morality takes precedence in northwest Ohio.

The political culture of Toledo is important to an understanding of the progression of race relations and the ebb and flow of racial tensions in the city throughout the mid-to-late twentieth century. If the city's majority-white residents generally believe that government actions should benefit everyone, it is to be assumed that government attention to race-specific issues will meet with suspicion.

### Early Black History in Toledo

At the time of the Toledo War, there were few black people in Toledo.[9] As in many other places in the urban North, black Americans began to arrive in Toledo in larger numbers during the Great Migration. Between 1910 and 1930 the black population in Toledo increased nearly 336 percent, to approximately 13,360 residents. During the same period the city's total population grew 64 percent.[10] The majority of the black newcomers came not from the Midwest, as the city's few early black residents had, but from the southwest and Deep South.

The growth of the black community in Toledo in the first three decades of the twentieth century was matched by a decline in the number of foreign-born whites settling in the city. Whereas upward of 12,300 foreign-born whites had arrived in Toledo around the turn of the century, this figure had dropped to around 2,200 for the period 1925–30.[11] Well before Toledo's black population reached significant numbers, Toledoans were expressing discontent with the city's black residents. In the Toledo Riot of 1862 a white mob of striking dockworkers attempted to drive blacks from the city.[12] Increased tensions resulted when the local NAACP was established in 1915. And in 1917 the city's leading newspaper, the *Toledo Blade*, lamented that its readers had to accept "Negro immigration as a permanent dilution of the white population."[13]

By 1930, when the significant migration of blacks to Toledo had nearly concluded, blacks were employed in semiskilled professions at increasingly high rates. Eighty-two percent of the city's porters were black, and 31 percent of janitors were black. Sixty-one percent of servants were black females, and 62 percent of elevator operators were black.[14] While these were blue-collar positions, they were a step up for many blacks used to struggling in the agrarian South.

Only 4.6 percent of the total Toledo population in 1930, the black community began to institutionalize as its residents became more prosperous. The first black church in Toledo, Warren AME Church, was established in 1847 with a few members, purchased a new building in 1943, and moved into it in 1950 with over one hundred members and a fanfare from twenty-five automobiles.[15]

Meanwhile, African Americans became increasingly visible in public roles. James Slater Gibson, installed in 1934, became the first black attorney in the city law department. James B. Simmons Jr., a Toledo resident since 1935, a member of Warren AME Church, and a recent graduate of the University of Toledo Law School, was elected the first black city councilman in 1945. He remained on the council until 1961, serving as the city's first black vice-mayor for the final two years. A founder of the Mass Movement League, an organization devoted to pursuing the civil rights of African Americans, Simmons was active in the early days of civil rights protests in Toledo. At a picket line in November 1942 fifty police officers stood watch, and a pregnant black woman was injured. The incident was a catalyst for the civil rights movement in Toledo, and later Simmons's call for justice drew a crowd of over fifteen hundred to a local black community-service agency, the Frederick Douglass Community Association.[16] Simmons is credited with forcing local hospitals, cab companies, telephone companies, and manufacturers to hire more African Americans and to promote them to more prominent positions. Other early black trailblazers include Emory Leverette, who was chosen as a principal within the Toledo Public Schools in 1955.[17]

*Race and Politics in Toledo in the Late Twentieth Century*

Though the city's black population had increased by the 1970s and black Toledoans served in some key roles, the city was not immune from the setbacks of the tumultuous post–civil rights decade, and socioeconomic problems persisted in Toledo's black community. In 1987 the *New York Times* chronicled the work of Rev. H. V. Savage, a white Toledoan who opened the Kitchen for the Poor in 1969 as a "free food center in the heart of Toledo's black district." The kitchen was intended to be "a temporary measure until economic gains took root from civil rights laws and Government antipoverty programs."[18] In 1970, 10,531 of 52,925 Toledo blacks—that is, about 20 percent—lived in poverty. By 1980 the number of black poor in Toledo had grown to 16,019, and it has since increased.

The times in which Savage created the Kitchen for the Poor in Toledo were volatile. On September 18, 1970, thirty-three-year-old white police officer William Miscannon, a three-year member of the force, was killed by a gunshot at point-blank range while on duty in front of the Toledo Black Panthers headquarters.[19] Shooting continued for over an hour. Troy Montgomery, a sixteen-year-old Panther, was injured. Panther John McClellan, twenty-five, was arrested and charged with the shooting following a "raid" in which fifty police officers participated.[20] McClellan was tried twice, but both trials ended in hung juries. A federal judge then eliminated the possibility of a third trial, citing double jeopardy. McClellan has always maintained his innocence. The police raid on the party headquarters resulted in several arrests, including that of Mike Cross, a leader in the chapter.

The 1970s and 1980s saw increased black political activity, which had largely been in abeyance since Simmons began to focus on his legal career in 1962. In 1971 an African American, Bill Copeland, was elected business manager of Laborers' International Union of North America, Local 500, a construction-based union with approximately one thousand local members. In 1974 Copeland ran for Toledo City Council and won. That same year George Davis Jr. was elected president of the American Motors Inter-Corporation Council.[21] In 1983 Copeland was elected vice-mayor, becoming the second black person to hold that title. Two years later he became the first African American elected to a county office when he became Lucas County recorder. In 1990 he became the first African American commissioner for Lucas County.

In 1986, a year after Copeland left the city council, forty-year-old Jack Ford, the executive director of Substance Abuse Services and president of the Mental Health Agency Insurance Trust, was nominated by the Lucas County Democratic Party to fill a vacancy on the council.[22] After a tie vote on the council regarding the vacancy in January 1987, Ford withdrew his name from consideration and decided to run for election to the council in November.[23] At the time of his election, he supported the development of "more and different" recreation programs for youth and an increased police focus on drugs. He said, "I'm a social worker and I'm interested in getting a little bit more of a social worker's philosophy on Council in delivering services."[24]

Though Toledo's black residents had advanced politically in the 1970s and 1980s, the city had grown increasingly racially polarized. With the advent of a new self-appointed black community leader in Rev. Floyd Rose, who founded Family Baptist Church in 1979 and served as its pastor, blacks in Toledo began to mobilize. One year after Ford assumed his role on the council, a group of ten local black ministers, two non-clergymen, and representatives of the NAACP were arrested at a city council meeting for occupying the seats reserved for city officials and refusing to leave for ninety minutes on June 28, 1988.[25] The group was protesting the suspension of four black city workers in the Community Development Department for alleged mismanagement of funds: the renewal commissioner within the department, Bernard "Pete" Culp, who was the brother of a locally prominent black pastor, had been fired, and the director of the department had been demoted. The protesters claimed that the accusation of mismanagement was really about a dispute between the city's priorities for the distribution of the federal government's Department of Housing and Urban Development (HUD) funds and those who supported the federal government's stated priorities for the money. According to Culp's supporters, "The men who got fired had actually been in charge of award-winning urban renewal developments, like Washington Village, which was what the funds were supposed to be used for." A white councilman complained to the *Toledo Blade* with a distinct lack of sympathy: "It's an old story that they can't do any wrong because they're black. We have to hire blacks because of affirmative action, but the problem is, once you do and they screw up you can't get rid of them." Five black Toledo ministers were arrested and charged with obstructing official business, and they went on trial over the bias protest.[26]

For many in the black community the suspension of workers in the Community Development Department was the climax of a host of other complaints. The Associated Press reported in the *New York Times* on August 14, 1988, for example, that a federal lawsuit had been filed on behalf of nineteen-year-old Walter Wade Jr. of Toledo with the purpose of "seeking an end to a new Police Department policy of randomly stopping and questioning black teenagers"—otherwise known today as the infamous "stop and frisk" policies within law enforcement departments nationwide. The policy's inception began with a letter from then police chief Martin Felker to members of a historic neighborhood association, the Old West End, informing the community that a deputy chief had been instructed to "pay close attention to groups of black juveniles." The letter explained, "Officers are to stop and identify these youths so that in the event an occurrence does take place, investigators will have the names of the juveniles." Republican mayor Donna Owens and city manager Philip Hawkey supported the policy. Melvin Jenkins, the acting staff director of the Federal Commission on Human Rights, called it "Neanderthal."[27] City council member Jack Ford tried to take a moderate approach in an effort to defuse the situation. According to a *Toledo Blade* editorial, Ford attempted to encourage the protesting black ministers to abandon their "counterproductive" strategy while at the same time urging Mayor Owens, Manager Hawkey, and fellow city council members to reach out to the black ministers, the black community, and their concerns.[28]

In a separate incident in 1989 a group of approximately seventy-five protesters attended a city council meeting on July 18 to highlight the "alleged discriminatory hiring and promotion by the city and alleged racist statements by Fire Chief William Winkle." Ford took action in that effort too, saying at the time, "There clearly is underutilization of women and minorities."[29]

The result of these incidents in the late 1980s was twofold. On the one hand, the Ohio State Advisory Committee of the U.S. Commission on Civil Rights launched an investigation and produced a report on race relations and municipal black employment in Toledo.[30] In 1988–89 blacks and other minorities accounted for 22 percent of all city employees in Toledo and women for 21 percent.[31] Dividing the city workforce into eight categories, the report established a template for future measurements of city personnel. Not surprisingly, it found that women were underrepresented in the administrative, protective services, skilled crafts, and service maintenance categories, while they were overrepresented in the office/clerical category. Similarly minorities, mostly black, were underrepresented in the administrative and professional category. The largest percentage of minorities worked in maintenance, followed by police and fire departments, where 18 percent of the workforce was African American.

The commission's plan recommended that the city administration "direct all city departments, divisions, and agencies to develop one-year and five-year affirmative action goals and objectives along with their budgets. The human resources director would correct problems [and] ensure compliance."[32]

While Toledo's black leaders considered this to have been a successful outcome, they continued to bring attention to issues in the black community. Hence an additional result of the council incidents was a ministers' boycott of local businesses, beginning with a major hotel chain in a key shopping district that had no blacks in upper management. This boycott resulted in the exodus of black bowlers from the National Bowling Association convention staying at the hotel in November 1988.

### Jack Ford on the City Council

At the time of the 1980s and 1990s racial incidents in Toledo, Jack Ford was either on the city council or a member of the Ohio House of Representatives, and in both cases he was an active advocate of the interests of African Americans. His service on the council is most significant, however, as many of the programs and policies he supported while on the council remained in place once he was elected mayor. As a councilman, Ford supported inclusion, diversity, fairness, and social justice, especially as these related to employment with the city, youth programming, and the health welfare of Toledo. Ford's positions on these issues were not only a result of strained race relations in Toledo, however; his background as a social worker also drew him to them.

Immediately after taking office in 1987 as the sole minority legislator on the city council, Ford started advocating on key issues on behalf of blacks. His first major proposal was to rename the downtown Cherry Street Bridge, which connected Toledo's east and west sides over the Maumee River, for Rev. Dr. Martin Luther King Jr. According to the *Toledo Blade*, in so doing, Ford "succeeded in a few minutes in accomplishing what others had failed to achieve for a year or more—winning agreement on naming an appropriate civic memorial for Dr. King."[33]

In addition, Ford cited the city manager system as a structure that limited opportunities for women and minorities, and he supported a grassroots strong-mayor movement to change Toledo's form of representation. Ford said the following of the city manager role: "What a lot of citizens want is a rock'em-sock'em mayor. Toledo is not a city manager town. Not in the 1980s. . . . Under a city manager form of government . . . the black community is tolerated, but is treated to reservation-type politics where they're lumped together and told this is your thing to do, just don't jump the fence. . . . The city manager can say 'I don't give a damn what the public thinks.'"[34] Ford did not get his wish in 1988. He even encountered resistance from members of the black middle-class community, who felt that earlier attempts to bring strong-mayor governance to Toledo had been ignored by city officials. Kenneth Spruce, founder of a "community-oriented black think tank," commented to the *Blade*, "I would be very careful about giving too much power to the folk downtown without them giving something back to us in the form of a district plan." Recognizing the skepticism of fellow blacks, Ford replied in a community gathering: "[A] strong mayor brings our political and administrative government closer to the people. But there is a responsibility that has to be matched by the electorate. The black community will not only have to register strongly, it will have to vote more. The day that black folks stop being foolish about not voting and begin to meet their civic duty, you'll see an automatic turnaround in responsiveness from city hall and county government because candidates look at that closely."[35] The issue went before voters on November 8, 1988, and was not passed. Toledo voters had rejected earlier strong-mayor plans in 1937, 1946, 1957, 1959, and 1986. The margin of defeat shrank from 33,809 votes in 1957 to 8,137 votes in 1986, however.[36]

Meanwhile, Ford actively discussed race relations in the city during his first year on the council. In a speech to the Jewish Federation of Greater Toledo, two weeks before the strong-mayor vote, Ford commented that race relations had never been "at as low an ebb" as they were at the time. Rekindling support for a failed 1984 effort to establish an Urban League, Ford said in 1989 that without "opportunities . . . for black men and women to exercise control," Toledo would "never be strong."[37]

Key agenda items of Ford's first year on the council included proposing an ordinance to make it illegal to sell drug paraphernalia, promoting a "guerilla-type war" against drugs, and increasing police efforts to tackle communities plagued by drugs. Also, when an estimated thirty people were affected by HIV/AIDS in Lucas County, he proposed an ordinance—the first for any Ohio city—that outlawed discrimination against victims of HIV/AIDS and those who cared for them.[38] Other initiatives included encouraging the Board of Community Relations (an independent organization chartered by the city that promoted social justice and intervened in conflicts by investigating allegations of discrimination) to urge the city manager to hire more minorities and women in administrative and managerial positions.[39]

While preparing to run for reelection to the council in 1989, Ford was nominated by local Democrats to run for mayor. He declined, citing the need to raise nearly $300,000 to unseat a "formidable" challenger in just eight months, the lack of mayoral power under city manager government, and his concern about the lack of minorities on the council should he win. Ford did indicate an interest in the office, however: "It is the mayor's office where the real action is at in dealing with local problems. I think anyone who is in politics at the local level would at some point entertain the idea of occupying the mayor's seat." He felt at the time that a black person could be mayor "if that candidate has everything that is required"; "everything" included "the ability to raise $250,000, the political organization, and the deep name recognition that comes from ballot longevity."[40] Though Ford concluded that 1989 "wasn't my time," he suggested he would run for mayor in the 1990s if the position were strengthened and included a four-year term.

Ford's key legislative initiatives on the council in 1989 included advocating that the city make a more sustained investment in affordable housing, especially in three thousand "abandoned homes," which he wanted the city to offer "at low cost to the working poor and welfare recipients."[41] In addition, Ford supported an initiative with minority contractors to "withhold support of the 0.75 percent income tax renewal"; he indicated, "Minority contractors were receiving less than $10,000 of about $30 million of business from the city annually."[42]

In pursuit of the initiatives that mattered to his legislative agenda, Ford developed a reputation for not being camera-shy. The *Toledo*

*Blade* wrote of Ford: "His news conferences are so frequent that some of Jack Ford's colleagues on Toledo city council have asked for copies of his press releases so they can respond to reporters' questions about them," and "Mr. Ford is not the sort of old-boy politician who plays the game quietly behind the scenes. When he's got something to say, he likes to say it in front of a camera."[43] In his early political career Ford used the media to his advantage. In his 1989 council reelection campaign, for example, he candidly answered questions posed by the *Blade* in reference to the city's "racial problems." Ford's responses indicated five steps he thought needed to be taken: "(1) Resolve the Pete Culp firing via settlement fair to both sides, (2) Shake up the Fire Department and the Police Department, which is more racist than the fire division, (3) Continue to hire quality minority candidates in visible jobs, (4) Strengthen the Board of Community Relations by making good appointments and heeding its recommendations, and (5) Develop a bottom-up community sense of obligation by black residents around the issues of housing maintenance, curtailed drug trafficking, and getting our children to stay in school and engage in more positive recreational and other civic activities."[44] These priorities indicate the social issues on which Ford would build his political career. The *Blade* offered him a strong endorsement for the council post on October 29, 1989.

After winning reelection, Ford continued to work on behalf of the black community. In 1990 he opposed the development of two construction projects off separate ends of Dorr Street, a historic street connecting downtown to outlying suburbs. Ford argued that the proposed projects—a 180-unit apartment complex and a shopping center—would negatively impact the character of several middle-class black neighborhoods.[45] He also successfully sought to increase the power of the Board of Community Relations. Finally, he proposed a ban on cigarette vending machines in most public places, especially where youth under the age of eighteen could access them.

The year 1991 saw Ford's introduction of legislation to require signs in bars warning of alcohol dangers for pregnant women, a revised plan for strong-mayor government in Toledo that included district council seats, and a proposal to establish a commission on youth to provide jobs, leadership training, and recreation for area young people. Up for reelection in 1991, Ford again won the endorsement of the *Toledo Blade*.

During Ford's third term on the council he became a media personality, hosting a local weekly cable television show called *Minority Monitor*. The program focused on such issues as the increase in the number of black males hired in ranking administrative roles for the city.[46] Ford also led a successful effort to create and pass a ballot issue establishing a youth curfew; he formed a committee to focus on lead-based paint; and pushed for more funding to eliminate lead poisoning, which disproportionately harmed poor children living in older, deteriorated homes in the inner city.[47] Along with other council members, Ford proposed a change to the city manager–council proportional representation system in which the mayor would be elected chief executive and an expanded council would include representatives from districts. Voters finally passed the amendment in 1993, electing former council member and vice-mayor Carleton Finkbeiner as the city's first strong mayor. Jack Ford was elected council president by his peers.[48] Running for one of six at-large council seats, Ford was again the only black candidate and was the top vote getter. African Americans were also elected to two of the six district seats.

With three blacks on the city council and Ford as council president, black Toledoans enjoyed a newfound political power, just as the city's demographics began to change. As table 4 shows, Toledo's African American and Latino/a populations have grown considerably since 1990, while the white population has declined. These conditions made local elected office viable for blacks in Toledo through the remaining decade of the twentieth century and into the twenty-first.

As the demographics began to shift locally and soon after Ford's election as city council president, Mayor Finkbeiner, with whom Ford had a "hot and cold" relationship, announced that he wanted Ford to run for the vacated state representative seat in district 48, a largely black district in central Toledo.[49] Casey Jones, the only black per-

TABLE 4. Toledo population changes, 1990–2010

| YEAR | TOTAL POPULATION | BLACK | WHITE | LATINO/A |
|------|------------------|-------|-------|----------|
| 1990 | 332,943 | 65,598 (19.7%) | 256,239 (75.9%) | 13,207 (3.9%) |
| 2000 | 313,619 | 73,854 (23.5%) | 220,261 (70.2%) | 17,141 (5.5%) |
| 2010 | 287, 208 | 78,073 (27.2%) | 186,188 (64.8%) | 21,231 (7.4%) |

*Sources:* Toledo population, 1990: U.S. Census Bureau, *Population of the 100 Largest Cities and Other Urban Places in the United States: 1970 to 1990,* table 22; Toledo population, 2000: U.S. Census Bureau, *County and City Data Book: 2000,* table C-1; Toledo population, 2010: U.S. Census Bureau, "2010 Census Interactive Population Search."

son from Toledo to have reached the state legislature, was retiring after twenty-six years. Ford, who had long acknowledged that he coveted the position, had promised voters that if elected council president, he would not seek the state representative seat. He reneged on this promise, however, and after eleven months as president of the council, Ford won the seat to the Ohio House of Representatives in November 1994 with 80 percent of the vote.[50]

### King Street?

While Jack Ford was often in Columbus, the state capital, Toledo experienced another racially polarizing incident around Mayor Carleton Finkbeiner's suggestion to name a major street after Dr. Martin Luther King Jr. in 2001. At the time Toledo was the only major city in Ohio that had not dedicated a street to Dr. King. The effort was welcomed by Toledo's blacks, yet not by many others. In 1986 civil rights leader Rev. Floyd Rose had pushed to rename Dorr Street—named for the city's tenth mayor, Charles Dorr, and home to one of the city's Fortune 500 companies and a major country club— after Dr. King. In preparation for the city's 2001 King holiday celebration, Mayor Finkbeiner announced his pursuit of the renaming: "We'd like to have total community support of it and to do it in the right way," the mayor said.[51] He appointed an all-black, seven-member advisory committee, chaired by the president of the local NAACP branch, to make recommendations within ninety days, and hold public meetings to gather input. The mayor also had an all-white committee of his own within city hall to review the all-black committee's recommendations.[52] In effect, then, an all-black committee was charged with making recommendations to an all-white committee, and then the mayor was to make the final suggestion.

Soon thereafter Mayor Finkbeiner suggested that the change be made on Cherry Street, a 2.5-mile street platted in 1827, ten years prior to the city's founding.[53] His recommendation was to rename the street "King-Kennedy Parkway" in honor of Dr. King and President John F. Kennedy. The recommendation had broad support, though not from some of the major businesses on the street. Yet Cherry was initially considered a better choice than Dorr Street, as Cherry was not named on behalf of an individual but for a tree that once grew along its length. Reverend Rose did not support the recommendation, saying: "I've traveled the length and breadth of this country; I have seen boulevards straight through the center of town in communities in the South. I've seen portions of expressways named for Dr. King, major thoroughfares for Dr. King. And I have never, ever seen nor heard of Dr. King having his named shared with anybody else—never." Without the support of key figures in the black community and select businesses along Cherry Street, the bid failed. Rose instead reargued his position that Dorr Street should be the choice, rejecting the claim that removing the name of a street for a former mayor was significant: "The irrelevant past must always yield to the relevant present . . . in any progressive society," he remarked.[54] Rose noted that Dorr Street made a good candidate for renaming given its surrounding concentrated black population.

In the end the all-black advisory committee made three formal recommendations to the mayor and ranked them accordingly. The first choice was to rename Toledo Express Airport the Dr. Martin Luther King Jr. International Airport. That recommendation would have required the approval of both the mayor and the board of the Toledo–Lucas County Port Authority, which operates the airport under lease with the city. Also, the Federal Aviation Administration would have had to weigh in. It would have been the first airport named for Dr. King. The recommendation had little support. The mayor noted that the airport was in Swanton Township and was "located far from the heart of Toledo's minority community."[55] This recommendation died.

The second suggestion was for the renaming of Collingwood Boulevard, a street that ran through a large section of the black community, crossing Dorr Street and passing through the city's historic Old West End neighborhood. Collingwood was also home to one of the largest majority-black public high schools in the city. Members of the Old West End Association, a majority-white neighborhood group, appealed to history and cited the street as the site where the famous phrase "Holy Toledo" was uttered, and it sidetracked the Collingwood recommendation. Moreover, Collingwood, the association pointed out, once was known as the "avenue of millionaires," as it ran through the neighborhood with the largest collection of Victorian and Edwardian homes east of the Mississippi River.[56]

The Collingwood Street recommendation resulted in racially polarized arguments. The all-black committee's recommendation was confronted by an all-white resident protest at a community gathering to discuss the issue. "I don't know any streets that have four words that I have to write out. For me, it's a huge burden," claimed one resident. Other residents insisted at length that their opposition was not about race and took issue with what they believed to be the suggestion of some black members on the committee that Dr. King was not important to whites.[57] At a subsequent public meeting in an overcrowded public library largely frequented by Toledo's black community and located on Dorr Street, blacks asked why Collingwood was not an appropriate choice. One resident, Dr. LaRouth Perry, a visiting assistant professor of Africana Studies at the University of Toledo, said, "I'm suspicious that there is camouflage about the reason. And I would like to have those things be aired. What is the real problem? I'm feeling, I'm sensing that whatever happens tonight, most of us will go out the same way we came in, and that will not be any progress. But I really want to hear why Collingwood is not OK. I hear that it's not. I just want to know why."[58] Some opponents at the gathering responded that Collingwood had history too. Many residents organized and placed yard signs in neighborhood association members' yards reading, "Keep it Collingwood." In addition, the *Toledo Blade* published an editorial rejecting Collingwood.[59]

The final recommendation of the committee was to rename Cherry Street after Dr. King but to drop the "Kennedy" portion of the mayor's proposal. St. Vincent Mercy Medical Center, a large hospital on Cherry Street, did not accept this proposal, nor did representatives of Central Catholic High School, located across the street. Both Catholic-based institutions were attracted to the King-Kennedy Parkway idea because Kennedy had been Catholic. The committee's suggestion that Kennedy's name be dropped also displeased major businesses. As a result, none of the committee's recommendations was accepted.

Mayor Finkbeiner later recommended naming Central Union Plaza, the city's Amtrak station, for Dr. King. While that decision also had to be accepted by the Toledo–Lucas County Port Authority Board, it received unanimous support from the board of twelve white men and one African American woman. The proposal garnered a mixed reaction from Toledo's black community, however. While Rev. Dr. Robert Culp, a member of the all-black committee, ultimately supported the mayor's recommendation, he noted, "The recommendation . . . was neither recommended by nor rejected by the [all-black] committee. It was just never presented to the committee." Culp added that his personal support was "lukewarmish, at best."[60] The compromise on the compromise was to incorporate other elements into the renaming, including the development of a circular street in front of the train station to be named in honor of Dr. King and a promise that space and facilities would be provided for an African American history museum. The amendments were accepted, and the recommendation was approved.

In *Multicultural Manners*, journalist Norine Dresser profiles the compromise as a major event and an example of race manners. Dresser highlights how the compromise resulted in positive discussion about race relations: "Public hearings and community debate ensue[d]. Rather than change the [Collingwood] street name, the committee creates the Martin Luther King Train Station, which also has space set aside for a future civil rights museum. From this resolution, a workshop is born called 'Building Relationships toward Racial Harmony' (BRRH) an organization of cross-racial conversation. Since May 2001, the fifty-member BRRH has met monthly, working on race issues in Toledo."[61] Dresser details how the group used *Race Manners*, Bruce Jacob's book about confronting race-related issues in the United States, as its guide. The group later invited Jacob to Toledo, and group members were so inspired that they created a *Race Manners* reading project, with over a dozen local agencies promoting the text and training facilitators, leading to over three hundred readers. Dresser uses the Toledo King Street controversy as an example of a "method [that] could serve as a model for other communities dealing with racial dissension."[62] Nonetheless, the city has named only a short street in front of the Amtrak station in Dr. King's honor, and the train station has yet to build a museum.

## Mayor Jack Ford

In 1992 Ohio voters adopted an amendment to the Ohio Constitution that limited state lawmakers to eight years in office. Thirty-six members of the Ohio House were prevented from seeking reelection to the House that fall. After two successful terms Ohio House minority leader Ford, who had been elected as leader of the Democratic Caucus in 1998, was term limited. Thus in the midst of the King controversy, state representative Jack Ford decided to run for mayor. He announced his candidacy in May 2001, only seven months before the election. Ford entered the race at the urging of Lucas County Democratic Party chairwoman Paula Ross, who did not want to support the better-funded, more conservative Democratic candidate, Lucas County treasurer Ray Kest. In a city where a Republican Party-endorsed candidate for mayor was intermittent at best and nonexistent in 2001, the Democratic Party's endorsement of Ford was significant. Ford's 2001 campaign theme, "Serious Leadership for Serious Times," was meant to address the pending impact of the

2. Ford's 2001 mayoral campaign literature. Courtesy Jack Ford.

shrinking national economy and the limited state and federal funds available to the city.

When he announced his candidacy, Ford indicated that his administration would be so inclusive and focused on diversity that an affirmative action office would not be needed. He said, "I believe in diversity, I teach it, I work it. I live it. A mayor should appoint directors and commissioners who believe in diversity and hold them accountable. I plan to work toward abolishing the office of affirmative action. If directors and commissioners do not hire, train, and promote fairly, they won't stay on my team."[63] Ford's comments were misinterpreted by some as suggesting that he wanted to literally abolish the affirmative action office. Hence he fielded calls from the president of the local NAACP and the city's affirmative action commissioner, to whom he explained that he was speaking figuratively.[64] Given Ford's long history as an advocate for social services, it is surprising that his campaign began with such a misunderstanding.

Such racial misunderstandings were largely absent from Ford's campaign for mayor, though the historic nature of his candidacy was obvious. Ford successfully courted votes from Toledo's white liberal

3. Ford's 2001 mayoral campaign literature. Courtesy Jack Ford.

community and from African Americans and other minority groups. Kest was initially believed to have won the Democratic primary, but a later recount indicated otherwise. In 1994 Ford had defeated Kest in the race to sit on the Democratic Party's state central committee. This time, however, Kest had the support of some African Americans as well, including an endorsement from a major black newspaper, the *Toledo Journal*.[65] Much of his support came from more conservative whites and select members of the business community. Ford, on the other hand, was endorsed by another black newspaper, the *Sojourner's Truth*, which had only recently been launched.[66] The city's main newspaper, the *Toledo Blade*, also endorsed Ray Kest. In fact in its November 4, 2001, endorsement of Ford's opponent, the *Blade* editorial board wrote, "A strong mayor is by definition his or her community's most outspoken advocate and cheerleader. But Mr. Ford simply does not appear comfortable in front of the cameras, and though he is not the sullen, wollen [*sic*] individual in person some believe him to be, neither is he at ease with the public relations obligations of the job. That could mean that he is better to be a legislator than a chief executive." The paper that a decade earlier described Ford as "not camera-shy" now labeled his 2001 mayoral campaign both "lackluster" and "benign": "Image is almost everything these days, but neither Ray Kest nor Jack Ford gives the impression of running on all cylinders. There's been no discernible or creative varooming of their mayor-wannabe engines. They lumber about, lowering the bar on what 50-somethings are supposed to look like, neither evincing the pizzazz or the healthy glow we're grown accustomed to seeing our current mayor exude." The *Blade*'s description of Ford was an apparent attempt to describe his professorial style of communication and perhaps his weight as well.

In a later acknowledgment of Ford's overwhelming victory, however, the *Blade* commented: "Race . . . clearly was not an issue in this campaign. When a candidate wins a head-to-head match-up with 60 percent of the vote in a city that is roughly 28 percent minority, he obviously appeals across the board and across the city."[67] The *Blade* is largely accurate in its assessment of the campaign's racial dynamics. Ford's victory was a landslide, as he won nearly every one of the city's twenty-four wards; Kest carried only one. Ford won 61 percent of the vote to Kest's 39 percent. In the predominantly black wards (8, 10, 13, and 14) Ford won 88.8, 85.8, 87.9, and 89.5 percent of the vote respectively. Yet even in the heavily white wards (3, 7, and 23) Ford won more than 50 percent of the vote: 50.7, 50.7, and 52 percent. (See appendix 1 for more analysis of the ward results.)

As table 5 indicates, content analysis of the *Blade*'s coverage of Ford's election campaign confirms that he did not suffer from an excessively racially divided portrayal or perception. Articles were coded on a Likert scale of 1–5, 1 being a negative mention of race, and 5 being a positive mention. Analysis of 192 *Toledo Blade* articles for the campaign period February 23, 2001–January 31, 2002, produced a mean rating of 3.51. This rating suggests that Ford's candidacy was not viewed by the media—and by extension the public—in overtly negative racial terms. The media seem not to have detracted from Ford's agenda-setting plans and goals related to diversity.

**TABLE 5.** Newspaper coverage of mayoral candidates Ford and McLin

| NEWSPAPER | NUMBER OF ARTICLES | TIME PERIOD | MEAN LIKERT SCALE RATING[a] |
|---|---|---|---|
| Toledo Blade | 192 | February 23, 2001–January 31, 2002 | 3.51 |
| Dayton Daily News | 61 | March 30, 2000–January 8, 2002 | 3.66 |

Sources: Toledo Blade articles were derived from a search at the Toledo–Lucas County Public Library by typing in keywords "Jack Ford" in the database of Newsbank and searching for articles discussing Ford's potential candidacy, candidacy, and swear-in ceremony. Dayton Daily News articles were derived from a search using the archival search database Lexis-Nexus by typing in the words "Rhine McLin" and searching for articles discussing the candidate's potential candidacy, candidacy, and swear-in ceremony under column headings "Full Text."

a The Likert scale runs 1–5, 1 being a negative mention and 5 being a positive mention.

While the *Toledo Blade* accurately identified Ford's broad appeal, much of his support came from the black community. As noted, where African Americans resided in higher concentrations, Ford received a larger portion of the vote.[68] As the election data suggest, Ford's broad appeal and black support were significant in 2001, a year that Ford labeled a high point in his first state of the city address.[69]

Though Ford's campaign was not itself racially polarized, Toledo's polarized racial and political history informed the conditions under which Mayor Ford entered office as the city's first black mayor. As figure 1 indicates, Ford's 2001 election results mirror the residential racial patterns in Toledo. Analyses indicate a statistically significant relationship between the percentage of black residents in a given ward and the percentage of the vote that Ford received in the 2001 election.[70]

As Ford campaigned, not only were the city's blacks and whites feuding over whether to name a street after Dr. Martin Luther King Jr., but a nearby community and parish in Sylvania, a Toledo suburb, was considering moving a house that had historic ties to the Underground Railroad.[71] That racial and political history did not determine Ford's agenda as mayor, however; it only highlighted the importance of it.

Ford understood he could not rely only on those who supported him if his administration was to be successful, so he was careful to quickly establish the relationships needed to support his agenda af-

FIG. 1. Relationship between Ford 2001 victory and black population

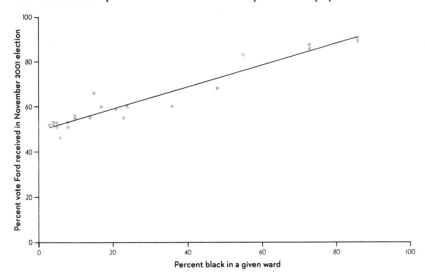

ter winning election. The twelve-member city council, meanwhile, elected an openly gay Latino as president (a Ford supporter). The council also included two black members elected from the districts. One of the first actions of the mayor-elect was to organize support in the business community. Claiming, "We're going to have a more business approach at city hall," Ford explained that he needed the support of business to govern effectively.[72] At the same time, his decision to tout the importance of business support may have been an acknowledgment of the expectations of many of his black supporters. One supporter told a *Blade* columnist that she "found a lot of comfort in Mr. Ford's plans." She explained: "He is setting out to deal with people, not things. The way his agenda sounds, 'things' might be taken care of because 'people' are addressed."[73] Hence Ford acknowledged that if major changes were to occur—principal among them filling budget shortfalls without cutting services—the business community would need to be involved.

Ford pledged to make Toledo "an elegant city."[74] In addition, he campaigned on a promise to spend 30 percent of his time on youth issues. His administrative priorities—perhaps best understood as an extension of his previous experience in social work, on the city council, and at the Ohio House of Representatives—reflected his interest in improving the socioeconomic condition of African Americans. Early in his term he verbally criticized the black school superintendent's performance. Citing a report that indicated the Toledo public schools had not moved up in a single performance indicator, achieving satisfactory performance on only five of the twenty-seven indicators used by the Ohio Department of Education to rank districts, Ford took issue with the superintendent's claim that the district was still identifying weaknesses: "He [the superintendent] should know [these] now," Ford remarked, "and I expect him to fix the weaknesses, pronto."[75] Other early initiatives included appointing a black woman minister to serve as executive assistant, an important feature in his efforts to involve churches in community service and government affairs. He also appointed a black chief of staff, another first for Toledo. Though he promised when announcing his candidacy that his chief of staff would be a woman, he appointed a male to the role.[76]

The racial climate under which Ford entered office was less than ideal. As he pursued an aggressive social improvement agenda over the course of his term, that climate arguably never improved. When Ford prepared to run for reelection, the county Democratic Party had a change in leadership, as Ford supporter and chairwoman Paula Ross was defeated by a more conservative faction led by former mayor Carleton Finkbeiner.[77] The loss of Ross as the head of the party meant that Ford was not likely to receive the party's endorsement. Perhaps sensing the shift in the party's direction, Ford never sought the endorsement. The party endorsed Finkbeiner, who organized a campaign, complete with yard signs, on the theme of "Carty Gets Results."

Meanwhile, Ford, along with other liberal Democrats, formed a PAC to raise funds and organize independent of the Lucas County Democratic Party. The party rift was labeled the "A-Team versus the B-Team" by media sources, the A-Team being those who supported a more liberal agenda and who had controlled the party for several decades and the B-Team being the more conservative Democrats who had filled vacant precinct committee seats in an effort to gain enough support to take over the position of chair.[78] Ford's A-Team lost its footing as one member of the team defected to run against him and Finkbeiner in the September primary. Ford placed a distant second to Finkbeiner. Though Ford's own campaign polls suggested that he would lose the upcoming election by a large margin, he nonetheless felt obliged to run, wanting to finish many projects already begun. His serious commitment to the race was questioned by members of the media and residents alike; many concluding that Ford had no enthusiasm for the job.[79]

Two weeks before the November election, on October 15, 2005, the National Socialist Movement, or "America's Nazi Party," a neo-Nazi organization, planned a march to protest alleged black gang activity in north Toledo. Ford spoke to a gathering of about two thousand people at a local black church the night prior to the planned march, urging people to ignore the neo-Nazis. His pleading fell on deaf ears. The next day, the planned march never began because the members of the organization were met by hundreds of protesters, most of whom were black youth, described as gang members in news reports.[80] The Toledo police and fire departments attempted to preempt the volatile environment by monitoring the situation in riot gear. Mayor Ford and the fire chief, Michael Bell, both African Americans, attempted to explain to the crowd that the group had the legal right to march and that the best response to the demonstration would be no response. Just as it seemed that Mayor Ford would calm the audience, however, isolated protesters began to set fire to nearby businesses and to loot, throwing bricks at police cruisers and yelling at Ford and Bell.[81] Dozens were arrested, and the rioting was broadcast on national television.

In the black community many people felt that Ford should never have allowed the neo-Nazis to enter the city or to plan a march in neighborhood streets. The riot proved a precursor to the inevitable defeat of Mayor Ford by his predecessor in November. Finkbeiner won the contest with 61.89 percent of the vote to Ford's 38.11 percent. In the predominantly white wards (3, 7, and 23) Finkbeiner won 76.48,

73.80, and 75.80 percent of the vote respectively. In the predominantly black wards (8, 13, and 14) Ford won 80.80, 80.55, and 86.7 percent—an average loss of 7 percent of support in the black community from 2001.

After Mayor Ford lost his reelection bid, other key African American leaders left Toledo and/or resigned their prominent positions in the city. Toledo public schools superintendent Eugene Sanders left to become the CEO of the Cleveland school district. Toledo school board president and vice-president Larry Sykes and Deborah Barnett chose not to seek reelection. Johnnie Mickler Jr., the founding director of the Urban League in Toledo, returned to South Carolina to run the Urban League of the Upstate and to attend to family matters. Fire chief Michael Bell was selected as the state of Ohio fire marshal and moved to suburban Columbus. At-large councilwoman and attorney Karyn McConnell-Hancock lost her reelection bid. And in 2008 the first black president of nearby Bowling Green State University, Dr. Sidney Ribeau, left the area to become president of Howard University. Whites replaced African Americans in all of these key Toledo leadership roles except for the director of the Urban League.

Meanwhile, three black employees whom he had fired sued Mayor Finkbeiner; they filed complaints with the Ohio Civil Rights Commission. After an investigation the commission found probable cause to believe that discrimination had occurred for engaging in "prior protected activity" in the firings of those three individuals, one of whom had been the director of affirmative action for the city.[82] In the midst of these racial conflicts between blacks and city hall, local civil rights leader and Baptist minister Rev. Floyd Rose returned to Toledo. Rose led a movement to establish a Toledo chapter of the Southern Christian Leadership Conference, with the director of affirmative action whom Finkbeiner had fired serving as head of the organization. Rose also pressed Toledo's blacks to reject the city's 0.75 percent tax renewal on the ballot on March 4, 2008. He argued—unsuccessfully—that the city was not worthy of the support of blacks because blacks did not receive fair treatment from the city: "This isn't about black and white. It's about what's wrong and right."[83]

*Black Municipal Employment*

While black community leaders like Rose fought for blacks' interests in Toledo's newspapers, neighborhoods, and churches, Mayor Ford attempted to help blacks sustain gainful employment with the city. His efforts and his successor's lack of a similar commitment are another example of Toledo's fluctuations in black political advancement.

Municipal employment, an example of political incorporation, is often cited as a key way in which mayors can exercise a substantive impact on the lives of black constituents. The number of blacks Mayor Ford employed during his term in office offers one example of efforts to sustain black political advancement in Toledo. After Ford took office, blacks' share of Toledo's municipal workforce increased in significant categories.[84] Data in table 6 confirm Browning, Marshall, and Tabb's findings that the presence of a black mayor has an impact on municipal employment.[85]

The table shows that from 2002 through 2005 blacks were well represented in the categories that tend to require more skills and training (i.e., executive and administrative, professional, technical, and protective service positions). While the largest percentage of blacks was found in the laborer category, blacks also made up a significant portion of protective service workers, for example. The average proportion of protective service workers from 2002 through 2005 was 18 percent, comparable to the result for the 2007–2009 years under Ford's successor, Mayor Finkbeiner. Though the percentages are equal, the salaries were not. While 28 percent of protective service workers in 2002–2005 with salaries of $43,000 to $54,999 were black, only 12 percent with salaries between $55,000 and $69,999 were black. Although the 2007–2009 data are not reported in the same detail, the salary discrepancies indicate that if the subcategories had been divided as in 2002–2005, the percentage of black protective service workers in higher salary ranges would be significantly lower than in 2002–2005.[86]

While Ford was mayor, blacks were also very well represented in the executive/administrative and professional categories, the two

**TABLE 6. Employment of blacks: Toledo city government, 2002–2005 and 2007–2009**

FORD YEARS: 2002–2005

| JOB CATEGORY | NUMBER OF WHITES | NUMBER OF BLACKS | PERCENTAGE OF BLACKS |
|---|---|---|---|
| Executive/ administrative | 60 | 24 | 27 |
| Professional | 140 | 29 | 17 |
| Technicians | 181 | 31 | 14 |
| Office and clerical | 276 | 93 | 23 |
| Craft workers | 109 | 21 | 16 |
| Operatives | 296 | 84 | 21 |
| Laborers | 106 | 136 | 54 |
| Service workers (protective: firefighters) | 252 | 80 | 22 |
| Service workers (protective: fire command officers) | 99 | 24 | 18 |
| Service workers (protective: police officers) | 392 | 101 | 19 |
| Service workers (protective: police command officers) | 110 | 19 | 14 |
| Service workers (non-protective service) | 77 | 35 | 29 |

FINKBEINER YEARS: 2007–2009

| | | | |
|---|---|---|---|
| Official and administrative | 79 | 23 | 21 |
| Professional | 294 | 54 | 15 |
| Technicians | 257 | 37 | 12 |
| Protective services | 646 | 165 | 18 |
| Paraprofessional | 0 | 0 | 0 |
| Administrative support | 203 | 80 | 27 |
| Skilled craft | 191 | 73 | 26 |
| Service: maintenance | 223 | 185 | 44 |

*Source:* City of Toledo, Office of Affirmative Action and Contract Compliance, Underutilization and Workforce Analysis Data, 2002–2005 and 2007–2009.

highest-skilled and highest-wage classifications. The percentage of black employees in both categories decreased in the 2007–2009 period, after Ford left office, with the largest decrease occurring in the category of executives and administrators. In Mayor Ford's years in office 27 percent of the administrators were black; near the end of Mayor Finkbeiner's last term in office, only 21 percent were black.[87]

These data are illuminating. Given that both Mayor Ford and Mayor Finkbeiner governed during poor economic times when layoffs were threatened, increases in taxes were debated, and the delivery of city services was downsized, the decrease in the number of blacks in higher-level job classifications under Finkbeiner cannot be blamed solely on economic conditions. Both mayors faced dim economic prospects, but only Ford aggressively diversified the city's workforce while balancing the budget annually. Ford's increased hiring of blacks as a black mayor supports evidence from earlier studies that found that "black employment and black labor force participation increase, black unemployment rate decreases, and the income of blacks rises after a black mayor takes office."[88]

*Resident Views on Black "Problems" in Toledo and Ford's Reaction*

Although the hiring of African Americans increased in Toledo's government under Ford's administration, it was not continued at the same rate once Carty Finkbeiner took office. Moreover, after Ford left the mayor's office, residents recalled Ford's ability to address "problems" in the African American community in a way that Finkbeiner did not. While details are discussed in chapter 7, I include some resident responses here because they add to our discussion on fluctuations in black political advancement. The varied responses in part explain why there has been an inconsistent effort to advance issues of the African American community in Toledo.

During 2008 I conducted a series of interviews in Toledo's black community. Interviewees included current elected officials and staff members in Ford's administration. Given prompts to describe life for African Americans in Toledo and the "major problems" facing them, most pointed to limited education and employment opportunities and—strikingly—"blacks themselves" as the problems. These individuals, whom most would describe as black leaders, initially had significant difficulty identifying "active and important" black organizations in the city at that time and people they would consider "black leaders." None of the people interviewed chose to identify themselves as leaders in the black community.

Despite some varying responses as to the "major problems," I categorized most respondents' comments in three areas: the economy, educational attainment, and black community values. Notably each of the respondents would be considered middle class, and arguably many of their commentaries on other blacks in Toledo were not so loosely veiled references to lower-class blacks. Black city councilman and former council president Michael Ashford, who represented a largely black downtown district, argued that the city had the oldest housing stock in the state of Ohio and that roughly forty thousand working poor were without health insurance, most of whom were African American. Ashford credited Ford's historic CareNet program as a significant boost to African Americans, giving them access to health care, but he suggested it was not well known through the black community as a program initiated by Ford or one that had a significant impact. CareNet, the first in the country, was a public-private partnership Ford initiated in his relations with hospitals when he was the director of diversity at ProMedica, one of the area's two major hospitals. With CareNet the two major hospitals came together to develop a health-care plan for those who did not have the resources to afford insurance.[89]

Ashford also indicated that competition for jobs between whites and blacks in Toledo, a blue-collar-based manufacturing city, heightened negative race relations during the Ford years and contributed to whites' views that Ford did too much for African American Toledoans. Meanwhile, blacks felt he did not do enough. Emphasizing that the state of Ohio lost more than a quarter million manufacturing jobs before 2008 (largely during Ford's years as well), Ashford suggested that many blacks and whites became fearful of losing their jobs, although most did not lose them. However, fear alone was enough to lay blame on Ford for a perceived poor local economy. Concerning people's perceptions of black problems in Toledo, Ashford said, "I realize right now especially in mid-sized cities you can't have a dumb president and a dumb leader at the same time," referring to former president George W. Bush and former mayor Carleton Finkbeiner. For Ashford leadership was key in improving the black experience in Toledo, and neither Republican Bush's federal policies nor conservative Democrat Finkbeiner's policies effectively addressed black problems. While in Ashford's view Ford's policies did effectively improve the black condition in Toledo, "No one knew it." Ashford blamed the local print and television media portrayals of African Americans, believing that these were "adding to the problem." Citing as an example a case in which a former black city councilwoman received front page news coverage in the *Toledo Blade* for not paying a parking ticket downtown, Ashford highlighted cases of white political executives and politicians who were convicted on more serious offenses and received little or no press coverage. Ashford summed up his perceptions of Toledo's black community this way: "There's limited opportunity in employment and anything else, [and there's] a perception that Toledo has not moved that far in race relations in the past two or three decades."[90]

Despite the major problems facing blacks in Toledo, in Ashford's view Ford did "very well" in addressing such issues. Ashford cited Ford's "weekly checklist on neighborhood issues" as an example of Ford's being "very present" on the ground in Toledo, surveying vacant houses, checking on progress on street cleaning projects, and ensuring neighborhood quality by ticketing home- and landowners for high grass and ordering city crews to cut it. For Ashford, Ford's biggest contribution to blacks in Toledo was helping them to receive a higher percentage of the $100 million in annual city contracts. Prior to Ford's tenure, "less than 3 percent of contracts went to minorities.... [Ford] made sure there was a fair playing field." In addition, Ashford, who labeled Finkbeiner as "racist and rude" and noted that he was regularly sued for discrimination while mayor, suggested that Ford was the focus of constant "negative attacks" from former mayor Finkbeiner, who benefitted from a weekly local television show on an *ABC* affiliate station in Toledo; the former mayor hosted *Carty and Company*, a Sunday morning public affairs show; and had a Monday television commentary entitled "It's Just Not Right" to promote his ideas. He kept these positions until May 2005 as he prepared to run against Ford. Ashford believed Finkbeiner used the platforms mainly to criticize Ford: "There's a good old boy network . . . but Ford did what Obama is doing right now—he surrounded himself with smart people, and he made sure blacks were included." Ashford suggested that Ford's efforts with blacks led to a significant group of construction trades people working hard to remove Ford as "the street repaving industry was against Ford's . . . goals."

For Wilma Brown, a longtime former district 1 city councilwoman and city council president, the major problems facing blacks in Toledo were "African Americans themselves . . . Anytime there is someone trying to improve the city, there are still a lot of naysayers. If you have a black business, they would rather go to the suburbs than support their own. We don't support our own." Brown felt that blacks had abandoned the very politician who had helped them the most simply because "Jack was not outgoing." As a result, Brown surmised, "Some people were not following his lead. I don't think the black community gave him as much support as they should have. He really believed in education, entrepreneurship for the young. He created a program where they were given lawnmowers, but most did not pay back loans. He believed in diversity and gave a lot of African Americans chances to work for the city. . . . He believed in people, and I think he still does."[91]

Describing Toledo politics and black opportunity in Toledo as being largely governed by unions and their significant financial influence on political campaigns, Brown insisted, "They [Toledoans] really are not ready for blacks to be in charge. . . . You always have to be 150 percent better than a white person to get any position, and then you always have to prove yourself." Describing the opinions in the black community on Ford, Brown commented that "after [Ford] got in there, it [was] like a barrel of crabs—anytime you start to get ahead, they pull you back. They always want more. They criticized him that he didn't smile. . . . Whites thought he was getting too much power; blacks were just jealous."

For Yulanda McCarty-Harris, Ford's director of affirmative action, the major problems in the black community were "unemployment, education, and access." Charged with leading Ford's effort to help ensure that minorities received a significant share of city contracts, McCarty-Harris noted that projects under $40,000 would not have to get a bond. "But [Blacks] can't get bonded, credit's horrible, no assets, no capital."[92] Thus despite early efforts to lower the bond threshold, Ford's administration yet had to work to increase the likelihood that black contractors seeking city contracts would get bonded.

Jay Black, the chief of staff for Ford and the first-ever black chief of staff, described the problem in the black community in Toledo as a bifurcation between education and income, indicating that "after the 1980 census, Toledo had a per capita income above the national average and was the highest in Ohio; meanwhile, the average educational attainment was below the national average."[93] Black noted that because of the manufacturing, union-based industry that dominated Toledo, the area for decades had done well when many other cities, particularly during the Reagan era, had not. He felt that African Americans were too poorly educated yet made a livable wage, resulting in active but ill-informed politics and policies regarding blacks.

For Fletcher Word, the editor of the *Sojourner's Truth*, Ford's efforts to ensure black progress may have been viewed by whites as too aggressive, leading to a significant effort to unseat him. Word described Ford as very bright, much brighter than Finkbeiner. He suggested that people understood that Ford had good political judgment and "they liked that," but he also "had a picture of Malcolm X in his office; I think he rapidly lost the backing of white leaders when he got into office."[94]

As the above interviews indicate, in the views of black leaders in Toledo, Ford made significant progress in addressing black problems on education, unemployment, and neighborhood issues. However,

Ford was hindered by a poor economy and a volatile political environment, including a fracturing of the local Democratic Party, which, when unified, had assisted his win in 2001 but, once divided, largely contributed to his loss. In addition, Ford's characterization as a man who was "not outgoing" and one who "didn't smile" was regularly contrasted with that of Carty Finkbeiner, who hosted two energetic weekly television shows on Toledo issues that highlighted his own controversial personality. For these interviewees the contrast in styles between Ford and Finkbeiner was significant. Ford's subdued style allowed him to get much accomplished for the black community through quiet political judgment, whereas that same style hindered his effectiveness as a candidate for reelection against a boisterous Finkbeiner. (Chapter 5 revisits Ford's efforts to address major problems in the black community, with a focus on his minority contracting program.)

The oscillations of race relations and the presence of effective and mobilized black leadership in Toledo are profoundly affected by certain macro-level factors affecting Toledo and other rust-belt cities. According to one report, Toledo in the recent past has had the third-highest rate of black unemployment in the nation.[95] Unemployment for the city is the highest of all the major cities in the state of Ohio.[96] Meanwhile, blacks' share of the total population increased from 24.5 percent in 2001, when Mayor Ford took office, to over 26 percent in 2006, when he left office.[97] The poor economic conditions in Toledo—the home of Jeep, Libbey Glass, Owens Corning, the Toledo Ticket Company, and other nationally known companies—have resulted in a poor economic outlook for the city in the future. If history is any precedent, the likelihood of race relations improving depends largely on the economy.

# CHAPTER 4

# Are We "to Be" or Not?

## The Push and Pull of Race in Dayton Politics

---

It is a struggle; for though the black man fights passively, he nevertheless fights; and his passive resistance is more effective at present than active resistance could possibly be. He bears the fury of the storm, as does the willow tree.

James Weldon Johnson

---

The history of race and politics in Dayton has been marked not by gradual progress toward better social and political harmony but rather by the push of racial progress alongside the pull of racial prejudice. During the 1970s and 1980s, when other medium-sized and large Midwestern cities with minority-black populations elected black mayors, Dayton did too, first appointing James McGee in 1970 and then reelecting him through 1982. McGee would become Dayton's longest-serving mayor. McGee, an attorney, had previously served as a city commissioner, replacing the city council's first black member, Don Crawford, who had been elected in 1961. Dayton also sent black politician C. J. McLin Jr., Rhine's father, to the Ohio House of Representatives in 1966. A powerful black politician in the state of Ohio, McLin would later become a special adviser to Ohio governor John Gilligan and an active voice on behalf of the black community in Dayton and throughout the region.[1] Alongside this progress in black political empowerment, however, a number of incidents revealed the extent of racial prejudice in Dayton. In 1963, when the black family of James Fuller moved into the Townview section of Madison Township, a

Dayton suburb, a small riot by white protesters ensued, to which a hundred riot-trained members of the police department responded. In September 1966 a black Dayton resident named Lester Mitchell was killed while sweeping his sidewalk at 3:00 a.m. He was shot in both eyes, and witnesses claimed that Mitchell was the victim of a drive-by shooting by white assailants. Race riots ensued, with more than a hundred black protesters and over one hundred arrests.[2] Following an investigation that showed a drive-by shooting to have been impossible, the riots inflamed again and were only calmed after Mayor Dave Hall called in a thousand members of the Ohio National Guard to maintain the peace.

### Dayton's Political and Social Culture

Like Toledo, Dayton is marked by the individualistic political culture of the state of Ohio. According to Elazar, however, Toledo's political culture is more deeply embedded than Dayton's.[3] A marked difference between the two cities is that Toledo is known to have more of a general commitment to all things communal, whereas Dayton does not. Thus the conditions under which a black mayor may successfully advocate for and implement policies of interest to black residents may be different in Dayton than in Toledo.

Phineas Myers describes Dayton as a city with a southern culture and a northern geography: "It has been said that Dayton is a northern city with a southern exposure. . . . We are close to the Mason-Dixon Line and have absorbed some of the South's prejudices. But we are far enough north so that these hot prejudices are tempered by the cooling breezes of racial tolerance and understanding."[4] For Myers, a white founding member of Dayton's chapter of the National Urban League, the city's geographic location and emotional context have fostered a unique environment that could potentially serve as a role model for better race relations in other cities. Noting that Dayton race relations in the 1940s and 1950s were tense, Myers explains how they subsequently developed, indirectly highlighting Dayton's differences from Toledo: "What has made the race situation in Dayton more tense than in cities farther north is the fact that with

the Negro migrants who came seeking not only employment but freedom from persecution as well, came also the Southern whites seeking employment in our factories and who found competition from
Negro workers here. And the mountain whites of Kentucky and Tennessee are perhaps the most race conscious of all southerners."[5] Myers believes that this confluence of southern blacks and Appalachian
whites migrating to Dayton in the 1940s and 1950s helps to explain
the city's contemporary racial unrest.

Other scholars agree that the presence of Appalachian whites has
contributed to racial tension in Dayton. Bertram Levine notes, for
example, that "thirty-five thousand newer white immigrants from
Appalachia reinforced a solid core of people opposed to [school] desegregation [in the 1970s]."[6] While proponents of segregation were
numerous in Dayton, the city's segregated culture was not systemi-
cally organized. Writing in 1959, Myers describes the segregation of
Dayton in the 1940s and 1950s as largely random, following northern
custom in some areas and southern Jim Crow practices in others: "In
line with most cities so close to the south, we practice segregation in
housing, schools, churches, recreation, and hospitals. Transportation has never been restricted in Dayton. We have never had Jim
Crow cars even though hotels and restaurants are definitely segregated. We are southern in our eating but northern in our riding. Our
prejudices are all mixed up with our emotions, a difficult psychological background. Reason plays no part."[7] While Dayton's buses
were not segregated, the city had no black bus drivers prior to 1960.
In accordance with its conflicting racial environment, Dayton's mid-
twentieth-century political and social culture can be appropriately
described as in flux between understanding and prejudice.

### Early Black History in Dayton

The presence of African Americans in Dayton dates back to 1798,
when a Dayton township tax document mentioned "William Max-
well and his negro."[8] While there were few blacks in Dayton, free
blacks were migrating to cities elsewhere in Ohio in large numbers.
In 1804, therefore, the state passed the Act to Regulate Black and

Mulatto Persons, requiring blacks entering Ohio to provide documentation proving their freedom. In addition, no white resident could employ an African American without a certificate of freedom, as slavery was forbidden under the provisions of the Northwest Ordinance of 1787.

Many scholars have noted the significant role that the "free" state of Ohio played in the freedom quest of enslaved African Americans who tended to cross into Ohio via the Ohio River on their flight from the South. According to A. W. Drury, the location of Dayton made the city a popular stop on the Underground Railroad, and this factor in turn "tended to keep at high tensions the excitement over the slave issue." Drury cites race riots in 1836 and 1841 "in which Negroes were driven away, their houses destroyed, and the sympathizing abolitionists mobbed."[9] In 1841 a white mob attacked "a disreputable colored resort" in southwestern Dayton, and one attacker was killed in the fray. Subsequently "a number of houses occupied by Negroes were burned." In this atmosphere of riot and tension, some blacks were forced to leave the Dayton region altogether.[10] Even beyond the threat of violence and property damage, early black Daytonians' lives were severely restricted. As a consequence of the so-called Ohio Black Laws, no free black could enter Ohio until two white freeholders posted a $500 bond guaranteeing his or her good behavior. Black residents of Ohio could not testify in trials involving white people, serve on juries, enter the state common schools, or serve in the militia. First enacted in 1804, Ohio's Black Laws sought to severely limit the freedom of free blacks.

These restrictions did not deter some blacks escaping slavery from stopping in Dayton and making the city home, however. By 1820 the U.S. Census reported 141 free blacks in a city with 1,139 residents.[11] By 1875 the Dayton black population had grown to 548 persons, while the city's population stood at 30,473.[12] As the population grew, so did the number of black organizations. During the period between 1820 and 1875 blacks in Dayton developed the American Sons of Protection, the Wayman Chapel AME Church, the Prince Hall Masonic Ancient Square Lodge No. 40, the United Daughters of Zion, and the

Lincoln Guards, among other organizations. The black population of Dayton continued to grow during the latter part of the nineteenth century and the early decades of the twentieth. By 1920, 9,052 blacks were recorded in the U.S. Census, a significant increase from the 901 reported in 1890.[13] With this population growth came the founding of churches such as Allen AME Church, St. Margaret's Episcopal Church, and Bethel Baptist Church, as well as the West Area YWCA, associated with Eaker Street AME Church. Dayton's first black police officer, William Jenkins, was hired in 1897. By 1910 the city had three black police officers.

The city's first black newspaper, the *Dayton Forum*, was published in 1913, the same year that a great flood severely damaged the property of black businessmen and the homes of many blacks. With three days of rain totaling over nine thousand gallons of water, the flood, which killed seventy-nine people, covered much of Dayton with twenty feet of water. According to Myers, the flood had a great impact on race relations: "It made little difference then whether or not the man who was rowing a boat to take you out of the second story window was white or black. You got in to the boat and prayed that it wouldn't be swamped before it got to the nearest riverbank, which looked miles away across the swollen yellow torrent. And you thank God that a Good Samaritan whether yellow or red white or black had braved the flood to rescue you."[14]

By 1940 the black population had reached 20,273, and black participation in community organizations had increased; by 1944 Dayton's black population had grown by nearly 50 percent compared to 1940.[15] Dayton's League of Colored Women Voters was established in 1921, the Delphinium Garden Club in 1931, and the Omega Chapter of Alpha Kappa Alpha Sorority in 1934. By 1960 Dayton's total population had grown to 262,332, with 57,288 blacks, 95 percent of whom lived in West Dayton.[16] During 1940–1960 the all-black Regal Theater was opened, the Southern Christian Leadership Conference and Dayton Urban League were formed, and blacks were admitted to the apprenticeship program at National Cash Register. Early-twentieth-century race relations in Dayton were generally calm and respectful. While racialized incidents did occur, they were comparatively infrequent. Blacks slowly built their community west of the river in Dayton, apart from whites. The DeSoto Bass Courts, a segregated apartment complex, was developed in the 1940s.[17] More organizations formed, including the South Side Civic Association, the Dayton Alumni Chapter of Kappa Alpha Psi Fraternity, and the West Dayton Area Council.

The early-twentieth-century expansion of black social and political activity, as evidenced through the rapid development of a black cultural community, was tempered by the ongoing influence of racial prejudice. In 1945 a riot brewed but was successfully averted. After a young black woman was hired as a drill-press operator at a local war plant producing materials for World War II, white citizens went on strike in protest. Myers references the event as a racial setback. Later that same year a white guard killed a "Negro elevator operator." According to Myers, while both incidents could have resulted in riots, they did not. Instead a biracial ministerial alliance calmed Dayton's West Side black community. In response to the incidents, mayors appointed race relations committees to address the problem, but such efforts were short-lived.[18]

With the civil rights era dawning, blacks in Dayton began to push for racial tolerance and to more actively and successfully engage in politics. In 1947 C. J. McLin Sr., Rhine's grandfather, became the first black person to run for Dayton City Commission. In 1950 Fred Bowers was elected to the Ohio House of Representatives. And in 1952 Rev. J. Welby Broaddus became the first black elected to the Dayton Board of Education. Offsetting these early political successes, a faction of blacks protested in front of city hall in 1954 over the lack of fair treatment and equal employment opportunities for blacks in Dayton. While the group was credited with increasing loan activity and jobs for blacks, its organizer lost his dry cleaning business after white suppliers "refused to sell to him."[19] Most black businesses, which were located on Fifth Street in West Dayton, remained strong, however. Fifth Street became known as the "center of black life," with more than seventy black-owned and -operated businesses by 1940.[20]

In the 1950s the push-and-pull pattern of Dayton race relations became even more evident. By 1950 Dayton's black population stood at 14 percent of the total population: 34,151 out of a total of 243,872 residents.[21] The 1950s was an era of the "omnipresent reality of race" in Dayton, according to native Daytonian and scholar Manning Marable.[22] A "predominantly blue-collar, working-class town, situated on the banks of the Great Miami River," Dayton was, according to Marable, divided by class and race. "Beneath the divisions of income, religion, and political affiliation," Marable writes, "seemed to be the broad polarization of race." He explains: "There appeared to be two parallel racial universes which cohabited the same city, each with its own set of religious institutions, cultural activities, social centers, clubs, political organizations and schools. African Americans generally resided west of the Great Miami River. The central core of the ghetto was located along the corridors of West Third and West Fifth Streets."[23] For Marable, who grew up on Dayton's West Side in the 1950s and 1960s, race was a prominent aspect of life. While the West Side black community "existed largely in its own world, within the logic of institutions it had created to sustain itself,"[24] race relations on the other side of the river were tense: "White taxicab drivers often avoided picking up black passengers at the train station. Very few blacks were on the local police force. Black children weren't permitted to use the public swimming pool on Germantown Pike. In most aspects of public and private life, whites acted toward African Americans as 'superiors,' and usually expected to be treated differently. . . . There was always an unbridgeable distance between us. . . . Whites were omnipresent in our lives, frequently as authority figures. . . . Race existed as a kind of prism through which we understood and saw the world, distorting and coloring everything before us."[25]

*Race and Politics in Dayton in the Latter Twentieth Century*

By 1960 Dayton's black population had reached 74,284, 28 percent of the total population, which was decreasing due to white flight.[26] C. J. McLin Jr. and Crawford were again elected to key political positions, but racialized incidents and riots continued. In November 1964 Dr. Martin Luther King Jr., along with Andrew Young, visited the University of Dayton for Dayton's Freedom Forum, sponsored by Rev. George Lucas of Bethany Baptist Church. King delivered an hour-long oration to an audience of more than 6,500. The city commission's sole black member presented King with a key to the city, noting that "there were many streets and neighborhoods in the city that the key wouldn't open."[27] The comment, fueled in part by frustration with the Dayton City Commission's failure to pass an NAACP-proposed fair housing ordinance earlier that month, outraged fellow commissioners, who thought Crawford had embarrassed the city with the comment.

In June 1967, following a speech by H. Rap Brown, the new chairman of the Student Nonviolent Coordinating Committee, riots broke out in West Dayton. According to newspaper reports, Brown made inflammatory statements, including, "The honky is your enemy. . . . You better shoot that man to death. . . . That what he's been doing to you." These remarks triggered two nights of rioting, with police estimating damages of $150,000.[28] Ray Alexander, who was a high school student at the time, recalled in a newspaper article: "It was fiery. Folks were fired up. As soon as the speech broke up, somebody threw a brick. Next thing you knew, it just got out of hand. . . . They were opportunistic. They'd riot, burn, loot. Some people, that's all they know to do. . . . I remember police chasing us."[29] No injuries were reported as a result of the riots.

In September 1967 Robert Barbee was shot and killed by a vice squad detective in the city center.[30] Barbee was a black Social Security representative carrying a pipe that the white officer mistook for a weapon. A year later the officer was acquitted of manslaughter; the acquittal drew over five hundred protesters, mainly black, to city hall and nearby police headquarters. In addition, a North End black neighborhood was burned and looted in 1967.[31]

While 1970 saw the appointment of the city's first black mayor, 1972 brought the Dayton Public Schools bus desegregation case. The key issue was that Dayton's public schools exhibited de facto segregation in violation of Ohio law. In December 1971 a liberal school board attempted to institute a plan to desegregate the school system. It adopted a series of resolutions committing itself to an integrated system in the fall of 1972. The resolutions, many thought, were a necessary step to confront the school system's segregated culture. One such resolution was for "every reasonable and constructive measure" to be taken to "eliminate racial imbalance."[32] The resolution was followed by an aggressive desegregation plan for the district, which at the time had a 42.7 percent black student enrollment in 1971–1972 and in which 75.9 percent of black students were assigned to one of the twenty-one all-black schools.[33] Little action was taken on the desegregation plan, however, because voters in Dayton elected a more conservative school board. That board soon fired the superintendent who had helped to draft the integration plan and later rescinded the plan's implementation schedule. With the backing of the local NAACP, Dayton parents sued the board of education and related parties in U.S. District Court, claiming the board had created "a deliberate pattern of segregation" that violated the Fourteenth Amendment.[34] Although the district court dismissed the suit, ruling that there was not sufficient evidence that the racial separation was the fault of or caused by the school board, the case eventually made its way to the U.S. Supreme Court after the Court of Appeals reversed the district court decision.[35]

Sixth Circuit Court of Appeals chief judge Philips, writing for a three-judge panel, concluded that the district court's decision was within the law but rejected its desegregation plan as not aggressive enough.[36] The appeals court found that since *Brown v. Board of Education*, the Dayton board had operated a racially segregated dual school system. Moreover, the Dayton board had been constitutionally required to disestablish that system and its effects since *Brown* but had failed to do so. Finally, the court found that the school board's failure to uphold *Brown* had had widespread "segregative effects" across the district, and it mandated a system-wide remedy. On two separate occasions subsequently Chief Judge Philips remanded the case back to the district court on the grounds that its proposed desegregation plan was inadequate to eliminate all system-wide vestiges of the segregation. This decision was appealed by the school board to the Supreme Court.

At the Supreme Court the justices cited the lower Sixth Circuit Court of Appeals' prior ruling "that the racial separation had been caused by the Board's own purposeful discriminatory conduct." At the same time, the court affirmed the case of the parents and the NAACP and determined that certain actions by the Dayton board amounted to a "cumulative" violation of the Fourteenth Amendment.

In the end the case was remanded to the district court, which ordered the Dayton Board of Education to take the necessary steps to ensure that each school in the system would roughly reflect the system-wide ratio of black and white students. The appeals court approved the system-wide plan for desegregating the Dayton public schools in *Brinkman v. Gilligan*.[37] On appeal from the Dayton Board of Education, the U.S. Supreme Court affirmed the judgment of the Court of Appeals, finding the following in 1977: "The public schools of Dayton are highly segregated by race. In the year the complaint was filed, 43 percent of the students in the Dayton system were black, but 51 of the 69 schools in the system were virtually all white or all black. . . . Every school which was 90 percent or more black in 1951–52 or 1963-64 or 1971-72 and which is still in use today remains 90 percent or more black. Of the 25 white schools in 1972-73, all opened 90 percent or more white and, if open, were 90 percent or more white in 1971-72, 1963-64 and 1951-52."[38] At the time that the school desegregation case reached the Supreme Court, Dayton had a black mayor but a conservative school board, which had continued to file appeals to various forms of integration rulings as the NAACP pushed for a more aggressive desegregation plan. Hence the racial and political climate in Dayton encompassed both the pulling back of the school board's appellate process and the pushing forward of the local NAACP.

Finally, on September 2, 1976, schools in Dayton opened under the new court-ordered busing plan. The plan mandated that "each school must be balanced racially within a 15 percent margin of the overall racial makeup of the school district" and called for the "clustering and pairing [of] 37 elementary schools and four high schools. An estimated 13,230 students are to be bused to achieve desegregation." According to the *Dayton Daily News*, the plan had a negative impact on public school enrollment within ten years, as "the number of school-age children who did not attend public schools rose from 8 percent to 18 percent [and] fewer students overall were attending the city schools."[39] In 1987 the state of Ohio agreed to pay $25 million to the district and reimburse 50 percent of all future costs associated with busing.

In 1997 Dayton Public Schools sued in federal court to reopen the desegregation case, arguing that the state of Ohio should pay for a larger share of the cost of reform. In 1999 black Dayton city commissioners, with the support of state senator Rhine McLin and state representatives Tom Roberts and Dixie Allen, all African Americans, called for an end to the court-ordered busing. In February 2001, with the support of mayoral candidate McLin, the Dayton school board voted to ask a federal judge to lift the desegregation order that the city schools had been under since 1976. At a time when district enrollment was 73 percent minority, the majority-black school board and its supporters claimed that busing black children around town served little purpose and that the order's original remedy had exhausted itself. Detractors, including the black school superintendent and the local NAACP, argued that ending school busing would cost the district millions in state subsidies. After black parents and the NAACP expressed their support for an end to court-ordered busing in May 2001, however, busing officially ended in Dayton in April 2002.

While Dayton dealt with racial prejudice in the guise of the school desegregation case in the 1970s, the city also embarked on a comprehensive citizen participation program. It began a tradition of citizen involvement in city government decision making with its selection as a Model City in 1967. Model Cities was a program of President Lyndon Johnson's Great Society and War on Poverty initiatives. Authorized on November 3, 1966, by the Demonstration Cities and Metropolitan Development Act of 1966, the program originated to address urban violence and the reform of federal programs by emphasizing comprehensive planning, rebuilding and rehabilitation, social service delivery, and citizen participation.

With its selection as a Model City, Dayton developed elected neighborhood councils as part of its Planned Variation Program. In June 1975, when the city had its first black mayor, the Dayton City Commission officially adopted the neighborhood councils as "priority boards," and they subsequently emerged as the official mechanism for citizen participation in city government. The priority board system has evolved since its implementation. For the first ten years the priority boards provided a vehicle of communication between citizens and city government, primarily by identifying the needs and priorities of neighborhoods for city officials. The boards' elected representatives also assessed the city's service effectiveness. Dayton city government used the priority boards to funnel information to neighborhoods about its actions. In the 1980s and 1990s the priority boards expanded their scope. They fostered grassroots leadership development through leadership programming and established the Citizens Financial Task Force in 1994 to take an active role in the city's budgeting, strategic planning, and capital allocations. The turn of the twenty-first century brought additional changes to the priority board system. Boards included citizens from every Dayton neighborhood and representation from neighborhood groups, including business associations and neighborhood associations and clubs. Each board now has at least one official relationship with a Community and Neighborhood Development Corporation (CNDC). Dayton has several CNDCs, and each works as an independent community organization within its respective neighborhood to spur economic development. Each CNDC has an established task force and subcommittees to which priority board members are elected.

The role of the priority boards is to provide neighborhood representation in city administration decision-making activities. Given that each commission member is elected at large, the priority board system is designed to ensure that the city's neighborhoods are represented effectively. Through their chairpersons, the boards act as the official voice of the neighborhoods, identifying and prioritizing the goals and objectives of citizens within the neighborhood. The goals are annually submitted to city administration and to Dayton's state legislative delegation. The boards are also expected through various committees to provide official input from the neighborhoods on which public service activities function well and which need to be cut. Through partnerships with neighborhood development corporations, the boards play a role in most issues that affect the neighborhoods, including maintaining housing options by preserving the existing housing stock.

Though priority boards contribute to all Daytonians' effective participation in city government, they play a significant role in the representation of black interests. Many boards have offices in their communities, while others have them at city hall. The placement of offices in the community arguably gives black residents, who may have limited transportation options, immediate access to their priority board representatives. In theory, then, the boards can serve as great facilitators of black residents' interests and concerns. Three of the seven boards are representative of the African American community: Innerwest, Southwest, and Northwest. As noted, the boards have been recognized by the city commission as "the official citizen participation structure for the Community Development Program and such other activities where citizen participation is desirable to improve the quality of life of the residents of the City of Dayton."[40] Hence the introduction of the priority board system is a key development in Dayton's racial and political history, providing the tools through which black citizens may actively engage local government (and the mayor) on issues that matter to them.

The 1980s brought additional racial progress and strife to Dayton. The Dayton City Commission chose its first black police chief, Tyree Broomfield, in 1983 and elected its second black mayor in 1984. Newspaper reports suggest that blacks in Dayton recalled Broomfield's tenure as being marked by his struggle against police union racism, which took its toll in 1987, when Chief Broomfield fired two black majors, resulting in three hundred protesters at city hall. Making an appearance at the protest, the chief announced the two majors would keep their jobs. According to one Dayton historian, "That announcement caused Broomfield to lose city commission support and led to reports that he would be forced out of office."[41] The *New York Times* reported that Broomfield received six months' severance pay and $100,000 in private donations to leave his post.[42] Other newspaper reports indicate that some residents felt Broomfield was not effective as police chief. Dayton's majority-white police union was actively critical of his performance. Broomfield did have the support of black leaders, however, who claimed he was a "victim of racism."[43] In 1989 four black police officers and a group of ministers sued the city and the local Fraternal Order of Police, "claiming a ten percent black police force in a forty percent black city was unjust."[44] The Black Police Officers Association had previously unsuccessfully sued the city in 1976 with similar charges.[45]

The late 1980s and 1990s saw some improvement in Dayton's race relations. In 1989 the Greater Dayton Christian Connection held its first annual Peace Bridge event, in which participants walked across the bridge connecting West Dayton with the downtown area. The annual event is a symbolic "coming together of the two races."[46] In 1992 the Southern Christian Leadership Conference conducted a successful drive to name Third Street, in the heart of Dayton's black community and connecting through downtown, for Dr. Martin Luther King Jr. King's wife, Coretta Scott King, attended the event. In 1990, when Dayton had a black population of 38 percent, the city's second black mayor, Richard Clay Dixon, was the only black member of the city commission, and only 24 percent of the city's 2,689 employees were minorities. Dayton residents elected the city's first black woman to the city commission, and Montgomery County residents elected the county's first black commissioner, in 1991. Rhine McLin was elected to the Ohio State Senate in 1994, the first black woman to hold the office.

In 1990 a group called Citizens for a Fair Share, for which black city commissioner Dean Lovelace was a co-leader, organized Dayton's black community to oppose the city's 0.5 percent tax renewal, a $19 million source of income for the city at the time. According to a *Dayton Daily News* article, Lovelace argued that the city's black community deserved more attention from the city: "Before we should be asked to pay for more taxes, we want to make sure we're getting what we're paying for." *Dayton Daily News* staff writer Edwina Blackwell wrote, "The group wants the city to improve its record of hiring and promoting blacks in all city departments and parity for blacks in the police and fire ranks."[47]

*Mayor Rhine McLin*

Two years before the scheduled November 2001 general election, state senator and Democratic caucus leader Rhine McLin announced she would run for mayor of Dayton. Her early musings about the potential run did not have the support of the *Dayton Daily News*, which remarked in an editorial, "A couple of years ago, Sen. McLin was saying she did not want to be mayor. She said she watched the sometimes-raucous city commission meetings on television, and the job did not look like fun. Something has changed her mind. But this is not all good. After all, when Ms. McLin . . . first went to the legislature, [she was] not ready. . . . She was the neophyte daughter of a political legend who had died in office; she was uncomfortable under the public spotlight and not able to discuss public policy issues with any sophistication." The editorial was less of a critique of McLin than of the state legislature's term limits, which, according to the editorial, create "state legislators who don't know local government."[48] Admittedly McLin's announcement focused on these term limits: "Because of term limits and these types of things, you have got to let your plans be known early," she said.[49] At the outset, she indicated her interest in having the city manager foster better relations with the Dayton public schools.

McLin's decision meant, among other things, that she was prepared to take a pay cut of $20,000 in base salary earnings, as the mayor's position in Dayton is officially part time, with a salary of $36,000. Her opponent was the incumbent, two-term Republican mayor Mike Turner. Turner was credited with bringing downtown

**McLin**

**Real Leadership**
for a
**Better Dayton**

☑ Create new jobs while protecting existing jobs.

☑ Work to improve ALL neighborhoods, not just a privileged few.

☑ Reinstitute Community Based Policing to reduce crime.

☑ Work with our schools to ensure quality education for all our children.

**Rhine McLin**

**Democrat** for **Mayor**

**Tuesday, November 6**

4. Once McLin did decide to run for mayor in 2001, her campaign slogan was "Real Leadership for a Better Dayton." Courtesy Rhine McLin.

economic vitality to Dayton, as even McLin acknowledged when the Democratic Party endorsed her candidacy: "The major focus has been downtown and we're not knocking that, but it's the neighborhoods and residents that make a city great."⁵⁰

Dayton's downtown growth, McLin argued, had "happened on the backs of neighborhoods." Hence with her campaign theme, "Real

Leadership for a Better Dayton," and in her campaign literature McLin stressed that she would "work to improve ALL neighborhoods, not just a privileged few."[51] She framed her candidacy as being about jobs, neighborhoods, community-based policing, and better-quality schools.

The daughter and granddaughter of political veterans, Rhine McLin nonetheless seemed at first an unorthodox choice for mayor. She had become Democratic leader in the state Senate, the first black woman ever in that role, but she was barred from immediately seeking a third term because of term limits and had to find a new occupation. Dayton's form of government would not provide McLin with strong executive authority. As the *Dayton Daily News* suggested, however, the position could still be powerful: "The office of mayor can be influential depending on the occupant's ability to rally votes from other commissioners or to use the job's public stature as a soapbox to push for programs."[52] Perhaps it was the appeal of the soapbox that attracted McLin to a position in which she previously had little interest.

In any event, once McLin announced, she campaigned aggressively. By late July 2001 she had sent out her first mailing, which touted her family background and her "call for an end to court-ordered busing of our school children," an appeal that was initially directed at white voters but that also received black parental support and the support of the NAACP in its final stages.[53] In August McLin conducted business lunches with key groups in the community. In September she forcefully criticized the incumbent on his lackluster effort to retain Dayton jobs: "Job retention and creation in Dayton needs a mayor's attention. . . . Turner has not led on jobs for Daytonians. . . . The current mayor is front and center when a ribbon is cut or the business community announces good news downtown. But his silence is deafening when it comes to jobs moving out or neighborhood businesses closing."[54] McLin's attacks on the weaknesses of her opponent would not be enough to secure victory, however. As one political observer indicated, "Rhine has to show that she has an in-depth command—not just a rhetorical command—of the problems

5. Mayor Rhine McLin's famous round and square glasses and hats spurred both controversy and praise. Courtesy Rhine McLin.

facing Dayton."[55] In this regard McLin had an advantage. As the *Dayton Daily News* suggested, "Anyone who knows, or has ever met, Rhine McLin would agree she has personality aplenty—including a whimsical, often self-effacing sense of humor. What else can you say about a political leader who sports a Winnie the Pooh watch, prefers to roller-skate rather than ride in parades and keeps a stash of toys and coloring books in her office?" To the benefit of McLin, who called herself "vertically challenged" and "a kid" and thought she drove "a high-chair with wheels," her personality was an asset her opponent lacked.[56]

McLin made use of this asset, building relationships with those who initially mistrusted her and reestablishing relationships with those who thought her service as a state legislator had removed her from the inner workings of Dayton politics. One Republican politician observed, "Rhine McLin is seriously very street smart and politically savvy. She has a great ability to establish rapport with and work with diverse constituencies. And she's also very good at constituent relations."[57] McLin's personality was not enough to win victory against a two-term Republican who many thought was doing a fair job, but it helped in that she was able to carry over her reputation as a collaborator in the state Senate to skeptical voters. As one former Republican colleague in the state Senate suggested, "Rhine was a bridge-builder.... She always took a consensus approach." Another remarked, "I have great respect for her. She was always concerned, first and foremost, with her constituents."[58] McLin credits her ability to reach across ideological and racial divides to see commonality to her education at Parsons College, a small, majority-white liberal arts institution in western Iowa. In addition, McLin found that her training as a mortician helped guide her approach to addressing Dayton's historic racial problems: "When you open people up—and I don't care who it is, everybody—we're all the same."[59]

McLin's skills at bridging the racial divide in a city with a long racially divisive history proved a formidable challenge to the incumbent mayor. For example, she successfully courted the support of many of the city's largely white male unions. As one union official commented, "This is a new era in politics. They [white males] are going to vote for her. They're going to vote for a black female."[60] People recognized McLin as a serious "doer" on behalf of Dayton issues—a label her legislative colleagues from both political parties recognized and a reputation that she effectively carried over into the mayor's race.

Her ability to connect with voters individually was an important asset to McLin, as she was handicapped by her disadvantage in fundraising and by the lack of a key endorsement. Whereas Turner's re-election bid included $270,000 in television ads, McLin spent only $131,000 on television ads.[61] Moreover, the *Dayton Daily News*, the city's only major newspaper, endorsed her opponent, arguing, "[McLin's] message lacks a compelling theme and is delivered un-

# Rhine McLin
### Fighting for Dayton's Working Families

Doing what's right without regard to political considerations.

A proven leader who brings Democrats and Republicans together to get things done.

Committed to working for ALL Daytonians.

*"As a State Representative and State Senator representing Dayton, Rhine McLin has always fought for working men and women. Rhine McLin has a 100% record in support of labor issues."*

- Wesley Wells
Dayton AFL-CIO

**DSSMV AFL-CIO Community Services**

## Rhine McLin for Mayor
### Endorsed by
## Dayton AFL-CIO Regional Labor Council
#### Wesley Wells, Executive Secretary Director

*William Nix, President*
*Thomas J. Ritchie, Sr., Senior Vice President*

*Steve Culter, Recording Secretary*
*Randy Tackett, Senior Vice President*

6. Running for mayor in a Democratic-leaning city, McLin enjoyed significant support from area unions. Courtesy Rhine McLin.

convincingly." While the paper had some criticisms of Turner, it concluded that "[Turner] has represented Dayton well and has done much to improve the city. He has earned re-election."[62] However significant the newspaper's endorsement may have been, it was offset by the national attention McLin's campaign received. She held fund-raisers in Philadelphia and Cleveland, and her campaign received donations and borrowed staff from the Democratic National Committee, as well as getting visits from its chair, Terry McAuliffe.

In the end McLin managed to defeat Turner at the polls, a result the *Dayton Daily News* called an upset. She did so by championing education as her number one priority while making it clear that she would also attend to rising theft, the deterioration of the neighborhoods, and downtown business. The newspaper cited her reputation as "the largest factor in her victory," noting, "She has become somebody whom Daytonians—black and white—see as caring about people like them."[63] McLin's name recognition and scandal-free campaign and Dayton's history as a Democratic city all factored in her victory.

7. Rhine McLin with then Democratic National Committee chairman Terry McAuliffe. Courtesy Rhine McLin.

TABLE 7. Dayton ward returns for Rhine McLin, 2001 election

| WARD | VOTES FOR MCLIN (PERCENT) |
|------|---------------------------|
| 1 | 39.3 |
| 2 | 23 |
| 3 | 22.7 |
| 4 | 47.8 |
| 5 | 74.5 |
| **6** | **86.4** |
| **7** | **85** |
| 8 | 21.1 |
| 9 | 17.1 |
| 10 | 15.7 |
| 11 | 21.4 |
| 12 | 20.5 |
| **13** | **87.7** |
| **14** | **84.5** |
| **15** | **84** |
| 16 | 79.4 |
| 17 | 55.8 |
| 18 | 44.6 |
| **19** | **88.8** |
| 20 | 17 |
| **21** | **82.6** |
| 22 | 76.2 |
| *Total* | **50.07** |

McLin had stronger returns in Dayton's black wards than either the previous Democratic mayors or Turner in his previous elections. McLin and Turner both won eleven wards each. Voter turnout was at 44 percent. The *Dayton Daily News* claimed McLin had ten strong wards from previous elections, while Turner had eight strong wards based on previous elections and the advantage of more registered voters. In the ten wards that favored McLin, she received over 85 percent of the vote, whereas Turner compiled less than 80 percent in his favored eight wards.[64] Much of McLin's support was from the west and northwest communities of Dayton, where the majority of African Americans reside. As table 7 demonstrates, McLin's base of support was largely in wards 6, 7, 13–15, 19, and 21.[65] The former political director for the Republican National Committee pointed out the strength of this base: "I don't think you can count on turnout to ever diminish the strength of the African American community. They turn out, they vote, and they vote enthusiastically."[66]

As figure 2 indicates, McLin's 2001 election results mirror the residential racial patterns in Dayton. Subsequent analyses show a statistically significant relationship between the percentage of black residents in a given ward and the percentage of the vote that McLin received in the 2001 election.[67]

The *Dayton Daily News* conducted an analysis concluding that race had an important role to play in McLin's victory. It found "a significant correlation between her ward-by-ward vote totals and the ward's proportion of voting-age black residents": "For every 10 percent increase of voting-age African Americans, McLin gained a 100-vote margin over Turner," the analysis found. "The correlation is undeniable," [political scientist Robert] Adams said. "It certainly displays very clearly that race remains a very, very strong motivating force in Dayton politics." At the same time, the analysis noted that "voting-age blacks are still a minority in Dayton . . . making up 38 percent of the 18 and older population, while whites make up 59 percent. There was more to the election than race."[68]

While McLin's base of black support helped her defeat Turner, neither candidate made identity politics of race or gender key to their campaigns.[69] Content analysis of the paper's coverage of McLin's campaign demonstrates that she did not suffer from an overly racially divided portrayal or perception.[70] Analysis of sixty-one *Dayton Daily News* articles for the period March 30, 2000, through January 8, 2002, yielded a mean Likert scale rating of 3.66. This rating suggests her candidacy was not viewed by the media, and by extension the public, in overtly negative racial terms and that her candidacy did not suffer from press bias. That McLin received considerable support from East Dayton and more conservative wards, winning at least 16 percent in wards with a nearly 90 percent white population, also suggests that race was not a significant factor in her election. In the end McLin won by 1,096 votes.[71]

FIG. 2. Relationship between McLin 2001 victory and black population

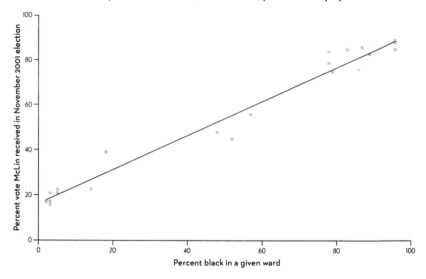

While Turner won many of East Dayton's white wards, he won them with a lower percentage of the vote than in previous elections. Newspaper reports do not indicate why McLin was able to cut into some of Turner's white support. It is reasonable to consider, however, that her experience in the state Senate, where she represented some majority-white neighborhoods in and outside of Dayton, as well as her status as a Democrat running in a historically Democratic city, helped her defeat Turner.

Elected mayor of Dayton on the same day that Jack Ford was elected mayor of Toledo, McLin took office in a similar atmosphere of hope for improvement in race relations—though, unlike Ford, she did not do so at a time when contentious racial events were at the forefront. While there was disagreement among black ministers and other black community members, including McLin, on a failed city commission bid to enact a gay rights ordinance for city employees, the issue itself was not racialized. McLin's victory over Turner coincided with the departure of the black city manager, who left office first to take a position out of the country and later to take one in nearby Cincinnati. The manager, who had close ties to Turner, had lacked the support of some of the newly elected commissioners. That issue was largely a personnel concern, however, and not a point of racial contention, as the city manager is appointed by the commission to oversee a government with 3,128 employees.

Like Ford, McLin soon organized a transition team of black community leaders, members of the local media, heads of nonprofits, and key business leaders. She chose a number of fiscally minded members for this team, as she was elected while the outgoing city commission was finalizing its budget for her first year in office. Immediately upon winning office, McLin and fellow commissioners-elect began assisting the outgoing commissioners with the new budget in anticipation of adopting a balanced budget by April 1, 2002. They debated how to continue basic services, such as trash pickup and recycling. Frustrated by the budget dilemma and the culture of city government in her first weeks in office, McLin lamented that "coming from the state level, we dealt in line items; here we speak in generalities."[72] Eventually, however, a $180 million annual general fund budget was passed. McLin subsequently took steps to separate herself from the contents of the budget, with which, media reports suggested, most commissioners had issues. She stated, "This is not my budget. I'm playing the cards I was dealt."[73]

In addition to these fiscal problems in her first weeks in office, McLin reached a stalemate with the city's commission-appointed civil service board concerning a commission plan to diversify the police and fire departments. Two black commissioners, who were Turner supporters, threatened to fire two members of the board for stalling the implementation of the plan. The commission's plan called for bonus points to be awarded on the civil service test for apprentices, a plan the civil service board found objectionable. The commission argued that the plan was necessary to diversify the ranks of the police and fire departments, which were 10 percent minority in a city with an African American population over 40 percent.[74] The commission ordered the board to submit a separate diversity plan within thirty days. After it did, the commission refused to accept it. The impasse resulted in firefighters picketing downtown.

Meanwhile, a *Dayton Daily News* article reminded readers that a center to honor Rev. Dr. Martin Luther King Jr. had been supported by a vote of the commission in 1992 and a forty-member committee recommendation in 1996, yet no center or memorial had been built, in large part due to a lack of funding and to organizers' concerns that the center's projected location on Dayton's West Side would cause some to view it as a resource only for Dayton's black community.[75] Hence the tensions between the city's east and west sides, though minimal, remained an issue for McLin upon taking office.

Much of McLin's attention was taken up with nonracial issues. She voted with the recommendation of the city manager and other commissioners to close a 414-bed jail that offered rehabilitation programs for nonviolent offenders.[76] The decision was a blow to the union supporting the jail workers, which had heavily supported McLin's election bid. The four commissioners who voted for the closing in May 2002 indicated they had little choice, however, as the county sheriff had pulled county inmates from the center, removing the center's largest paying customer. This decision was followed by more bad business news for the city when Elder-Beerman, a national department store, announced that it would be closing its location in downtown Dayton in the summer. Hence McLin's efforts to implement an agenda were thwarted by the economic realities she faced in her first year. She gave herself a "C" for her first six months.[77]

The city's civil rights leaders protested the promotion of a white Dayton police officer in June 2002. The officer had pepper-sprayed a black teenage girl during an arrest in 1998 and was initially fired for the offense. He was later reinstated, however, and acquitted of a criminal charge. He also was ordered to attend diversity training and received a one-year unpaid suspension. His promotion to sergeant angered the civil rights leaders, who labeled the pepper-spraying incident "a terrorist act." The city manager argued that the city had exhausted its ability to prevent the officer's reinstatement. McLin reacted to the event by saying, "When you see it from the outside in, it looks terrible, but everyone is entitled to their due process."[78] Her support of the process of law in this case mirrored Mayor Ford's recognition of the right of neo-Nazis to march in neighborhood streets. McLin's position in this case may have played a role in some Dayton blacks' decision not to support her reelection.

In February 2005 McLin remarked of her reelection bid: "I inherited a fragile budget when I became mayor and the economy changed and it hasn't gotten any better. The focus I've had has been to maintain the city's fiscal integrity while maintaining basic services. I welcome the opportunity to prove myself."[79] In the May primary she was the top vote getter, with 49.5 percent of the vote in a four-way race, while David Bohardt, the executive director of Home Builders, came in second, winning the slot to be her general election opponent. Bohardt, a Democrat, ran as an independent with the support of the former mayor and other key business leaders. He cited a lack of leadership as his reason for running: "I think it is difficult to overestimate how important the leadership issue is." Bohardt argued that Mayor McLin had become disconnected from the problems of the average citizen of Dayton. Barbara Temple, a fired police major who competed against Bohardt and McLin in the primary, argued that McLin had neglected the neighborhoods: "Mostly, the neighborhoods are feeling somewhat disconnected [from the city as a whole], which is not good. There's a high-level frustration with service delivery." McLin replied that the city's fortunes relied on the active participation of all residents, not only government officials: "We have a commitment to go out and do what we can as a city, but the community needs to go out and do what it can, too."[80]

McLin and Bohardt participated in a debate focused on public safety and the budget. Bohardt claimed McLin "confused the absence of bankruptcy with the presence of leadership" and called for more police officers. McLin responded, "It's not how many police people you have, it's how the police people operate."[81] She maintained that she should not be blamed for the fact that her election coincided with a downturn in the economy.

According to the *Dayton Daily News*, despite the dismal fiscal climate, McLin had presided over a drop in crime, a flat unemployment rate of 8 percent, reduced city spending on police and fire services, a 6 percent increase in public works spending, and a growth in airport revenue of 65 percent.[82] These accomplishments were sufficient for her to win the paper's endorsement for reelection. The endorsement noted, "There have been good things that have been going on during Mayor McLin's tenure—the University of Dayton's purchase of NCR property, Good Samaritan and Grandview hospitals' redevelopment efforts, to name a few."[83] In the end McLin was reelected with the support of "the same coalition of Democrats, blacks and labor" that had brought her victory in 2001.[84] She carried 55 percent of the vote, receiving 90 percent on the city's West Side.

*Racial Attitudes in Dayton*

Three surveys of racial attitudes conducted in the mid-to-late 1990s by the University of Dayton and the Dayton chapter of the National Conference for Community and Justice (NCCJ) found that "increased contact between the races reduces prejudice."[85] One survey of residents in 1979 focused on the quality of race relations in Dayton and the six-county Miami Valley region. Fifty-three percent of whites indicated that race relations were "good" or "excellent," whereas only 39 percent of minorities indicated the same. Eighty percent of whites indicated that race relations were "very important" or "important," versus 96 percent of minorities. The survey was repeated in 1989, when it "revealed a diminishment in the perception of racial quality among both groups."[86] Sixteen percent of whites stated that race relations were "poor" or "very poor," a 6 percent increase from a decade earlier. Thirty-six percent of minorities thought race relations were "excellent" or "good," a decline of 3 percent. Asked whether race relations were important, 96 percent of whites called them "very important" or "important," a 16 percent increase. Sixty-four percent of minorities considered race relations to be "very important," an 18 percent increase from 1979.

In 1994 the Dayton chapter of the NCCJ, in conjunction with the University of Dayton, conducted a telephone survey and held focus groups on racial and religious attitudes in Montgomery County. Survey results revealed that blacks and whites in the Dayton region con-

TABLE 8. Racial attitudes toward discrimination in
Dayton, 1994 (percent of respondents)

| GROUP PERCEIVING DISCRIMINATION | POLICE DISCRIMINATION | TEACHER DISCRIMINATION | STORE CLERK/ SALES DISCRIMINATION |
|---|---|---|---|
| Blacks | 13.2 | 4.4 | 32.5 |
| Whites | 1.5 | 0.9 | 3.3 |
| Appalachians | 1.1 | 1.1 | 4.5 |
| Other minorities | 6.8 | 6.8 | 6.8 |

Source: Mark Fisher, "Racial Attitudes Reported," Dayton Daily News, October 11, 1994.

tinued to view race through different lenses. Of the African Americans surveyed, 59 percent said they had experienced discrimination in the past year, and 76 percent said there were fewer opportunities for managerial promotion for blacks in Dayton, while only 36 percent of those in the white community agreed with the latter statement. In a variety of survey categories, including those on the hospitality and service industry and the career sector, whites perceived equal opportunity where blacks noted discrimination. In some cases, a nearly 40 percent differential was reported.[87] As table 8 shows, whites and blacks also had different perceptions of discrimination by the police force, teachers, and store and sales clerks.

The University of Dayton commissioned a similar survey in 1997 using comparable indicators from the earlier survey. It had similar results. The survey of 1,100 Montgomery County residents found that 89.4 percent of respondents believed that "discrimination against blacks is still a problem in the United States."[88] The findings indicated that blacks experienced discrimination six times more than whites.

Dayton's long history with push-and-pull race relations and the results of these racial attitude surveys led to the creation of several groups to address the issues in the twenty-first century. Michael K. Briand credits the "vision, commitment and goodwill" of some Dayton residents for trying to improve race relations. He notes that an interracial group of pastors, the Black-White Christian Clergy Dialogue, and members of several congregations created the Vineyard

Project to build relationships among people of similar faiths and with "shared spiritual and moral values that obligated them to show concern and respect for their fellow human beings."[89] According to the *Dayton Daily News*, the group formed in the late 1980s and early 1990s; it focused on "issues of common concern to people everywhere, such as the drug crisis, AIDS and day care," meeting monthly for six to nine months a year to discuss these issues.[90] Briand sees this civic partnership as an initiative that could be replicated across the country, not for its spiritual connection but for its "value commitments." Hence the effort to improve race relations in the Dayton community begins with community members, not necessarily government. Briand recognizes, though, that "healthy civic relationships are not sustained on goodwill alone." He explains: "People keep them alive by doing the difficult political work of recognizing the hard choices they face by struggling together, to find a way forward that everyone can live with." Briand calls these efforts a form of political practicality.[91]

Other groups have developed more recently in an effort to improve Dayton's race relations. In October 2000 the Dayton Dialogue on Race Relations (DDRR) was formed directly as a result of the 1997 racial attitudes survey in Montgomery County. The program is a coalition of community leaders that seeks to use intergroup dialogue to foster improved race relations. The city of Dayton and Montgomery County contribute approximately $60,000 annually to the program, with the Dayton Human Relations Council, the *Dayton Daily News*, the Kellogg Foundation, and other groups funding the initiative as well. The DDRR had the support of many area groups, such as 27 Good Black Men. According to the *Dayton Daily News*, "The DDRR has groups of eight to 12 racially diverse Miami Valley residents [who] meet in homes for six two-hour sessions to talk. Discussions range from personal experiences to observations about how people relate to each other."[92] The first home session took place in December 2000.

During McLin's terms in office the city and county's efforts to improve race relations seemed to suggest that the Dayton region was committed to moving forward on race. Not everyone believes McLin's terms produced positive changes in the community, however. In 2010, when McLin was running for reelection to a third term, for example, an influential group of black ministers announced they would not support her effort. The leaders cited a rising crime rate on the city's West Side and a dismal economy as the reasons for their decision.[93] Four other candidates also submitted petitions to run against McLin.[94] McLin lost her bid for a third term to Gary Leitzell, a white neighborhood activist who had never held prior political office and who was from the city's predominantly white southeast side. Leitzell, an independent who was endorsed by the Montgomery County Republican Party, won 51.5 percent of the vote, defeating McLin by less than nine hundred votes of nearly thirty thousand cast. McLin's support of gay rights and loss of key endorsements from labor unions and the black religious community likely contributed to her defeat. In addition to the reasons cited by the religious leaders mentioned above, others cited McLin's support of a city ordinance granting health and social benefits to gay city employees as reasons for the ministers' lack of support and McLin's subsequent loss.[95] Meanwhile, blacks' share of the total population has remained steady from when Mayor McLin took office in 2001 to the conclusion of her second term. According to the U.S. Census, the black population in Dayton was 42.9 percent of the total population in 2010. The total city population dropped from 166,179 to 141,527 between 2000 and 2010, and the black population reflected this drop, falling from 71,688 to 60,705, but its percentage of the total remained fairly steady, down slightly from 43.1 percent in 2000. The increase in crime in the city's black community, reported by the group of black ministers, combined with the poor economic conditions in the city, created a dismal environment for Dayton's fiscal health and McLin's support in the black community, her base of electoral support. Moreover, the less-than-liberal or welcoming East Side environment for Dayton African Americans, combined with the limited power of the office of mayor, made it difficult for McLin to actively pursue policies and programs designed to improve black quality of life.

# CHAPTER 5

# "Lowest and Best" (and Black) Bids

Mayor Jack Ford and the Active
Pursuit of Black Contractors

---

I see myself not as a politician, but a social worker.

Jack Ford

---

As Jack Ford closed his inaugural address as Toledo's first black mayor in January 2002, he quoted Isaiah 58: "House the homeless, clothe the naked, lift the yokes of oppression from the disinherited." He continued: "We are promised God's marvelous support and backup if we do these things."[1] Ford's biblical reference reflected the governing mode and priorities of his administration. Elected in November 2001 with the support of 45 percent of Toledo's black registered voters, the largest percentage in Toledo's history,[2] Ford shouldered responsibility for nearly 2,800 employees, a $400 million budget, and the health and welfare of approximately 300,000 citizens. He took office during an economic downturn wherein manufacturing-based, heavy industrial rust-belt cities such as Toledo were the first to feel the cuts. He also inherited a $15 million budget deficit from the previous administration. Thus, on the surface, the mayoralty of Toledo in 2001 was in every way the "hollow prize" that Friesema describes.[3] Despite Ford's own description of the contracting effort as a failure, he nonetheless made significant efforts to work on behalf of black interests while mayor, and he did so by presenting black interests as the universal interests of the people of Toledo.[4] This chapter considers Ford's two most significant efforts: the launching of the Center for Capacity Building and the merger of the Department of Affirmative Action and Contract Compliance with the Division of Purchasing in the Department of Finance.

## The Center for Capacity Building

What we're trying to do is almost revolutionary. What we're trying to do is develop the capacity of individuals who live in the core city, in the neighborhoods that ring the downtown area . . . [ so that they are] able to get their fair share of these billions of dollars that we know are getting ready to come into this economy.

Jack Ford, *Toledo Journal*, September 4, 2002

The creation of the Center for Capacity Building in 2003 was a major initiative by Mayor Ford to improve the quality of life of Toledo African Americans. Launched in conjunction with the University of Toledo, the Associated General Contractors of Northwest Ohio (AGC), the Northwestern Ohio Building and Construction Trades Council, and the Economic Opportunity Planning Association (EOPA), the center had its genesis in a long legal history. In December 1980, in response to a decade of "complaints regarding and statistics concerning minority group participation in state construction contracts,"[5] the Ohio House of Representatives passed House Bill 584, the Minority Business Enterprise Act, known as the Set-Aside Law. U.S. district judge Joseph Kinneary struck down House Bill 584 in 1982, but the Sixth Circuit reversed his decision in *Ohio Contractors Association v. Keip* in 1983. The decision established the Minority Contractors and Business Assistance Program (MCBAP) and designated that specific geographic areas be awarded grants from the Ohio Department of Development to establish programs to foster the development of minority business opportunities. The Minority Business Office determined the funding of each program on an annual basis, using U.S. Census Bureau data and zip codes to locate the highest concentrations of minority businesses.

The businesses generally referred to as minority business enterprises (MBEs) include individuals, corporations, or joint ventures of any kind. If the business has more than one owner and operator, those that have been 51 percent owned and controlled for at least one year by minorities (black, Hispanic, Asian, and American Indian) are considered MBEs. The focus of MCBAP is largely limited to the construction industry, though it has increasingly encompassed goods and services as well. The Ohio Department of Administrative Services listed 1,180 MBEs in October 1998.[6]

The Set-Aside Law established the requirement that MBEs be given the opportunity to effectively bid for and receive state procurement contracts with the private sector, setting quotas of 15 percent of contracts for the purchase of goods and services, 5 percent of prime construction contracts, and 7 percent of subcontracts for construction and materials.

In 1998 the AGC filed suit from its Toledo chapter, arguing that House Bill 584 was unconstitutional. Federal judge James Graham agreed with the plaintiff. The Ohio House of Representatives later amended the bill to remove the set-aside clause for construction and related projects. In addition, the state of Ohio filed an appeal to the Sixth Circuit, in which it argued that the law passed strict constitutional scrutiny because it served a compelling state interest. That the Toledo chapter of the AGC had brought the suit suggested that the large contractors the group represented in Toledo were discontented with the increasing resources and bidding tools being made available to minority contractors. According to a *Toledo Journal* article, Bill Brennan, president of the chapter, remarked, "Quite honestly, we're not in favor of set asides as administered by the state of Ohio. I guess I would have to see the evidence . . . that minority companies cannot compete."[7]

In this context Mayor Ford's creation of the Center for Capacity Building with the AGC as a co-sponsor and mentor of minority business enterprises on various aspects of the contracting process was a significant achievement. Just two years after Brennan's comments, the program's creation coincided with the planning of large-scale institutional, commercial, and industrial construction projects in Toledo, including city sewer construction, the Toledo Waterways Initiative Project, the I-280 Bridge Construction Project, the Toledo Public Schools Facilities Improvement Project, Toledo Hospital, and the development of the Marina Entertainment District, which was projected to cost $2 billion over a period of fifteen years.

The development of the Center for Capacity Building, which some observers labeled "the House That Jack Built," began at the suggestion of a project manager at EOPA, Weldon Douthitt, and the head of economic and community development at the University of Toledo, Ken Dobson.[8] The result was a cocktail party meet-and-greet initiative organized by Mayor Ford between minority contractors and large contractors at the elite, private Toledo Club. The early goal was that minority contractors would develop long-lasting relationships with some of the larger and more profitable construction companies that would result in wealth generation. As mayor-elect, Ford had been informed that one of the city's major projects for sewer reconstruction was set to begin without any goals or targets having been set for minority participation. Immediately upon taking office in January 2002, Ford placed a hold on the project agreement and sought out help in setting goals and building the capacity of minority companies to be qualified to meet them.

In his 2003 State of the City address, Ford introduced the program as an initiative to "build capacity within Toledo's disadvantaged business community." The first of its kind in the United States, the education program developed at the Center for Capacity Building was "created at the insistence of the Ford Administration and funded annually [with a pledge of five years of support] with $250,000 from the city," according to the *Toledo Journal*.[9] Ford was able to attract the support and partnerships from both the private and public sectors. Ohio Republican governor Bob Taft provided additional start-up support, with a $1.34 million grant toward operating costs; the AGC's valued in-kind contributions totaled $340,000. Pledging the support of the University of Toledo through the use of space and the contributions of the university's head of economic and community development as the center's director, the university president indicated at the announcement ceremony, "This is what it means to be a metropolitan university, to be engaged with the city, to be engaged with the state, to be engaged with the private sector industry and community leaders."[10]

Ford created the program in part because of the perception in the black community that the local state-funded MCBAP program, which is charged with providing assistance to minority contractors in an identical capacity, was not doing its job effectively. During Ford's tenure the EOPA, a community agency that oversaw the MCBAP process, lost its decades-long control over the grant that assisted minority contractors in bidding for and securing contracts. A largely black-run community action agency since its founding in 1964, EOPA aims to "develop and operate programs to advocate for low-income and moderate-income individuals and families to assist them in achieving self-sufficiency."[11] The loss of the grant was a blow to the organization.[12] The Toledo Regional Chamber of Commerce took control of MCBAP for the region. While the argument was that the chamber had greater resources than EOPA to ensure the sustained execution of the state-funded MCBAP, the reception of the shift in the black community was cold. The chamber had a reputation as a largely white organization that tended to favor elite businesses.[13] As a result, during Ford's tenure the services of the MCBAP in Toledo were largely delivered through the Center for Capacity Building and through the Department of Affirmative Action and Contract Compliance.

At its development stage the center enjoyed the best wishes of all involved. Mayor Ford recognized the program as a significant historical achievement wherein public and private partnerships were successfully arranged for the purpose of leveling the playing field for minority contractors. Taking personal pride in the center's development, he noted at its inauguration, "This is an historic moment in Toledo's history. There's some groundbreaking on economic development that is occurring here that can be a pattern not only for the rest of the state but for the rest of the country. . . . This is very serious business. I think this may be the strongest initiative that I'll have on my watch to empower entrepreneurs to live and work inside the city." Lee Moore, the president of the Toledo Minority Contractors Association, suggested of the program that "For anybody with any kind of future in their minds, who intends to move up and advance . . . it's one of the best opportunities they're ever going to get." Tom Manahan Jr., president and general manager of Lathrop Inc., a large contracting company in the Toledo area, said, "We have a unique opportunity in this community to make a difference over a long period, not just a single project." Ken Dobson, the director of the center, stated of his new responsibility, "We have such a great opportunity here to create wealth. For the businesses that develop the capacity, there is a world of opportunity waiting for them."[14] Strong words of support also came from a Republican city councilman, the president of the AGC, and the University of Toledo president. From all sectors and corners—private, public, and political—the center's development was lauded as a great step forward; many parties had big hopes for the center and had made appreciable investments in its success.

The center's forty-five-week program, called the Core Competencies in Construction Curriculum, was free to enrollees. It focused on the construction process, project management and scheduling, understanding financial statements, and insurance and bonding. In addition to classroom instruction, the director described participants as being "mentored," and there was individualized tutoring as well; participants were taken to offices and job sites, introduced to equipment, and "taught the business end of construction contracting" from the construction itself to "making money, retaining profits and reinvesting those profits back into their businesses." "This is a long path," he remarked, "but the right path."[15]

The sense that community members had a responsibility to assist in the effort was broadly understood and was evident in the design of the curriculum. University professors and major contractors were the instructors, assisted by graduate students, with the intent that the larger contractors would groom the smaller ones to develop into prime contractors in the future. Major contracting companies welcomed the opportunity to assist in the skill development and wealth generation of smaller companies. According to Bill Rudolph, president of Rudolph/Libbey Inc., "We think that's good for us, we think that's good for the community, we think it's good for the other companies and most of all it's good for our customers."[16] In addition, students had monthly meetings with officers from major contractors, bonding companies, insurance firms, and banks who assessed the capacity of each student's business and spent six months in on-site mentoring.

The program's primary goal was to enable minority-contractor participants to qualify for state contracts for larger construction projects. Organizers wanted minorities to procure more contracts at progressively higher levels, with the hope that graduates of the program would be able to increase their earnings and profitability. The process was designed to encourage the continued attraction and engagement of more-qualified minority construction workers with the construction industry.

In addition to the director, the center was overseen by a forty-seven-member board of advisers, an executive committee, and three advisory committees comprised of a coalition of local government, academic, and private industry officials. The advisory committees focused on construction contracting, engineering planning and design, and workforce attraction and development. This organizational structure was designed to ensure transparent oversight but also to keep in mind the center's mission.

Fifty-three minority entrepreneurs graduated from the program's first class. More than eighty individuals initially enrolled, and sixty-three completed the course requirements, but only those students who attended 90 percent of the course were permitted to graduate.[17] Councilman Michael Ashford, one of three black councilors at the time, called the graduation rate "better than high school, better than college, better than anything." A majority of the graduates were African Americans, as Mayor Ford had intended. The *Toledo Journal* reported, "Mayor Jack Ford said he wants as much [of $2 billion in pending area projects] money as possible going into the bank accounts of African American and other minority contractors."[18] The graduation of the first class, then, was a significant first step toward Ford's goal of generating wealth in the black community.

In his address to the graduates Mayor Ford touted the program's significance to the city and highlighted the role it was designed to play in assisting black contractors to expand their annual revenue: "This administration is committed—and I mean that—committed to diversity and to creating wealth throughout the city. As long as I am mayor, we're going to stay the course. . . . My role is see you get up to $200,000 or a quarter million . . . then a half-million and beyond. I'm talking about, in simple terms, big money. Serious money. That's where I want you to be."[19] While wealth generation was Ford's long-term hope for the graduates, in the short term graduates received a certificate, plaque, and memberships to both the Toledo Area Chamber of Commerce and the AGC.

Mayor Ford's development of the Center for Capacity Building raised the expectations of the largely black enrollees. At the program's genesis, many enrollees spoke very highly of it. Graduate Milton McIntyre, president and CEO of Peak Electric, said, "Most helpful has been the networking. That's been the best part of the program for me. Just to know where to go and who to call for what you need . . . being able to talk to some of the major players." Graduate Ruben Daniels, owner of Rules Piping and Fire Protection, was amazed at the improved efficiency resulting from the technology to which he was introduced in the course; he believed it would reduce the time he spent estimating the cost of installing fire suppression equipment: "They've got a beautiful system. Two hours—that's for the whole building. It's all computerized. That's something I didn't know. Something I wouldn't have known if I wasn't in this program." Graduate and African American contractor Thomas Bebley said that the program introduced him to contractors with whom he might not otherwise have been closely acquainted and allowed him to "pick their brains." Stan McCormick, a black contractor who owned an industrial supplies business, praised the "opportunity to get fully engaged in the business of construction."[20]

Many of those with high hopes undoubtedly expected to gain more business as a result of completing the program.[21] McIntyre indicated, "It's tough to make money in the bid industry. I'm looking to being able to actually make deals." According to the *Toledo Journal*, Daniels hoped to be "hired to install fire suppression systems in the buildings planned by Toledo Public Schools."[22] Those integrally involved in the program suggest that when such jobs did not immediately develop, program participants were more than disheartened: "Participants thought they were going to get jobs through their participation in the program. It was perceived that that was the number-one goal. However, participants failed to know that no one can guarantee goals. They may help you get opportunities, but they can't promise it."[23]

The dashing of such high expectations led to a community-wide misconception of the program's original goals and intent. While the city council increased the city's funding portion to $257,000 for the second year of the program, donations from major contractors like Rudolph/Libbey began to decrease after the first year.[24] As a result, the program that had begun as a history-making endeavor began to erode. The former president of the University of Toledo indicated in an interview, "The program was well conceived, yet it was poorly implemented."[25] The result, according even to Mayor Ford himself, was a failure. Although many African Americans may have gained skills from the program, most blamed the mayor when they did not receive contracts. The program lost steam once Ford was out of office. The minority contracting assistance once provided by EOPA and later the Center for Capacity Building is currently the responsibility of the Toledo Regional Chamber of Commerce. Meanwhile, the Center for Capacity Building at the University of Toledo has reframed its original mission to focus on energy efficient and alternative energy construction and technological development projects.[26]

Though the Center for Capacity Building was not implemented effectively, it is significant that Ford developed the program. Ford saw that Toledo, and the office of the mayor specifically, had a vital role to play in ensuring that minorities were actively and fairly engaged in the procurement of contracts from private entities and all levels of government. His decision to pursue this effort to improve the skills and connections of minority contractors is a clear example of his active efforts to improve the quality of life of blacks in Toledo.

## Merger of the Department of Affirmative Action and
## Contract Compliance with the Division of Purchasing

Generally, it's big businesses, same old companies most of which were owned by Caucasians, that got all the city contracts, big contracts, million-dollar contracts, and [Ford] wouldn't accept that as the status quo and made it very clear.

Mike Navarre, former Toledo police chief

In addition to his development of the Center for Capacity Building, Mayor Ford worked to change the Toledo Municipal Code in an effort to protect the interests of African Americans.[27] Making good on the promise he made in his 2001 campaign announcement speech "to increase the participation of minority firms as city vendors," in 2003 Mayor Ford merged the Department of Affirmative Action and Contract Compliance with the Division of Purchasing and funded one director. The result of the merger was the enforcement of minority good-faith goals that had been established as a result of the ministers' protests and boycotts in the 1980s and early 1990s (see chapter 3), as the merger gave the city the power to ensure that its goal of 12.3 percent minority participation in city business was met. In addition, it gave the director the power to issue contracts (or not) to companies that could prove they met the city's minority participation goals. Under the previous mayor's administration the Division of Purchasing had been able to overrule the Department of Affirmative Action and Contract Compliance.

As mayor-elect, Ford had introduced the "Ford Plan 2002," a comprehensive document detailing the priorities of his pending administration.[28] The plan, completed by April 2002, was based on the recommendations and observations of the Ford Citizen Transition Team and the goals and visions Ford established for his administration. The transition team was organized into several committees, and the members of the committees conducted surveys and interviews of stakeholders from within city government and the community at large. Subsequently the team prepared a report containing the information it had gathered and making recommendations for the Ford administration, and it presented the report to the mayor on March 1, 2002.

In part three of the plan, "Management Strategies and Objectives," the transition team made two key recommendations regarding affirmative action: "1. Enforce and encourage Affirmative Action in all hiring and promotion decisions, [and] 2. Move purchasing and contract compliance functions to the Affirmative Action Office." The team also recommended several goals for affirmative action, including but not limited to maintaining a current affirmative action plan and developing an effective monitoring process within one hundred days, developing interim effective working relationships with the Department of Human Resources and the Division of Purchasing within six months, and establishing a plan and process for ongoing coordination between the Department of Affirmative Action and Contract Compliance and the Department of Human Resources and Division of Purchasing for diversity-related matters within a year. In addition, it suggested that the Board of Community Relations might be merged with the Department of Affirmative Action and Contract Compliance, with the new board comprised of "community leaders/ activists and individuals with expertise and a skill set in specific economic/professional areas." Finally, the plan recommended the development of a report to the community, entitled the "State of Diversity in the City of Toledo," an annual publication to address all areas of responsibility under the aegis of the Department of Affirmative Action and Contract Compliance. Hence the plan to reorganize the Department of Affirmative Action and Contract Compliance grew out of the Ford transition team's recommendations.

On August 26, 2002, eight months into Ford's term, the Toledo City Council considered a first read of Ordinance 654-02. The ordinance, drafted by the city's law department at Ford's urging, called for a new Chapter 125 of the Toledo Municipal Code, moving "responsibility for Purchases and Supplies from the Department of Finance to the Office of Affirmative Action and Contract Compliance."[29] At-large Republican councilwoman Betty Schultz referred the ordinance to the Committee of the Whole. The ordinance sat in committee for a year, and on August 27, 2003, it was brought to council for a second read, at which time it was again remanded to the committee for another year.[30] On November 25, 2003, the ordinance was voted on, with eleven council members voting in favor and one, Betty Shultz, excusing herself. It passed as an emergency measure, meaning that it took effect and was enforced immediately after passage. According to the passage document, the emergency lay in the measure's necessity "for the immediate preservation of the public peace, health, safety and property."[31]

The creation of the Department of Affirmative Action, Contract Compliance, and Purchasing was significant. The responsibilities of the Division of Purchasing in the Department of Finance were relegated to the new office. The director of the new office was appointed by the mayor and given responsibility "for the City's Affirmative Action program, contract compliance activities and purchasing functions . . . [and] authority to perform the same functions and duties as those specified for the Commissioner of Purchases and Supplies and Administrator of Purchases and Supplies throughout the Toledo Municipal Code."[32] The new director of affirmative action and contract compliance, in short, controlled what got spent and how.

Significantly the merger also allowed the director to pursue legislation that would make it easier for minority contractors to bid on and ultimately receive city contracts. In December 2003 the director, at the mayor's request, asked the law department to draft legislation to amend the Toledo Municipal Code in respect to contracting, purchasing, and supplies. Ordinance 832-03 was designed to make a number of key changes. First, it increased the "local preference" criteria from 4 to 5 percent, meaning that local vendors and contractors would be eligible for a 5 percent discount in their bids for goods and services. Next, it raised the threshold for formal bidding and for performance bonds on city contracts from $10,000 to $40,000. Finally, it amended the criterion that required the lowest bid to be accepted to include a "lowest and best" criterion for construction contracts.[33]

The ordinance was designed to make it easier for small and minority businesses to bid for and therefore receive city contracts. Prior to its passage, according to small business owners, any contract over $10,000 required a lengthy bid process of over a dozen forms and a time frame of at least six weeks until notification. The formal bid process required that any contract over $10,000 had to be advertised, a step that government officials suggested usually took two to three weeks. Then bids had to be evaluated by the appropriate division or department and a recommendation made to the purchasing division. Only at that point could the purchasing division process contracts in bid form.[34]

By changing the threshold to $40,000, city government officials hoped to make it possible for small businesses—many without the time and resources to devote to completing multiple forms and appealing in person to the Division of Purchasing and city council for a contract—to access a larger amount of city business, enabling a more diverse group of vendors to bid on city contracts.[35] According to administration officials arguing in favor of the ordinance, the purpose of the $40,000 threshold was to expedite service to citizens and the review of all purchasing requisitions and contracts. Administration officials also suggested in the meeting of the Committee of the Whole that the $40,000 figure—at the time a threshold higher than that used in any major city in the state—was appropriately based on the needs of the divisions and departments.[36]

The "lowest and best" criteria that the ordinance sought to establish would allow the city to take into consideration a number of factors in awarding contracts, including related project experience, project familiarity, and construction experience generally.[37] Price would become only one of the factors considered, giving access to more local vendors and thereby increasing tax revenue and potentially allowing for better projects—so argued the officials.

In addition, the ordinance created a maintenance system whereby for one calendar year a potential vendor could volunteer to be listed as prequalified, eliminating the need for vendors to reapply for bids that opened throughout the year. Such a one-year listing would significantly reduce paperwork, better position small businesses to bid for contracts, and increase tax revenue to the city as a result of the local preference incentive. The ordinance also allowed the Department of Affirmative Action, Contract Compliance, and Purchasing to "hone in on" experience specific to the work needing to be completed and not only related experience.[38] Within the city bureaucracy the culture of contracts frequently allowed large companies that offered a variety of services to beat out smaller companies specializing in the work a contract specified, either because the smaller companies did not have the resources to apply within the designated time frame or because the large company could afford to make a lower bid. The new ordinance made it possible for such specialized companies' expertise to be a factor in the decision-making process.

As with the Center for Capacity Building, one of the merger's key successes was in improving the perception that the city had an active role to play in ensuring that minorities, and African Americans in particular, had equal access and opportunity to grow their businesses. In addition, the merger established one individual, the new department's director, as the contact for private-sector industries, like the University of Toledo, that sought to better prepare, educate, and train minorities to be competitive.[39] It also affected the way in which minority business enterprises were counted. The ideology of the mayor and those he appointed to the position of director was that "MBEs" largely referred to black contractors. Had the departments remained separate, confusion as to what constituted an MBE would more likely have remained endemic. The previous administration had included neighborhood organizations as MBEs, for example.[40]

The merger made the contract bidding process more efficient and improved tracking of the awarding of contracts. It also taught many in Toledo business and government that minority contractors were not inferior, unqualified, or inexperienced if given the tools and resources to bid confidently. As figure 3 indicates, the 2003 merger allowed for greater MBE participation in Toledo contracting.

According to interviews with members of the black business community in Toledo, prior to the merger the commissioner of purchasing tended to grant contracts to the usual members of a "good ol' boy" system.[41] The first director of the newly merged department,

FIG. 3. City of Toledo MBE participation for all contracts and agreements

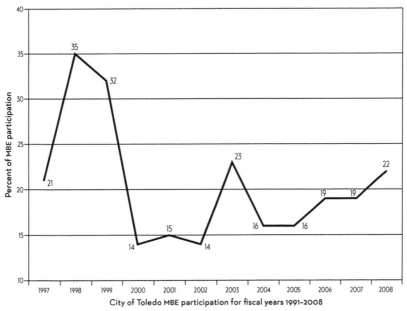

City of Toledo MBE participation for fiscal years 1991-2008

*Source:* "Request for Information" response letter from Commissioner Calvin W. Brown, Office of Affirmative Action/Contract Compliance, July 22, 2008.

Anita Lopez, stated, "When I was running the office, the majority of the people I worked with were African Americans, and the merger allowed me to force all city departments to seek out MBEs, not because they were minorities but because they were qualified. That never happened under the previous arrangement. As a result, bids were more competitive, and departments had to prove that the minority bid was not qualified." Lopez's comment suggests that the merger resulted in a significant shift in the purchasing culture of the office. Lopez highlighted the shift by implying that those previously in control of the funds had backgrounds that limited their understanding of the importance of fairness: "If you don't live in a diverse community, you can't break patterns of oppression. You have to make institutional change. There was this culture of graft, and I made a lot of enemies because of hiring."[42] The office gave Lopez substantial power to change the city administrative culture.

The department's second and last director (the merger functioned only during Mayor Ford's tenure), Yulanda McCarty-Harris, also spoke of the broad power of the position, indicating that enforcement was tracked more efficiently: "[The merger] allowed me to have direct control over everything that was bid out. If you didn't do minority inclusion, you couldn't bid." Calling the mayor "the smartest man I know" and noting that "blacks felt they had a voice and access within Jack's administration," McCarty-Harris specified that in her role as director, her job was to assist with efforts related to the black community. She had the support to aggressively pursue and ensure that minority participation goals were met. She lamented, "Jack was very committed to African American issues, yet he was misunderstood." She perceived the merger of the offices as a significant step toward changing the culture of city bureaucrats who viewed black contractors as inferior, just as it was an effort to change whites' perception that blacks were incapable of performing contract services. McCarty-Harris noted that Ford took a risk in making the merger, and he paid for it: "He did not get reelected, and I think a part of the reason why he did not is because construction is a good ol' boys' network."[43] Ford's efforts to hire more blacks in key administrative roles at city hall, who then assisted in the hiring of more black contractors, were not well-received by everyone.

When Mayor Finkbeiner took office following Ford's failure to be reelected, he removed the powers of the Division of Purchasing from the director of the Department of Affirmative Action, Contract Compliance, and Purchasing and demoted the office from department-level status. He later fired the director he had hired for the office, who had directed the office in Finkbeiner's previous administration in the 1990s. The fired director, along with two other fired black city employees, sued and filed a complaint with the Ohio Commission on Civil Rights, which later found probable cause to rule that discrimination was a function of their firings.[44]

Meanwhile, the commissioner of the affirmative action department Finkbeiner later hired suggested in an MBE participation chart that the second Finkbeiner administration's MBE participation rates were higher than they had been during Ford's term, an assessment that Ford disputed. In an article in the *Sojourner's Truth* former mayor Ford and former director McCarty-Harris took issue with the Finkbeiner administration's numbers: "Finkbeiner's figures have lumped together HUD monies, grants, and agency funds—those for community development corporations. . . . The Ford administration uses a measure of the amount of city contracts going to minority contractors . . . only money going to minorities. . . . Finkbeiner's figures included monies to contractors who then funneled parts of those contracts to majority contractors."[45]

Mayor Ford said bluntly in an interview, "I ran for mayor and had a clear position for blacks to be empowered. . . . I wanted to create wealth for blacks in Toledo."[46] Ford's major program development as mayor, the creation of the Center for Capacity Building at the University of Toledo, was a clear outcome of his avowed desire to empower African Americans. For Ford it was not enough to simply educate black contractors on how to bid for contracts—at least two organizations were already doing that at the time he took office. Rather he sought to create a more educated class of black entrepreneurs who would have the skills to effectively manage their businesses, positioning them for long-term sustained economic growth.

The Center for Capacity Building at its genesis had such a focus. Ford was initially successful in securing the support of private partners, many of them influential whites whom Ford had convinced of the program's potential benefits. Ford's success in obtaining the support of major white corporate and nonprofit leaders is an example of his ability to universalize the interests of blacks as interests that mattered to everyone. Given Ford's powers of persuasion, these leaders were initially convinced that their interests and those of the program, with majority-black enrollees, were mutually beneficial. As chapter 8 will explain, Ford framed his advocacy of black interests in such a way that he neither alienated key white leaders nor deemphasized the significance of race. In fact such leaders were initially drawn to efforts like the Center for Capacity Building because of the universalizing approach Ford utilized. While Ford believes the program to have been a failure in that it did not achieve the goals he had set out for it, the program's creation by a sitting mayor resulted in the city being an effective conduit for job opportunities for program participants.

The merging of the Division of Purchasing and the Office of Affirmative Action and Contract Compliance and the subsequent procurement ordinance are clear examples of Ford's active pursuit of the interests of African Americans, as the merger and ordinance provided the tools for black contractors to competitively bid for contracts. While the exact number of black contractors who benefited cannot be determined, the mayor's effort to change the public perception of minority business owners and his determination to act on the belief that the public sector has a role in private companies' development have few models. McCarty-Harris and others believe that the merger effort played a role in Ford's failed reelection, as it temporarily dismantled the "good ol' boy" network that had long ensured many white (and male) contractors of city contracts. (Chapter 9 will detail other reasons for Ford's 2005 failed reelection bid and present implications for the targeted universalistic approach toward governance.)

# CHAPTER 6

# Strong Housing Support and a Weak Mayor

## Rhine McLin's Efforts for Improved Housing

---

When you talk about all these issues, even though I'm the mayor of color, it's across the board. There is only in the city, to your constituency, an east and a west, but to me as the mayor, they're all my constituents.

Rhine McLin, interview, June 26, 2008

---

Having campaigned for improved schools, better neighborhoods, and reduced crime, Rhine McLin was elected mayor of Dayton in November 2001 with 51 percent of the vote, managing to defeat a popular two-term incumbent, Mike Turner. She became the first female mayor and third black mayor of a city with a long and sometimes difficult racial past. McLin herself was knowledgeable about race relations, having once taught college courses on the subject. Her self-identification as an African American and her familial political lineage also made her especially sensitive to racial issues. Shortly after taking office, McLin organized interracial "friendship lunches" as part of her effort to address the region's historic racial problems. Nearly three hundred people attended the first lunch, each donating fifteen dollars to a charitable fund she had established. "I wanted to do something a little different and let people have a relaxed atmosphere and have people understand friendship," McLin said of the lunches.[1] While she strongly identified with the black community, her role as mayor was to be the mayor for everyone. Indeed "mayor for everyone" best defined the approach McLin used in her efforts to improve the quality of life of black Daytonians.

*The McLin Years: Limited Powers and Economic Challenges*

Dayton's commission-manager form of government means that the city has a weak mayor. The city charter defines the commission as the city's "governing body" with the power "to pass ordinances, to adopt regulations, and to appoint a Chief Administrative Officer to be known as the 'City Manager,' and exercise all powers hereinafter provided."[2] The city's mayor has a number of ceremonial duties and is charged with leading the regular meetings of the city commission. Dayton's city manager, as "the administrative head of the municipal government," bears responsibility for submitting an annual budget and ensuring "the efficient administration of all departments," which includes hiring or appointing heads of departments. The city manager oversees sixteen departments, a general fund budget of approximately $170 million, and 2,400 employees. With the exception of making some board appointments, Rhine McLin had no more authority as mayor to implement policy and develop programs than did her fellow commissioners.[3]

Although McLin did not have the executive authority Ford had in Toledo, she had the ability to wield a great deal of informal influence, which she may have chosen to exercise on behalf of black Daytonians. On the other hand, the extent to which she actively pursued black interests may have been limited by her understanding that as mayor, she was to advocate for the interests of all of Dayton. Unlike her father, she was not the state representative of a majority-black district; rather McLin was the weak mayor of a majority-white city.

When she entered office, McLin faced a $16 million shortfall in the budget and a bleak projected regional economic outlook that was symptomatic of the state's economic condition. Between 2000 and 2007 Ohio had lost nearly 250,000 manufacturing jobs. Meanwhile, the poverty rate increased: in 2004 there were 580,021 more Ohioans in poverty than in 1998, an increase of 5 percent. Ohio was one of only seven states in which the poverty rate had increased between 2003 and 2004, and the situation continued to deteriorate. The state's poverty rate grew by 2.5 percent—or more than 293,000 people—be-

**TABLE 9.** Montgomery County's and area counties' population changes, 1960–2010

DECENNIAL COUNTY POPULATION

| COUNTY | 1960 | 1970 | 1980 | 1990 | 2000 | 2010 | 1970–2012 (PERCENT) CHANGE |
|---|---|---|---|---|---|---|---|
| Butler | 199,076 | 226,207 | 258,787 | 291,479 | 332,807 | 368,130 | 62.7 |
| Clark | 131,440 | 157,115 | 150,236 | 147,548 | 144,742 | 138,133 | 12 |
| Darke | 45,612 | 49,141 | 55,096 | 53,619 | 53,309 | 52,959 | 7.7 |
| Greene | 94,642 | 125,057 | 129,769 | 136,731 | 147,886 | 161,573 | 29.2 |
| Miami | 72,901 | 84,342 | 90,381 | 93,182 | 98,868 | 102,506 | 21.5 |
| Montgomery | 527,080 | 606,148 | 571,697 | 573,809 | 559,062 | 535,153 | -11.7 |
| Preble | 32,498 | 34,719 | 38,223 | 40,113 | 42,337 | 42,270 | 21.7 |
| Warren | 65,711 | 84,925 | 99,276 | 113,909 | 158,383 | 212,693 | 150.4 |

Source: U.S. Census Bureau, U.S. Census, various years.

tween 2000 and 2008. The number of elementary school students eligible for free lunches in the state, a commonly used measure of poverty, rose by 9 percent between 1993 and 2000. The high school graduation rate was 88.3 percent for whites and 61.9 percent for blacks in 2002. Sixty percent of Ohio's white students scored at the "proficient" level or higher on third-grade achievement tests in 2003, compared to 27.8 percent of black students. According to a report by *Education Week*, Ohio's black-white achievement gap was among the worst in the country in 2006, with 80.5 percent of whites graduating, as compared to only 50.7 percent of blacks.[4]

At the county level the economic picture also showed signs of distress. Between 1970 and 2010 Montgomery County, where Dayton is situated, lost more than seventy thousand residents (see table 9). Over a period of forty years the Montgomery County population decreased by 11.7 percent. Meanwhile, neighboring counties enjoyed a combined average increase in population of 43.6 percent during the same period.

The county's and state's poor economic outlook also negatively affected Dayton. When McLin was elected mayor in 2001, the city had a substantial unemployment rate of 9.2 percent.[5] Between 2000 and 2009 the region lost thirty thousand jobs.[6] Major Dayton manufacturing companies such as General Motors, Delphi, National Cash Register, the GH&R Foundry, and Mead Corporation all significantly downsized, closed, or left the region entirely in the first decade of the twenty-first century. In 2008, for example, General Motors announced that its plant in nearby Moraine would close in 2010. According to the mayor, many of the Moraine workers were black citizens of Dayton. Dayton was the fifteenth poorest medium-sized city in the United States in 2006, with a median household income of $28,630.[7] In that year 28.8 percent of the city's residents lived below the poverty line. According to the Ohio Department of Education, 65 percent of Dayton public school students qualified as poor, and the district ranked twentieth poorest in the state in 2007.[8]

Many of McLin's constituents, especially Appalachian whites and low-income blacks, lived in poverty. According to the 1999 "CitiPlan Dayton," Dayton's residents were "four times as likely to be living in poverty as residents living in the rest of Montgomery County." The report elaborated: "In Dayton, 25 percent of the people live in poverty while only 6 percent of the people in the rest of the county live in poverty. The most troubling are the statistics on children in poverty. In the nation, 18 percent of children live in poverty, and, in Dayton, 40 percent of children live in poverty."[9]

A 2007 National League of Cities report on Dayton's poverty and equity agenda did not reveal many positive changes in the poverty pattern from the 1999 CitiPlan report, and it found that elected officials, including Mayor McLin, had a "moral imperative" to address the issue. The report suggested that some cities were examples of "innovation, creativity and leadership" in their efforts to tackle the "problems of poverty, inequalities, and racism endemic to urban America." These efforts, which the report labeled an "equity agenda," would ideally make Dayton "more livable for residents and more attractive to people who want to move or invest there." The report's co-authors found that as a result of fiscal necessity and conviction, Dayton's city leaders had developed an equity agenda through partnerships and in collaboration with county agencies and nonprofit organizations. Yet Dayton city officials were limited in their ability to implement their equity agenda as "cities are increasingly expect-ed to do more with less." The report elaborated: "For every one-point increase in the poverty rate, cities spend $27.75 per capita more on non-poverty related services."[10]

Given these economic challenges, McLin faced an uphill battle from the beginning of her term to implement an agenda that served the interests of blacks. Her response to the economic conditions un-der which she took office was varied in scope and approach. Given the tight budget, she, other commission members, and the city man-ager were forced to streamline city services and lay off city workers for the first time in thirty years. Despite the layoffs, the *Dayton Dai-ly News* supported McLin's efforts to improve Dayton's economy: "With steadfast support from Mayor Rhine McLin and the other com-missioners, Mr. Dinneen [then city manager] has made sure Dayton didn't collapse financially. . . . Efforts by Mayor McLin . . . during the past three and a half years have mattered immensely."[11]

### Barriers to Safe and Affordable Dayton Neighborhoods

The severity of the city's budget shortfall and the economic chal-lenges McLin faced upon entering office in 2002 ought not be under-stated. Nevertheless, Mayor McLin's support for the development and continued funding of programs and policies that would improve the quality of life of Dayton's black residents was crucial to their pas-sage by the city commission. Housing and neighborhood redevelop-ment was not a major issue of the 2001 election campaign, though it received some attention. According to some observers, Mike Turn-er highlighted his record on housing and neighborhood development, among which was the attempted rehabilitation of designated areas citywide, including initial investments in many of the projects that McLin would continue. On the campaign trail the McLin camp took issue with Turner's claim to have invested in neighborhoods. One leaflet sponsored by the Ohio Democratic Party suggested that Turn-er's expenditures of $140,000 to $260,000 per house to fix seven-teen homes in two neighborhoods was not an effective use of rehabilitation resources. The literature particularly attacked Turner

FIG. 4. Foreclosures in Montgomery County, 1995–2008

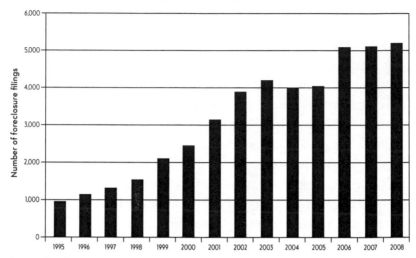

*Source:* "Foreclosure Growth in Ohio 2009," Policy Matters Ohio.

for introducing "an Emergency Resolution which gave a ten year tax break on property valued at $460,000 on Red Oak, the Estate Home of wealthy supporters of Mike Turner." It concluded, "Turner takes care of his wealthy supporters and calls it an investment in our neighborhoods."[12]

McLin's efforts to improve housing and neighborhood redevelopment were significant.[13] Safe and affordable housing was, and remains, a major issue for the Dayton region, as lagging housing and crime statistics demonstrate. According to a report on foreclosure growth in Ohio by Policy Matters Ohio, a nonprofit economic policy research organization, Montgomery County has experienced an unprecedented growth in the number of foreclosures since the 1990s. Between 2002 and 2008 an additional 1,313 foreclosures were reported in the county (see figure 4).[14] In 2007 Dayton had the fifteenth highest foreclosure rate in the country, with 8,493 cases, or 2.07 percent of households, entering some stage of foreclosure that year.

In November 2008 an amendment to Dayton's Neighborhood Stabilization Plan (NSP) identified the areas within the city that were most affected by foreclosures.[15] The city used the foreclosure and abandonment risk score system suggested by HUD to target the areas of greatest need within the city. The report found that while much of Dayton was affected by foreclosures, many in West Dayton also had tax-delinquent properties. This finding suggests that many of Dayton's black citizens had been disproportionately harmed by foreclosures and lived in areas in which many faced additional foreclosures and abandonment. Moreover, the report stated that non-payment of property taxes was a good predictor of future property abandonment.

Mayor McLin explained how the foreclosure crisis in Dayton created other problems:

> The foreclosure and the market crisis also breeds the abandoned properties, the nuisance properties that we have to try to tear down, which also increases the crime. Then you have the renters, the renters that are paying rent, and then the people that own the building are the owners of the building and are in foreclosure, so now immediately you have displaced people. . . . Then on the other hand you also have the people who are making the mortgage payments but they can't afford to fix up their houses, so then the cities are charging them with housing inspection violations. So . . . there are a lot of consequences. . . . The property values are going down. Who would have thought that the American dream of a home would devalue?[16]

McLin recognized that securing safe and affordable housing for Dayton residents was an important priority.

The confluence of a city budget shortfall, a declining tax base as a result of outmigration, disparities in education access and achievement, and the home ownership and affordability crisis caused the city's crime rate to escalate. Violent crime increased by 3.5 percent between 2007 and 2008. This increase was even more evident in African American neighborhoods. In West Dayton police districts 3 and 5, nearly every category of violent crime increased between 2007 and the rest of McLin's second term in office. Dayton ranked as the nation's nineteenth most dangerous city in CQ Press's annual report for 2007.[17] The FBI Uniform Crime Reports from 2003 through 2007 indicated that Dayton experienced an average of 1,627 violent crimes per year, or 4.5 per day (though Houston mayor Annise D. Parker, chair of the U.S. Conference of Mayors' Criminal and Social Justice Committee, lamented that the rankings involved "a gross misuse" of FBI data).[18] Low educational attainment in Dayton had arguably created an environment in which employment options were limited, home ownership was unattainable or unsustainable, and many could generate income only by illegal means; the crime statistics revealed the results.

Unemployment posed another barrier to the development and sustainability of safe and affordable neighborhoods. In November 2008, a year before McLin would go on to lose reelection, the city's unemployment rate was 9.0 percent, higher than the state's rate of 7.3 percent and higher than the national average of 6.5.[19] Dayton unemployment increased significantly over the next few months, reaching 12.2 percent in May 2009. The rate in November 2009 was 12.9 percent. In comparison, the rate was 8.8 percent when McLin won election to her first term in November 2001. Meanwhile, the Census Bureau's 2005–2007 American Community Survey Three-Year Estimates reported that more than 40 percent of the city's black population lived below the federally defined poverty level, versus only 20 percent of whites.[20]

The ability of the city's poor black residents to enter the housing market was and remains limited. Generally blacks are far less likely than non-blacks to be homeowners.[21] This is a significant disadvantage, as home ownership is the primary avenue toward building wealth.[22] It is particularly important in a region where thirty thousand jobs have been lost since 2000 as home ownership potentially creates a safety net that is not available to renters, including federal and state foreclosure assistance, home equity borrowing power, and rental income.

Given that homes have become increasingly affordable in Dayton, one might assume that black access to home ownership has improved. According to the Dayton Area Board of Realtors, the median home price in Dayton was $79,900 in February 2009, an 18 percent decrease from February 2008. That median price was much lower than the state median of $118,992 and the national median of $174,700. Given that 40 percent of Dayton's black residents live below the poverty level, however, even a purchase price of $80,000 requires a larger mortgage and down payment than the majority of Dayton's black residents could qualify for or afford. And while foreclosures due to job loss also provided opportunities for first-time homebuyers, the city's black population had for the most part not been in a position to benefit from these opportunities. It makes sense, then, that McLin chose housing and neighborhood redevelopment as an issue on which to focus city resources.

*Support for Affordable Housing and Neighborhood Redevelopment*

Recognizing the need, McLin gave priority to many different housing and neighborhood redevelopment projects. By partnering with nonprofit community development housing organizations such as Improved Solutions for Urban Systems (ISUS) and CityWide Development, she actively supported the construction of affordable and/ or mixed-use housing communities. Though these projects did not exclusively benefit African Americans, they improved the aesthetic image, business development, and market value of homes in many African American neighborhoods. Moreover, McLin's focus on housing was important because Dayton's population suffers from heavy housing segregation.

In her first State of the City address McLin commented that the Arcade, an abandoned historic landmark, should be redeveloped with affordable housing. Located in Dayton's central business district, the Arcade consisted of five interconnected buildings. When built in 1902, the main space was used as a farmers' market, with housing on the upper floors. Through the 1940s the Arcade's supermarket remained "one of downtown's prime attractions."[23] By the 1970s investors had begun to restore the Arcade as a retail shopping center, and it was reopened in 1980. Since 1990, however, the Arcade had been closed and vacant. In her 2003 address McLin stated, "I believe the site has the potential to include the kind of affordable housing we have pursued in our more traditional neighborhoods. . . . A proposal is being considered now to use the Arcade for affordable housing." Her approach was part of an effort to create a "walkable" urban community.

In an interview with MayorTV McLin commented that "affordable housing" meant housing that was affordable, not necessarily low-income: "Let's just face it; there's always been little buzz words out there, and you know when you start talking about affordable housing, people think you're talking about low-income housing. . . . [But] affordable housing . . . [is] something that whatever you're making, . . . you can afford to buy."[24] According to McLin, affordable housing was not simply government-subsidized housing, though her remarks were interpreted to mean this.[25] The *Dayton Business Journal* labeled her State of the City speech "strange," arguing that some downtown landmarks already included affordable housing: "As far as we know, 'affordable housing' is a euphemism for 'government-subsidized housing,' which is what the Biltmore [a former hotel turned senior-living apartment building] already offers." McLin's plea for affordable housing at the Arcade conflicted with plans for the continuing development of one of the Arcade's neglected buildings at a time when strategic investments of any kind were sorely needed. The *Journal* noted that a developer had invested millions in upgrades of the Arcade and that HUD "said it would be impractical to have a mixture [of affordable units and others]."[26]

Despite the criticism, McLin's pursuit of more affordable housing in downtown apartment buildings is a strong example of her active pursuit of the interests of blacks. According to the U.S. Census Bureau, 52 percent of the 2,156 persons living in downtown Dayton were African American in 2000.[27] The district had 931 households and 927 occupied housing units, compared to 77,321 housing units city-wide. More than 90 percent of blacks and whites living downtown were renters, and 2 percent fewer whites rented than blacks. Of the fifty-eight owners of housing units downtown, 60 percent were white. The mean household income for blacks in the district was $17,884, compared to $26,048 for whites. Ten percent of black households earned $50,000 or more, compared to 12 percent of whites. Seventy-eight percent of downtown black households earned less than $15,000 annually, compared to 56 percent of whites. Fifty-three percent of those who lived below the poverty level in the district were African American. McLin's focus on downtown housing development was also important because blacks were more likely than whites to face barriers to transportation access. Fifty-two percent of black workers sixteen years of age and older reported using public transportation as their means to work, compared to 10 percent of whites. Thus McLin's push to construct more affordable downtown apartment units, where public bus routes are more accessible, was geared to encourage blacks to move to or stay downtown in an effort to diminish travel times to places of employment.[28]

The city's 2008 and 2009 action plans detailed goals to support affordable housing. They explained the city's strategic efforts to continue to support public and private partnerships to construct new homes and invest in the maintenance and renovation of other properties "to suit the needs of low to moderate income households."[29] These plans included the development of affordable housing in the Arcade.

In her first State of the City address McLin actively supported Project SUN (Strong Urban Neighborhoods), a new city initiative she helped to establish. It involved training the city's community development staff to develop diverse housing and retail opportunities for Dayton residents through new construction and renovation. McLin explained that quality schools, diverse housing, and support for business development were all key to improving the city's neighborhoods. She used Project SUN as a vehicle to spur the development begun under her predecessor and to generate new initiatives.

As part of Project SUN, McLin supported Project Genesis, a comprehensive neighborhood redevelopment effort. Genesis was located in Dayton's Fairgrounds neighborhood, a racially mixed community in the South Park division on Dayton's southeast side. The 2000 U.S. Census reported that the neighborhood was 7 percent biracial, 10 percent African American, and 80 percent white. Blacks living in the

South Park division had a mean household income of $13,451 in 2000, whereas the mean income for whites was $31,555.[30]

Genesis was managed by CityWide Development Corporation, a nonprofit resource partner with the City of Dayton that offered financial, consulting, educational, and investment services with a focus on business, neighborhoods, entertainment, and downtown housing. CityWide also offered loans to businesses and homeowners alike to purchase and maintain their properties. Project Genesis purchased vacant houses and either tore them down and rebuilt new homes in their place or refurbished homes that were structurally sound. The developers have demolished at least forty homes and built or remodeled more than twenty homes and townhomes since the project's inception. Project Genesis received the Audrey Nelson Community Development Achievement Award from the National Community Development Association (NCDA) in 2004, an award established in 1987 to recognize exemplary uses of Community Development Block Grant (CDBG) funds that address the needs of families, homes, and neighborhoods.

Although McLin was not mayor during the initial stages of the development project, which began in 1996, her support of Genesis demonstrates her commitment to improve all of Dayton's neighborhoods. Her continued support of work in the majority-white Fairgrounds community also demonstrates her effort to improve the quality of life of blacks in Dayton regardless of where they resided. The project's low-interest loan program, for example, provided attractive buying options for moderate-income African Americans. Thus McLin's support of Genesis revealed her desire to be the "mayor for everyone." While the community had few African American residents and she arguably had no choice but to support the project given its inception prior to her election, McLin was under no obligation to publicly acknowledge her support in her State of the City address.

Through the Project SUN initiative McLin also supported the Wright-Dunbar Village project, a redevelopment of the historic Third Street corridor in West Dayton, once home to the Wright brothers' famous bicycle shop and poet Paul Laurence Dunbar. The ten-block-area redevelopment began as the Wright-Dunbar Urban Renewal Plan in 1995 under McLin's predecessor with a $24 million initial investment in a public and private partnership that would eventually cost more than $75 million. The city had identified local, state, and federal funding for the area's first housing redevelopment in over forty years and began awarding grants to individuals for home rehabilitation. At the time, the city sold $7.9 million in bonds, and the county, state, and federal governments provided the other contributions.[31]

Unlike Genesis, the Wright-Dunbar community, located on the city's West Side in Five Points, is primarily black. The 2000 U.S. Census reported that the Wright-Dunbar area is 95 percent black, with a mean household income of $26,237.[32] Of the 244 black residents twenty-five years of age and older who lived in Five Points as of 2000 and had attained some education, 12 percent had received a graduate/professional degree or higher, though the vast majority did not begin or complete college. The dozen or so whites who lived in Five Points in 2000 had a mean household income of $35,157, and none had achieved more than an associate's degree. Though blacks were and remain the majority, the neighborhood is increasingly diverse, according to a black community member within the district who chose to remain anonymous: "Wright-Dunbar is an 80 percent working-class community; however, it has the foundation in the making to become a middle-class community. Yes, it is majority African American. However, there is more and more diversity." The community member did not describe the increased diversity in the neighborhood or the business sector as gentrification, however: "The increased diversity is not gentrification—it is not [private and public partnerships] that have made a very big effort to make resources available to individuals who own their properties to stay in their homes."[33] This resident credited McLin's predecessor with initiating the Wright-Dunbar redevelopment efforts.

In preparation for the Dayton 2003 Celebration of Flight, a tribute to the historic accomplishments of the Wright brothers and poet Paul Laurence Dunbar, the city planned a Citirama "showcase of homes" event and purchased three demonstration houses as examples of the

8. To celebrate the Wright Brothers' event, Rhine McLin wore a dress reflective of the period. Courtesy Rhine McLin.

type of construction desired in the area. Competitively selected developers were chosen to construct the homes, and, significantly, 74 percent of the thirty contractors who worked on the three demonstration homes were minority firms.[34] The developers used $12 million to build new roads and utility lines, redeveloped five historic buildings and twenty owner-occupied homes, constructed eight new homes matching the late-nineteenth-century style of existing struc-

9. Mayor Rhine McLin (far right) in Wright-Dunbar Village with the Dayton Public Schools Construction Technologies Program to enable students to rehabilitate a property on Mercer Street. Courtesy Rhine McLin.

tures, and rehabilitated eight vacant lots. They also coordinated with the city to cut off street entrances and added streetlights to improve the perception of the safety of the neighborhood.[35]

As of 2004 forty-five new homes had been built in Wright-Dunbar and seventy-three renovated. According to one of the contracting companies, the success of the redevelopment project was evident in the value of homes being sold in the village: some went for $150,000 in 2003 that would have sold in 1995 for less than $10,000.[36] Among the contractors and organizations involved were ISUS, a charter school partially funded by YouthBuild USA;[37] the Innerwest Community Development Corporation; and the Ecumenical Neighborhood Development Corporation.

The Wright-Dunbar Village redevelopment project was recognized with much publicity and awards. The neighborhood became a locally designated historic district in March 2002. One of the village developers, the Miller Valentine Group, received the Associated Builders and Contractors' Award for Excellence in Renovation in 2003 for its work on the Victor Cassano Senior Health Center, located within the district. First Lady Laura Bush visited the village in

2003, and the project's leaders received the HUD Opportunity and Empowerment Award in 2004.

One anonymous community member noted that McLin continued the work in Wright-Dunbar that had begun under the previous administration, though not with the same level of leadership or resources. Another active neighborhood community leader within the village concurred, saying, "Really hardly anything has been done since she's been in office, nothing in particular has been done in Wright-Dunbar. ... With the ISUS program—they swooped up some land and are putting up some replica houses, but according to the National Trust [for Historic Preservation] it shouldn't have happened."[38]

Despite such criticism, the city made efforts in Wright-Dunbar under McLin's leadership. McLin purchased a home and moved into the primarily working-class neighborhood in 2004, commenting, "By purchasing a home in the Wright-Dunbar neighborhood, it gives me an opportunity to show my commitment to the restoration of this historic neighborhood. It is a win-win situation."[39] Her support of the redevelopment project was tied to the neighborhood's past as the cultural center of African American life in Dayton. She remarked: "Not only has the Wright-Dunbar Village been revitalized after years of disinvestment, but the surrounding neighborhoods are also starting to benefit as well. We are creating vibrant neighborhoods and new housing choices for residents that were not available before."[40]

In addition to moving into the neighborhood, McLin had the opportunity to support the funding of some of the redevelopment project's final stages. She voted with the commission to fund the last two phases of the project and its showcase of urban homes in 2003, providing more than $300,000 in marketing and loan interest support for area corporations.[41] She also voted in 2005 to give Wright-Dunbar Inc. a $994,100 grant provided by HUD to rehabilitate the interiors of six historic buildings within the village that were ready for commercial tenants. McLin's support of the development effort in this historic African American community was thus both symbolic, as evidenced by her move to the neighborhood, and substantive, as shown by her votes to fund the project's final stages.

Subsequently other successes came to the village, including rising home values and more home construction; the final two stages of the project called for nineteen new homes and thirteen renovated homes. Students built many of the homes from ISUS; many Dayton-area minority youth were employed while they were being trained in the construction industry. Moreover, PriMed, a local physicians' group, renovated space in the village for a new office at a cost of $801,000. WDAO Radio, the country's first full-time rhythm and blues station, moved into the district as well, with support from the City of Dayton.

Comparable efforts supported by McLin include the Phoenix project, a housing development investment near Good Samaritan Hospital in West Dayton adjacent to downtown, where there are no income restrictions for homebuyers. The initiative, modeled after Project Genesis, was an effort to remove dilapidated homes and build new ones in Dayton's Fairview and Mount Auburn neighborhoods, near the hospital. After voting in 2003 to give $5 million to the project, McLin remarked, "I'm pleased we could come together as the catalyst for the improvement to the Good Samaritan Hospital neighborhood."[42] The $5 million investment was to be used for affordable housing subsidies. In addition, in January 2008 McLin and fellow commissioners voted to approve funding for the new construction of forty homes in West Dayton, where most of the city's black population resides. The three-to-four-bedroom homes were an $8.1 million investment billed as lease-to-own properties with monthly rents averaging $485.[43]

In a city that offered the most affordable housing in the state at a time when the city was facing an economic shortfall, McLin lobbied aggressively for improved housing and neighborhood redevelopment. She opposed a state Senate bill to change municipal residency requirements in an effort to keep a middle-class tax base. Her supportive actions, particularly in the area of home construction, reaped some substantive rewards. In 2002 and 2003 there was an increase in home construction in Dayton and throughout the region. In 2002 housing construction was at its busiest in Dayton since 1986.[44]

The housing redevelopment projects examined herein were not specifically targeted at African Americans, as the homes constructed with the Phoenix, Wright-Dunbar, and Genesis projects sold for market value at approximately $150,000 each. These homes cost more than the average Dayton African American could afford. The new and renovated constructions in formerly dilapidated areas changed the image of the neighborhoods, however, and as a result positively affected the quality of life of neighborhood residents, both black and white.

*Support for Vacant Demolitions, Victims of*
*Predatory Lending, and Low-Income Families*

In addition to supporting various housing and neighborhood redevelopment projects, McLin lobbied local and federal officials for assistance in tearing down nuisance properties. Between 1999 and 2003 the city received $2.5 million in federal funds to demolish 171 single-family homes and 58 commercial buildings. Moreover, McLin voted with the city commission in 2004 to spend $1.1 million to demolish approximately 14 commercial and apartment buildings, saying, "We agree it's tough to stimulate new housing or economic investment in areas where vacant eyesores exist, so we are taking a much more aggressive approach to removing them from our community."[45] McLin saw the removal of vacant properties as an extension of the broader housing and neighborhood redevelopment agenda she advocated. In 2008 she lobbied the federal government, with the assistance of Commissioner Nan Whaley and U.S. senator Sherrod Brown, for $5.5 million in foreclosure assistance to knock down blighted properties, including 25–30 apartment buildings.[46] With the additional federal funds, McLin aggressively supported city efforts to tear down nuisance properties.

While not targeted directly at Dayton's black community, McLin's support of these demolition efforts affected it. The efforts were citywide, but many of the properties were located in West Dayton.[47] When left standing, vacant and abandoned structures often become sites for illegal activity, arson, and other concerns that eventually may cost the city more in services.[48] Thus the demolition of vacant West Side properties in particular had positive effects for black quality of life in Dayton.

In addition to the demolition effort, McLin announced the development of a "weed and seed" program to encourage downtown businesses and area homeowners across city neighborhoods to better maintain their properties. The city's Housing and Neighborhood Strategies Task Force, with the support of the mayor, conducted litter campaigns and sent inspectors to areas to warn owners about property upkeep. McLin's efforts thus involved not only the construction of new homes and the tearing down of dilapidated structures but also efforts to more effectively deal with yard violations. She commented: "This is an area where citizens have requested help from City Hall, and we are giving it to them."[49] McLin understood that citizens demanded that the broader housing and neighborhood redevelopment effort include the demolition of vacant structures and the enforcement of the city's housing regulations.[50]

McLin also helped to lead the fight against predatory lending practices. Such practices are particularly relevant to blacks, as there is a geographical concentration of subprime mortgages in neighborhoods with high concentrations of low-income and minority households.[51] Understanding that blacks are often targets of such practices, McLin actively supported taking legal action in Dayton. In 2001, for example, her Dayton City Commission colleague Dean Lovelace introduced the first anti-predatory lending law for a municipality in Ohio, and McLin supported the ordinance in her first campaign. In 2005, as a candidate for reelection, she accused her opponent, a key figure in Dayton's home construction industry, of not acknowledging the targeted effects of predatory lending.[52] At a joint event with other Ohio mayors in 2008 McLin exclaimed, "Unfortunately today's economic times are causing more and more people to fall prey to the lure of the so-called payday loan operations."[53] With these comments McLin expressed her continued support for safer lending opportunities for low-to-moderate-income families.

On the national level McLin supported the creation of housing opportunities for low-income families. As of 2008 McLin was one of only two public officials in Ohio who supported the National Housing Trust Fund Campaign, an effort by the federal government to establish sources of revenue to build, rehabilitate, and preserve 1.5 million units of housing for the lowest-income families over the next ten years. President George W. Bush signed the Housing and Economic Recovery Act in July 2008, establishing the National Housing Trust Fund, and a February 6, 2009, *New York Times* editorial supported the project and encouraged even more federal funding. The fund—as well as McLin's support of it—is significant to black Dayton residents because one of its primary goals is that at least 75 percent of it should be used for housing that is affordable for extremely low-income households.[54] These funds indirectly benefit low-income black residents of Dayton.

As the examples above demonstrate, McLin's focus on housing and neighborhood redevelopment was broad in scope. From her support of construction projects such as Wright-Dunbar and Genesis to support for the increased enforcement penalties for housing violations to support for commission and state legislation affecting housing and the demolition of properties, her efforts were multiple and significant. Some observers hope that initiatives to improve housing conditions and the development of more housing opportunities may improve race relations in the city. According to the former president of the Dayton Urban League, housing segregation has a negative effect on race relations: "Look at how people live. They don't go to church together. They're not at a lot of social events together. If you had more instances where people were being together more than apart, there would be more community and better understanding of the [racial] issues."[55] McLin's support of the Wright-Dunbar Village, for instance, may help over time to improve the city's culture of housing segregation since the once primarily black low-income neighborhood is increasingly becoming more diverse and more populous.

*HOPE VI and the Dayton Metropolitan Housing Authority*

The mayor's support for housing and neighborhood development did not have a good beginning. According to custom, the mayor of Dayton has the power to make two appointments to the Dayton Metropolitan Housing Authority (DMHA), the agency with countywide jurisdiction over the research, development, and recommendation of policy and programs to assist citizens in obtaining affordable housing. (DMHA was changed to Greater Dayton Premier Management in October 2011.) DMHA is also responsible for the operation of the public housing projects in the Dayton region. In her first year in office McLin asked two DMHA employees appointed by her predecessor to resign. She initially claimed they had not contacted her or reported on their progress or duties during the eight months she had been in office. The *Dayton Daily News* did not support the dismissal, commenting in an editorial that "for someone who says her forte is building bridges, Mayor McLin's missives were clumsy and insulting."[56] The paper did support McLin's efforts to get updates regarding the agency's progress, however. Specifically McLin wanted to know where the agency planned to rehouse the residents slated to be affected by a DMHA plan to raze more than four hundred units of public housing.[57]

Formed by the state of Ohio, the DMHA received federal support to raze the buildings through the HUD HOPE (Housing Opportunities for People Everywhere) VI program. HOPE VI was a $5 billion federal public housing program enacted by Congress in 1992 as a result of the recommendations of the National Commission on Severely Distressed Public Housing.[58] That commission, established by Congress in 1989, had been charged with identifying severely distressed public housing developments and assessing strategies to improve their condition. The commission's national action plan to address the problem included the creation of HOPE VI. According to HUD, the program was designed to affect "revitalization in three general areas: physical improvements, management improvements, and social and community services to address resident needs."[59]

The DMHA attained HOPE VI funding following a long application process. With 3,500 units of public housing in Montgomery County, the DMHA often has plans to rehabilitate or demolish several structures at any given time.[60] The agency had succeeded at winning smaller grants, such as an $800,000 HUD demolition grant in 1998 to tear down Summit Court, a public housing complex. Earlier in the decade of the 1990s however, the agency was less successful at securing significant grants. By 1999, after several unsuccessful applications, the agency was finally awarded an $18.3 million HOPE VI revitalization grant to finance the demolition of three public housing units in Dayton: Edgewood Courts, Metro Gardens, and Metro Annex. The grant also provided funds to rehabilitate or rebuild one hundred Old Dayton View homes. (Old Dayton View is a neighborhood within the Northwest Priority Board area on Dayton's West Side that was 86 percent black as of 2000.)[61]

The various HOPE VI project developers were sued in 2002 by the Dayton chapter of the National Association of Minority Contractors, who alleged that the developing partners had failed to follow federal guidelines to create an open and competitive bidding process.[62] David Abney, the president of the local chapter, claimed, "In my capacity as the president of Wise Construction, I have been denied the opportunity to bid as the general contractor or joint venturer in the HOPE VI housing initiative."[63] Jeff Payne, the HOPE VI project manager, replied that Wise Construction did not respond to a DMHA request for qualifications issued in August 2000. The suit had the potential to stall the project, which had a December 2003 completion deadline because low-income tax credits were being used to finance the initiative.[64]

McLin actively supported the DMHA's procurement of HOPE VI and other grants for public housing development in the Dayton area. In 2003 the DMHA began demolishing 1,200 public housing units in Dayton, a project that was still ongoing four years later. The agency developed approximately one thousand affordable housing units throughout the city during the same time period.[65] In July 2008 McLin voted with fellow commissioners to purchase and dispose of a property on Negley Place, on Dayton's West Side, a HOPE VI project.[66] Through her support she lent her political capital to the physical plan for the new developments. Many new developments were built with a sense of community in mind, replacing a popular yet outdated superblock design.[67]

In addition to advocating for the redevelopment of neighborhoods through public-private partnerships and supporting the construction of new public housing projects with the DMHA, in 2005 McLin helped initiate the ORION (Organizing Resources to Improve Our Neighborhoods) Solution to "address the undesirable circumstances" affecting Dayton residents.[68] Through the collaborative efforts of city departments, neighborhood organizations, and other private entities, the ORION Solution sought to increase civic participation in neighborhood projects by gathering information about the issues negatively affecting the quality of life in neighborhoods. According to the *Dayton Daily News*, the ORION Solution aimed "to reduce crime and generally improve quality of life," coordinating "neighborhood organizations and citizens to help focus services such as police, fire, building inspection, recreations and public works to provide some extra help."[69] After the appropriate data were gathered, the city departments used them to allocate resources over a concentrated four-month period. Throughout the period work teams comprising members of city government, neighborhood groups, and other community-based organizations served as guides to a neighborhood's development. The idea was that at the conclusion of the period of concentration, the neighborhood would be better positioned to continue to address the quality of life issues that most negatively affected it. The city then evaluated proposals from neighborhoods that competed to be a part of the next round of intensified efforts.

Four neighborhoods were chosen for the first round of concentrated resource support, two of them within Dayton's primarily black Innerwest and Northwest Priority Board areas: Wolf Creek and Old Dayton View. The other two neighborhoods were located in the adjacent, racially mixed Fair River Oaks Priority Board area northwest of downtown. Subsequent rounds of targeted impact focused on neighborhoods throughout the city. In the end, while the ORION Solution was designed to stabilize challenged neighborhoods throughout the city, the neighborhoods chosen included significant minority populations such as Mount Vernon and Roosevelt. A fall 2007 report identified the improvements made to those neighborhoods as a result of the ORION Solution, including the removal of forty-five tons of debris and an increased police presence that resulted in hundreds of traffic violations.[70]

Like the projects discussed above, McLin's support of HOPE VI similarly benefitted black communities in Dayton. While McLin's predecessor was instrumental in assisting the Omega Baptist Church, a predominantly black congregation, with securing the city's first HOPE VI grant in February 1999, valued at $44 million, McLin was instrumental in securing its completion as a project to revitalize a twelve-block area with 150 new mixed-income, single-family homes, the rehabilitation of current housing, and reconfigured streets and infrastructure in one of the city's most crime-ridden neighborhoods.[71]

### West Dayton Retail and the Role of the City Manager

Mayor McLin noted in interviews that Dayton's economic vitality was a function not only of improved housing opportunities but also of improved neighborhood aesthetics. She remarked that investments in neighborhoods were unlikely to occur if those neighborhoods suffered from an image of decay. Hence McLin actively supported the investment of retailers in the West Dayton community. Understanding that the relationship among housing, neighborhood redevelopment, and economic development in the neighborhoods was symbiotic, particularly in Dayton's black community, she worked to preserve the presence of West Dayton retail giants Rite-Aid and Kroger.

Many of McLin's efforts on behalf of Dayton blacks took place behind the scenes. An interview with Dayton's then city manager, Rashad Young, suggested that McLin wielded much informal power. Addressing how well McLin responded to major problems facing the black community, Young indicated that she exercised her influence "in very subtle ways." Young elaborated: "She's not at the podium and might not even make [the issue] very pronounced with me. . . . She's on the phone."[72] For example, in 2007 Rite-Aid, a national drug store chain, announced that it would be closing Dayton-area retail stores, many in West Dayton. McLin and Young had a difference of opinion concerning the commitment of city resources for the stores' retention, but Young said McLin took an aggressive behind-the-scenes approach. She called Rite-Aid executives to determine how many stores were slated to close, where, and when. She pressed company executives to provide convincing marketing evidence to support their decision to close, asking what the revenue numbers were, what the shrinkage variables were, and why Rite-Aid had chosen not to invest in store facades. According to Young, McLin asked the senior vice-presidents of Rite-Aid and of other businesses threatening to leave West Dayton, "What's your commitment to African Americans in Dayton?" She followed up her attempts to retain these retail stores in Dayton's black community by asking the presidents of the companies to visit Dayton to discuss the retail drain in the community.[73]

While McLin's efforts to support the black community were not always exercised publicly, Young argued that she actively pursued the interests of blacks (and not at the expense of the primarily white community in East Dayton): "[McLin is] one of the hardest working mayors I've ever seen. She walks around regularly at 10 p.m. just talking to people. She gives rides to strangers—blacks normally . . . but she is in a difficult spot, caught in the middle a lot. To some black leaders, she's not doing enough on the West Side; from the East Side the perception is that all she does is cater to the West Side. Kroger is a classic example."[74] In 2007 Kroger, a national grocery chain, announced it would be closing a West Dayton store by January 2008 and opening an East Dayton store at a cost of $16 million. A coalition of West Dayton civil rights leaders, residents, and black ministers protested. They garnered nearly three hundred signatures for a petition submitted to the city commission asking it to cease future dealings with the company. Black Dayton minister Rev. Jerome McCorry said, "We try not to make it a racial issue, but West Dayton is not treated like the rest of the city."[75] McCorry asked other clergy to use their pulpits to express support for a boycott and to utilize church transportation to help residents travel to other West Dayton area grocery stores. Earlier McCorry's group had held a community meeting with more than one hundred residents calling for a boycott of all Kroger stores. At the meeting McCorry also asked residents to make copies of their grocery receipts and pass them on to their church secretaries to be collected and tabulated in an effort to estimate the black community's buying power. Kroger officials who attended the meeting stated that their decision to close the store was not about the community it served: "We have operated a store at that location for 20 years. It has not been profitable for us. It is very hard for me to stand in front of you. We felt it was our responsibility to come and speak with you. Our intention, be that as it may, is to close in January."[76]

The black ministers' boycott of Dayton Kroger stores was highly visible. Rather than publicly support the boycott, McLin again opted to work the phones, questioning Kroger officials' commitment to the black community and demanding that they document their lack of profit.[77] The Kroger store closed nonetheless, and the construction of the proposed East Dayton store was delayed as a result of the economy.

Young's references to McLin's behind-the-scenes efforts on behalf of blacks demonstrate the working relationship between the city manager and the mayor. Young directly credited McLin for his hiring as an assistant city manager, interim city manager, and later selection as city manager. When asked whether McLin made key personnel changes within her appointment powers that benefitted blacks, Young responded, "Hiring me."[78] Although Young noted that McLin had very limited appointment powers according to the city charter, his reply suggested the informal mechanisms at play. An interview with McLin corroborated her use of informal influence on Young's hiring as she indicated that she wanted to be mayor long enough to ensure his tenure was successful.[79]

### Black Perceptions of McLin's Behind-the-Scenes Approach

Perceptions of McLin's efforts in the black community were mixed. Black supporters such as Alvin Freeman, a grassroots organizer, and B. Cato Mayberry, a higher education official, were quick to point out the constraints of the economic climate and the unrealistically high expectations of some blacks. Freeman and Mayberry claimed that difficult economic circumstances prevented many African American Daytonians from perceiving McLin as doing her job effectively.[80] Others, such as the anonymous Wright-Dunbar community member quoted above, felt that McLin did not do a good job of improving black quality of life in Dayton. The editor of the only black newspaper in the city, Don Black, commented that all he saw of McLin was "the mayor cutting ribbons in other parts of the community," rather than someone working "to keep economic vitality."[81] For some blacks, then, McLin's front-and-center approach on initiatives such as housing and neighborhood redevelopment contrasted with her seemingly quiet approach toward retaining black neighborhood retail.

Leaders in one of the city's primarily black priority board areas felt that McLin's efforts in the black community had few tangible results. Annie Bonaparte, the first vice chairperson of the Innerwest Priority Board, argued, "The black community doesn't have any businesses. Nobody is trying to create anything, especially in the black community."[82] The president of the same board, Claude Bell Sr., could not name any important policy ideas directly affecting blacks that McLin introduced or implemented. Bell felt that McLin needed to communicate better with the black community: "I should not have to be president of the NAACP to get attention," he said. He noted of McLin, "She's likable, [but] she doesn't touch her father, who always had time [for the black community]."[83] As Bell's statement suggests, McLin faced the high expectation from some blacks that she would devote as much time to their community as the mayor of a majority-white city as her father had as the state representative of a majority-black district. Clearly, given such expectations, she fell short.

Regardless of the community perceptions, Mayor McLin did give attention to issues that had a positive effect on blacks' quality of life in the racially divided city of Dayton. Unlike Mayor Ford, whose efforts focused on a small number of major priorities, McLin's efforts were many and varied. They included the development of programs such as the ORION Solution and support for a variety of efforts, from the public housing initiatives of the DMHA to the attack on predatory lending and the state senate municipal residency bill. McLin supported blacks in Dayton mostly indirectly, through her pursuit of priorities that affected Dayton citizens more widely. Given McLin's more diffuse approach, it is reasonable to expect that her efforts on behalf of the black community may have been less effective than Mayor Ford's. It seems, for example, that her behind-the-scenes approach to representing black interests was not effective in retaining businesses in West Dayton.

Even still, for the housing initiatives she backed, McLin was successful in securing the support of significant private partners and public officials. Many of these private partner organizations were led by influential whites, such as the leaders at CityWide Development Corporation and the Dayton Area Chamber of Commerce and a number of the public officials she successfully courted to support various legislative initiatives. McLin convinced many influential whites that they would benefit from supporting the efforts, and each of them had a stake in the city's housing efforts under McLin's leadership; among such leaders was Gregory Johnson, CEO of the Dayton Metropolitan Housing Authority, and members of the Housing Appeals Boards. McLin's effort to obtain the support of white public officials and corporate or nonprofit leaders is an example of her ability to universalize the interests of blacks as interests that mattered to everyone. As chapter 8 will explain in more detail, largely through her rhetoric in State of the City addresses and in behind-the-scenes conversations, McLin framed her often-indirect advocacy of black interests in a way that did not alienate the potential support of key white leaders. In fact it appears that white public officials were initially drawn to support preestablished city efforts on housing and related initiatives under McLin in part because of her universalizing black-interests approach.

McLin's approach to representing black interests within Dayton's non-majority-black context did not deny a racial dilemma, nor did it advance racialized policy appeals. While McLin was moderately successful with the approach, her efforts and actions on behalf of blacks were quite different from those of Ford in Toledo. Whereas he was often able to propose and implement policies and programs almost unilaterally, McLin's role as a weak mayor limited her to supporting others' already initiated actions and taking additional symbolic actions.

# CHAPTER 7

# Trickle-Up Public Opinion

## Universalizing Black Interests Perceptions

I think the mayor is 100 percent dedicated to what she feels is right, but is it the right path? Could that energy be used elsewhere?

Ken Sulfridge, AFSCME-Dayton Region union leader

Mayor Ford of Toledo and Mayor McLin of Dayton were both first elected under similar conditions in 2001. In both cities severe budget shortfalls, struggling public schools and downtowns, and a lack of corporate leadership posed serious challenges. And both cities elected black mayors who were "firsts," surmounting significant historical barriers to public office: Ford was the first black mayor of Toledo, and McLin was the first female mayor of Dayton. Even given these and other constraints, however, Ford and McLin were able to introduce policies and programs that had an impact on the quality of life of black residents.

Chapters 5 and 6 showed how the presence of a black mayor led to an active pursuit of black interests on select issues: contracting for Ford and housing and neighborhood development for McLin. In this chapter after defining what is meant by "black quality of life," I will detail the extent to which the mayors' actions are examples of the pursuit of black interests. In addition, I examine the responses of eighty-one interviewees to three questions to reveal white and black citizens' differing perceptions of their mayors' efforts. I will then draw conclusions regarding which of the hypotheses of this book have been confirmed by the data.

*Assessing Black Quality of Life*

In an effort to better code and define particular mayoral efforts as substantively meaningful attempts to improve "black quality of life," I created a political typology that classifies mayoral activity. The representative efforts range from the largely descriptive to the seminally substantive. This range serves as the frame for describing what constitutes quality-of-life improvements. I conceptualized five essential categories. For any mayoral effort, a value of one is low, indicating that the mayor made only a relatively insignificant attempt to improve black quality of life, while a value of five is high since activities placed in category five were more difficult to pursue. Each category contextualizes how a mayor achieved his or her goals and indicates how he or she prioritized policy decisions through administrative management.

*1. The Politics of Shared Racial Experience.* Evidence of mayoral responsiveness and recognition of black constituent concerns is manifested in symbolic gestures situated within the context of shared racial experience. One example in which a mayor expresses such shared racial experience with constituents is Harold Washington's 1983 campaign slogan, "It's our turn."[1] Another might be the mayor's officiating in the marriage ceremony of black constituents.[2] Noticeably in these examples the mayor and the constituents are drawn together by African Americans' common experience of slavery and institutionalized racism. Within this context blacks are also diverse, and there are individual differences in how much intensity African American mayors exercise in addressing black constituent interests.

*2. Access and Opportunity: The Policy Incorporation of Black Interests.* Evidence of black mayors' attempts at incorporating and mobilizing blacks includes their appointment and hiring of qualified African Americans in visible, significant positions across the spectrum of city government. In the example of hiring practices the black mayor is making a political and economic contribution to the lived experiences of qualified African Americans. Identifying employment opportunities for blacks is an expression of shared racial experience since blacks may not have been given the same level of access and opportunity in prior or subsequent administrations. A mayor's active hiring and appointing of qualified African Americans makes a difference for politics and power.

*3. The Politics of Constituent Service.* Constituent services range from neighborhood street cleaning, paving, and development to trash removal and snowplowing to tree stump removal and improved street lighting and signs.

*4. Programs for Black Middle-Class and/or Low-Income Residents.* Evidence in this policy or program arena is multilayered as the beneficiaries might extend beyond the black community. In the allocation of city contracts, for example, are contracts awarded according to the percentage required by the city's good-faith goals? Does the mayor monitor the allocation of the contracts in a way that is fair and equitable to ensure that minority contractors have access and opportunity to apply?[3] In a community where African Americans are disproportionately poor, moreover, what programs has the mayor introduced that may have broad appeal and at the same time strongly meet the particular interests of blacks? Policies that are designed to provide neighborhood redevelopment and renovation—for example, HUD's HOPE VI programs—may have broad appeal to low-income residents and at same time significantly meet the interests of blacks. This area of policy concern is considered community development as it focuses on social welfare–defined policies and programs.[4]

*5. Substantive Management Priorities.* Evidence of policy and program effectiveness herein includes social welfare policies and programs that improve access to health care, such as the introduction of a health care network for the uninsured or a citywide smoking ban, increased employment opportunities for minority youth, and the substantive support of the financial and academic status of the city's public school system.

Each category in the typology reflects a different level of responsiveness to African American citizens' interests. The typology provides a structured mechanism from which to evaluate the extent and breadth of Ford's and McLin's active pursuit of policies and programs that worked to improve the quality of life of black residents. In combination with respondents' answers to interview questions, as well as content analysis of city council minutes and agendas, I use the typology to frame each of the mayors' activities designed to improve the quality of life of blacks (see chapter 8).

*Interview Methodology*

Thirty semi-structured interviews were performed in Dayton and fifty-three in Toledo.[5] These interviews assisted in the identification of policy actions and program developments introduced and/or implemented by the mayors and the formal and informal mechanisms they used. Four separate interview schedules were conducted with different categories of persons, wherein respondents generally answered thirty of the same questions. The four categories of persons interviewed were labeled General Influentials, Public Officials, Mayors, and Community Activists.

The category of "General Influentials" included members of campaign and administration staff, journalists, academic and business leaders, friends and opponents of the mayor, and other relevant actors with knowledge of the mayor's efforts. "Public Officials" encompassed elected officeholders in varying roles at the time of the interviews. Dayton's unelected city manager was also included. Former elected officials were categorized as "General Influentials." The "Mayors" category included the two mayors, Ford and McLin, and their immediate predecessors, though McLin's predecessor chose not to be interviewed. "Community Activists" included members of the black community, pastors, leaders of race-advancement associations, and neighborhood activists. The interviews were conducted from June 10, 2008, through August 7, 2008. Appendix B includes a list of the questions asked in each category of interview.

Data from the interviews and content analysis of city council/city commission minutes and agendas were coded to identify the extent of each mayor's active pursuit of black interests.[6] The city council in Toledo meets biweekly, whereas the city commission in Dayton meets weekly. Therefore content analysis was performed on a total of 108 minutes/agendas for the entirety of Mayor Ford's term in Toledo. In Dayton a total of 386 city commission minutes and agendas were analyzed, from the beginning of Mayor McLin's term in 2002 through August 1, 2008, as McLin began her attempt at reelection to a third term.

The combined data show that Mayor Ford actively pursued more substantive black interests than Mayor McLin. This finding is especially significant as it suggests that a larger black population has little effect on a black mayor's policy and program efforts in the black community, as previous research has determined in congressional and state-level politics.[7] Given the typology referenced above, I coded the number of activities the mayors pursued in the interests of blacks. Figure 5 indicates the amount of time the mayors spent in said activities across five defined typological categories in the model.

Both McLin and Ford spent a substantial majority of their efforts to aid black constituents on category 3 activities (constituent services). This type of effort is significant as city culture often dictates that neighborhoods that are better served in terms of service delivery are often those associated with the mayor.[8] Hence the presence of a black mayor had an impact on the delivery of city services to residents of poorer neighborhoods.

The data also show that Ford spent 43 percent of his time conducting substantive efforts in categories 4 and 5. McLin made no efforts in category 5, suggesting she was limited in her powers to impact the quality of life of blacks in Dayton. McLin spent a larger percentage of her time on the more symbolic efforts of categories 1 and 2. These findings suggest that government structure has a significant influence on the introduction and implementation of policies and programs that are designed to improve African Americans' quality of life in Toledo and Dayton.

*Perceptions of Mayors' Efforts Regarding Black Interests*

Three interview questions specifically aimed to identify how McLin's and Ford's efforts were perceived by city residents: "From your perspective, what do you see as the major problems facing African Amer-

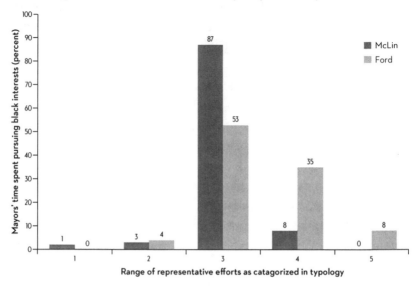

icans in City X, and how were/have these issues been addressed by Mayor X?"; "Are/were there important new policy ideas directly affecting the African American community implemented by Mayor X's administration?"; and "How would you characterize Mayor X's efforts at pursuing programs designed to improve the quality of life of black residents?"[9] The demographics of the interviewees were representative of the cities' populations, as 56 percent of the respondents were white, 40 percent were black, and 4 percent were Latino.

Figure 6 displays how well Dayton and Toledo respondents thought their mayors addressed major black problems that the respondents identified. The data refer to the questions, "From your perspective, what do you see as the major problems facing African Americans in City X [and] How were/have these issues been addressed by Mayor X?" While 58 percent of white respondents indicated that their mayor had responded very well to major black problems in the city, only 39 percent of black respondents felt the same—a difference of nearly 20 percent. This finding suggests that whites were more likely than blacks to see their black mayors as responsive to black problems. Noticeably 12 percent of blacks found the mayor had addressed black

FIG. 6. How well Mayor Ford (Toledo) and Mayor McLin (Dayton) addressed major black problems

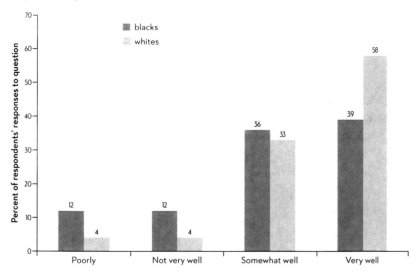

problems poorly or not very well, versus only 4 percent of whites. Hence the black respondents were less convinced of the success of their black mayor's efforts to address problems in their community.

In reply to a question asking respondents to identify a policy or program of the mayor's that directly affected the black community, more than 90 percent of whites and blacks were able to respond with the details of a particular policy or program (figure 7). Blacks and whites overwhelmingly indicated that the black mayor implemented important new policy ideas directly affecting African Americans (97 percent and 91 percent respectively). Blacks did so almost unanimously, suggesting blacks had a greater knowledge of issues than did whites. Moreover, the high response rate of both black and white constituents suggests that the mayors were effective in communicating to their constituents. The fact that such a high percentage of whites could identify such policies or programs, however, could potentially be detrimental to the mayor's efforts as well. If a majority of those white respondents were prejudiced, their recognition of the mayor's efforts might cause them to throw their support to a different mayoral candidate.

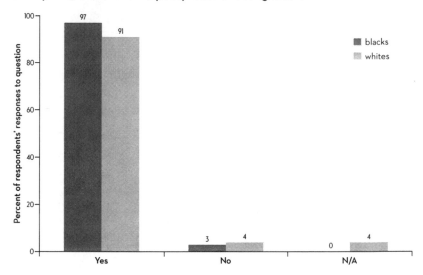

**FIG. 7.** Dayton and Toledo respondents' recognition of mayor's (Ford or McLin) policy ideas affecting blacks

Figure 8 identifies Dayton and Toledo respondents' responses to a second question that asked how they would characterize their mayor's efforts at pursuing programs designed to improve the quality of life of black residents. The pattern is the same, with whites responding more positively: 42 percent of whites indicated the McLin and Ford did "a lot" in terms of pursuing programs to improve black quality of life, versus only 33 percent of blacks. At the same time, 30 percent of blacks indicated that the mayor either "did not do enough" or "did not do nearly enough," whereas only 9 percent of whites responded in this way.[10]

The respondent data for Dayton and Toledo indicate that while whites and blacks were equally able to identify their mayor's pursuit of policies in the interests of blacks, whites consistently viewed these efforts as more successful than did blacks. When I examined the cities separately, I found similar results, with the distinction that Mayor Ford's black and white constituents perceived him to be notably more successful than Mayor McLin in addressing black concerns. Sixty-two percent of Toledo respondents indicated that Mayor Ford had addressed major problems facing the African American com-

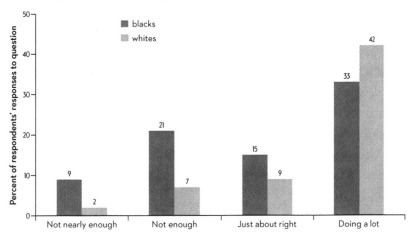

FIG. 8. Respondents' perceptions of mayoral leadership to improve black quality of life

munity "very well," as compared to only 34 percent for Mayor McLin in Dayton. Furthermore, 46 percent of Toledo respondents characterized Mayor Ford's efforts as "doing a lot," whereas only 21 percent of Dayton respondents indicated so for McLin. Sixty-five percent of the white leaders interviewed in Toledo indicated that Mayor Ford had addressed major problems facing African Americans "very well," as compared to 44 percent of whites in Dayton regarding Mayor McLin. On the same question 50 percent of blacks in Toledo responded "very well," compared to 23 percent of blacks in Dayton. In both Toledo and Dayton African American respondents perceived their black mayors' efforts more negatively than did whites.

A clear majority of white and black respondents in Dayton and Toledo indicated that the black mayor had implemented important new policy ideas directly affecting African Americans, yet their assessments differed in degree. Twenty-five percent of white Daytonians characterized Mayor McLin's efforts as "doing a lot," versus 15 percent of blacks. Fifty-one percent of white Toledoans responded that Mayor Ford was "doing a lot" for his black constituents, as compared to 45 percent of black Toledoans. In general Mayor Ford's constituents were more likely to recognize and approve of his efforts on behalf of blacks than were Mayor McLin's. Mayor McLin compared less favorably in every category according to the respondents.

### Assessment of Findings

The evidence from Dayton and Toledo supports earlier literature. That black mayors who had the institutional and formal powers of a strong-mayor system were more likely to actively pursue policies designed to improve the quality of life of black residents was confirmed.[11] While both Ford and McLin pursued black interests, Ford did so more substantively, and this difference was due to the institutional and formal powers of a strong-mayor system in Toledo but not in Dayton.

That black mayors who governed in cities with a large white middle-class population were more likely to actively pursue policies designed to improve the quality of life of black residents was also confirmed.[12] Toledo had a higher household median income and higher white median family income (in 1999 dollars) than Dayton. Mayor Ford was found to more actively pursue black interest policies and programs.[13]

That black mayors who served on city councils in which African Americans were a majority or a substantial minority were more likely to actively pursue black interests was also confirmed.[14] When Ford was mayor of Toledo, the city council had three black members, two elected from districts and one elected at large. Their presence had a significant impact on the passage of the few mayoral agenda items that needed council approval, though Ford also needed the support of white liberal council members.[15] Dayton's city commission had two black council members in addition to the mayor, though one was not an avid supporter of McLin's 2001 election. Moreover, on some issues, such as the mayor's support of a gay rights ordinance, the black commission members did not support McLin, whereas two liberal white members did. Hence the presence of black council members was a necessary but not sufficient criterion for the success of Ford's and McLin's agendas.

As I was nearing the process of completing field research in Dayton and Toledo, it became increasingly evident that the mayor's style and approach toward governing and the presence (or not) of effective professional relationships with members of the business community were two key variables significant to Ford's and McLin's efforts to improve black quality of life. Interviewees reported that McLin's personality was an asset (at times), while Ford's was considered to be a detriment In both cities members of the business community had good personal relationships with the mayors. These positive personal relationships had little effect on the mayors' policy actions and program developments, however. The result in each case, arguably, was the business community's limited support of the mayor and the mayor's efforts. Such limited support from business interests had a greater effect on Ford, who failed to be reelected, than on McLin, who had an extensive base of support in Dayton's African American community for her first reelection bid.

## THE INFLUENCE OF BUSINESS LEADERS IN TOLEDO

As reported in interviewees' many reflections, Mayor Ford generally suffered from weak relationships with the business community. The combination of what the *Toledo Blade* described as Mayor Ford's lackluster personality, his perceived lack of attentiveness to some business community members' concerns, and his perceived active promotion of black business at the expense of downtown economic development projects played a role in his failed reelection, particularly as it related to a loss of support from leaders in the construction trades as a result of his active promotion of minority contracting.

Many of the interviewed members of Toledo's business community familiar with Mayor Ford's administration lauded his efforts in the black community. Mayor Ford's creation of CareNet, interviewees agreed, was "his legacy."[16] Ford's purported desire to "create wealth" through the establishment of the Center for Capacity Building was also cited as significant.[17] Those two projects were the most often cited examples of his efforts to improve black quality of life. Nonetheless, respondents in Toledo's business community also found that Ford's style of governing suffered from "[a] lack of communication."[18] Hence Ford's professional relationship with the largely white business community was poor overall, though many business owners and union representatives personally liked him. Ford was credited with being knowledgeable on business-related issues, but his approach was viewed negatively. One member of the business community indicated that while Ford had "good personal relationships" with business leaders, he "did not come across as somebody who was leading the city." That same individual claimed that "as much as [Ford] wanted to be, he was not a good communicator."[19]

When pressed about Ford's one-on-one relationships with business leaders, another respondent replied that his relationship with Ford was "personally, very good."[20] When probed about Ford's professional relationship on behalf of the city, another key respondent said, "It's not his style to champion [issues]."[21] For these leaders Ford's approach, while not uninformed, "[came] off as really laid back," and it resulted in their perception that he was not as serious about meeting business needs as he was about some other goals. In addition, one business leader felt particularly snubbed, suggesting, "I infrequently felt I had access."[22] Thus Ford's professional relationship with members of the business community was not ideal. His approach to meeting business needs was challenged, his staff members' willingness to return phone calls was questioned, and many felt that what they perceived to be a lack of one-on-one meetings to discuss economic concerns only further highlighted his disinterest.

Mayor Ford responded to the criticism by acknowledging he could have done more to court the business community. He countered, however, that "Because I was a black man, I think when they saw me, they saw a black guy—quiet, overweight—who didn't care much about kissing their ass."[23] Yet even given their criticisms of Ford, the business leaders who were interviewed recognized his efforts to improve blacks' quality of life in Toledo. When asked to share their perceptions of the mayor's leadership in this area, most responded favorably. Many indicated Ford did "a lot" or "everything he could do" and described his work as "superb," saying, "He always supported the children." Moreover, one business leader even suggested that Ford "did not do enough."[24] The suggestion that Ford's active pursuit of black interests was extensive yet still not enough for the black community is compelling and implies that even when interviewees did not find Ford to have positive working relationships with the business community, they still recognized his efforts on black issues and thought that he could have done even more.

Ford's approach toward business was apparently different from what community leaders were accustomed to. Toledoans had only Ford's predecessor as an example of a strong mayor, as the city had changed its city charter to allow for a strong mayor only in 1993. Since Ford was only the second strong mayor under the new city charter, many residents, business leaders included, arguably compared his style of governance to that of Carleton Finkbeiner, his predecessor. Such comparisons likely caused Ford to have a weak professional relationship with the business community, given the significant personality differences between the two men.[25] These comparisons turned out to be significant, as many of these leaders, who may have voted for Ford in 2001, actively campaigned against his reelection bid in 2005.[26] The outcome suggests that a black mayor needs to maintain positive relationships with the business community to be most successful in pursuing policies and programs designed to improve black quality of life.

## THE INFLUENCE OF BUSINESS LEADERS IN DAYTON

Interviews with business leaders in Dayton revealed that many of them also compared Mayor McLin with her predecessor. According to one respondent, Mayor Turner "had been a strong mayor in [the] sense of [having] opinions [and being] able to articulate a vision." He then stated that "Mayor McLin does not come out of the same mold as her predecessor, an approach many in the business community are familiar with"; this respondent also felt that McLin did not understand business or the business community as well as her predecessor had.[27] Conversely a union leader with AFSCME–Dayton Region, when asked of McLin's relationship with civic leaders, responded with the comment recorded in the epigraph above. He continued: "She's a likable person, has energy, loves her job, but with a legacy like her father's, she could have done much more but [has been] wined and dined by big business."[28] These excerpts suggest that members of the business community who cast McLin in the shadow of her predecessor argued that she was not knowledgeable about business issues, while others who compared her to her father, a former member of the Ohio House of Representatives, perceived her as catering to business interests. While business leaders generally characterized their personal relationships with McLin as good, the interviews overall suggest that McLin was viewed as weak on business issues. Acknowledging this view, Mayor McLin replied that "the city's a conduit for businesses. We don't make businesses. But they don't understand that."[29]

Phillip L. Parker, the president and CEO of the Dayton Area Chamber of Commerce, reported that McLin supported a preexisting effort to build the capacity of minority contractors so that they would have the "wherewithal, information, and understanding of projects in a couple areas in Dayton." Yet Parker observed that "most businesses do not perceive doing business with the city as business friendly—they are concerned with the cost of doing business in a city with taxes when there is less regulation in townships." While McLin and members of her administration supported the chamber's contracting capacity program, Parker stated that many in the business community "do not think she gets business issues as well as she should."[30] Parker suggested that McLin was perceived as making an effort to support business but lacking in critical business knowledge.

Another active business community leader who chose to remain anonymous found McLin's efforts in the business arena acceptable: "On the housing front [McLin] is taking down a lot of vacant housing, [and she conducts] good community development work with businesses to develop neighborhoods [where] youth and gang violence are very visible." Furthermore, "McLin is in—in the inner city—with neighborhood watch programs and police; crime is not big in Dayton, but the perception is it is bad, [and] McLin asked to look at police and fire hiring within ranks at parity with the city's demographics . . . to look at how to get qualified blacks to apply." In addition, this business leader pointed out that McLin "used informal influence to help with fund requests for projects in the black community," though he noted that "she doesn't distinguish between white and black; when we talk about issues, it's not black or white; it's everybody." While this respondent noted McLin's efforts in the business community for blacks and the general public, he also stated, "She is not using the power of her political position yet."[31]

Thus it appears that while some in the business community pointed to efforts by McLin to spur economic development in the black community, the perception remained that she was weak politically and not competent when it came to business issues. McLin's relationship with business leaders appeared to be one of paradox and shadows. She lived in the shadow of her politician father and her Republican predecessor. She was viewed as likable and personable but also as "wacky" and "capricious." Such diverging perceptions foster tenuous business relationships at best.

MAYORAL PERSONALITY AND STYLE: TOLEDO

Mayor Ford also lived in the shadow of his predecessor, Carleton Finkbeiner, who, as noted, became his successor. Community members viewed Finkbeiner as more direct and confrontational than Ford. As the city's first strong mayor, Finkbeiner crafted a host of expectations concerning the position. In an editorial endorsing Ray Kest in the 2001 campaign, the *Toledo Blade* stated, "A strong mayor is by definition his or her community's most outspoken advocate and cheerleader."[32] Mayor Ford's approach to governing was different. He countered the criticisms of his personality, style, and governing approach in his 2005 State of the City address: "I have been criticized for what one pundit recently called my lumbering style. That I seem to be in perpetual hibernation and that nothing gets done or will be done. Fellow citizens, my style has been to work hard, work quietly, and have the work I've done speak for me. . . . I ran for mayor on the stated platform of serious leadership for serious times. You will never see me substitute frantic ravings in place of thoughtful planned-out action."[33] Constituents and the mainstream media expected a different style of governing—one that Mayor Ford was unwilling to deliver.

Because of Ford's style, the community's perception was that not much was accomplished during Ford's term. Election return comparisons demonstrate that many who supported Mayor Ford in 2001 chose not to support him in 2005.[34] As a result, he lost his reelection bid, which essentially destroyed his ability to implement the "quiet" agenda to improve black quality of life or to "create wealth" in the black community. This perception also led to a loss of power for the county Democratic Party, as Ford did not aggressively work with the chairwoman to ensure that vacant committee seats were filled by like-minded supporters of his agenda and administration. Ford indicated, "I was never really a leader in the [Democratic Party]; I was just the one willing to run—almost like I was a sacrificial lamb."[35] Meanwhile, a more conservative faction led by Finkbeiner was reported to have quietly filled vacant seats, enough to oust the party leader who supported Mayor Ford shortly before his reelection bid.[36] Mayor Ford's reportedly "lumbering" approach to governing was perceived as ineffective. Mayor Ford admitted that his personality had some political deficiencies: "I did my job and thought people would be able to see that I did it. I mistakenly and naively thought that if I fixed the $15 million deficit, most folks would reelect me just on that. I really wasn't a smiling type of guy. Toledo has a history of black politicians that tend to be more easy-going."[37] Mayor Ford's choice not to promote successes other than the balanced budget apparently backfired; his political deficiencies made it difficult for him to relate to voters and ultimately cost him reelection.

## MAYORAL PERSONALITY AND STYLE: DAYTON

Dayton's Mayor McLin was described in the interviews as "very likable," "very accessible," and "passionate"; one respondent stated that "everybody loves her." Yet it seems that not everybody did—another interviewee called her "wacky" and "not serious." Nonetheless, Mayor McLin's personality seems to have served her well. It was said that the former teacher "often ha[d] three or four kids with her at different city events," suggesting that her approachability made her a favorite of some young citizens.[38] Mayor McLin recognized the significance of her attention to youth: "When these kids see me, they see the mayor, and especially for black children and little girls, they feel as though they can become the mayor one day."[39] For Dayton youth she organized annual events like a Valentine's Day Jam and a Showcase of Talent.

While the respondents complimented her interactions with Dayton's young people, they also pointed to some of her personality deficiencies as mayor—deficiencies that McLin herself acknowledged: "I hate giving the State of the City [speech]," she said. "I am a workhorse, not a show horse."[40] For McLin achieving progress behind the scenes was a better use of time than giving State of the City speeches. It appears she understood her approach was foreign to many, and she saw much of the criticism of her style and approach as based in sexism. McLin believed that as the city's first female mayor, she was seen by the black community, her base of support, through the lens of sexism. She indicated, "People don't realize how sexist the black male establishment can be." In respect to her father selecting her to take his seat in the state House upon his death, she mused, "I didn't even think my Daddy thought that much of me."[41]

While McLin's personality was perceived as an asset in her symbolic work with youth, it was perceived as a detriment with the business community, causing some not to take her seriously. Such perceptions, particularly among black leaders and business leaders, hindered her ability to work on behalf of black quality of life, limiting the substantive progress she was able to make.[42]

### Additional Variables of Influence

While personality/style and business influence was shown to be significant, two additional variables also influenced the governing outcomes of the Ford and McLin mayoral administrations. Observation and analysis of Ford's and McLin's professional behavior revealed that the structure of the political system in which they governed and the extent to which each had ideologically similar council supporters significantly impacted their efforts to improve black quality of life.

STRUCTURE MATTERS

Ford and McLin's active pursuit of policies and programs designed to improve the quality of life of blacks in the non-majority-black cities of Toledo and Dayton was in part determined by the governmental structure in which the mayors governed. This finding confirms previous research that found mayoral structure to be significant.[43]

In Toledo the strong-mayor form of government equipped Mayor Ford with substantial authority concerning the city's economic development and businesses, permitting him to introduce and enact various policies and programs. Mayor Ford's personal visits to businesses, many unscheduled, to ask how the city could have helped and to evaluate their minority participation as listed on their contract applications, serve as an example of his use of strong-mayor authority.[44] His ability to directly hire dozens of city personnel and his responsibility to submit a proposed budget to the city council annually are additional examples of how he was able to use his strong-mayor powers to benefit African Americans.

In Dayton Mayor McLin suffered from her inability to make direct efforts to improve black quality of life. Though she was reported to have influence over some black appointments, such as the city manager, director of water, and director of public works, such influence was not transparent.[45] Generally McLin's power was limited. While she had the power to convene summits with private and public partners to devise strategies for making substantive changes, she had only one vote out of five on a city commission that enacted such changes. The limitations of a weak-mayor system caused McLin to be seen as unable to directly address major problems, despite her commitment to being a full-time mayor. In fact interview respondents frequently answered questions with the qualifying phrase "to the extent that she can . . . ," suggesting that many were cognizant of her limited powers.

McLin benefitted from her political family lineage, and she could heavily influence the all-Democratic commission to vote with her on major issues. Her influence extended only so far, however. On the controversial decision to extend rights and benefits to gay city employees, for example, she was forced to cast the tie-breaking vote to enact a policy that would further prevent discrimination against gays and lesbians.[46] She supported the ordinance despite negative community backlash, largely from the black religious community. McLin was unable to influence the other black Democratic commission members to vote with her on the ordinance, demonstrating that her influence was not all-encompassing. This vote came to be detrimental to McLin's reelection to a third term as it was regularly cited by African American pastors as a significant reason she did not earn their support in 2009.[47]

Given the tenuousness of McLin's influence, however, she was not entirely prohibited from making major contributions on behalf of blacks. As noted above, she moved into a newly redeveloped, predominantly black neighborhood. She introduced symbolic activities for the city youth, many of whom are black. Moreover, her personality arguably helped the average Dayton black citizen feel more connected to the mayor's office, as she continued to wear glasses with a square lens and round lens, and she occasionally skated to work—all in an effort to connect to Daytonians on a "street level" basis they could understand.[48] The limited powers of Dayton's mayor, then, leave the interests of African Americans to be determined in part by the occupant of the office. Yet even for those who may fairly actively pursue black interests, like McLin, limited powers hinder a mayor's ability to implement substantive changes.

## THE ROLE OF IDEOLOGICAL CONGRUENCE ON COUNCIL/COMMISSION

A second observation that emerged from the field research is that the presence of like-minded members on the major legislative body—

council or commission—played a significant role in the mayor's efforts to improve black quality of life. This finding confirms previous research that found that the presence of black council members had an impact on black political representation.[49]

Mayor McLin had some influence over members of the city commission, who are elected on a non-partisan ballot in at-large elections every four years. While she was mayor, all members of the commission were Democrats, and as she sought reelection in 2009 three of them (including the mayor herself) were black and two were white. While it was possible for Mayor McLin to achieve the necessary three-person majority with the support of her two fellow black Democrats, the aforementioned vote on extending benefits to gay employees serves as an example of how ideology may matter more than shared racial experience. The vote demonstrates that where blacks in the commission disagreed, Mayor McLin benefitted from having like-minded white members to support her positions.

Mayor Ford, on the other hand, led a city council of twelve members, ten Democrats and two Republicans, with the support of the council's three black members. This support was not sufficient to get the mayor's agenda implemented. Therefore it was equally significant that Ford had the support of the sole Latino member of the council (who served as president) and the support of at least two white members as well. Without their support many of Mayor Ford's initiatives would have failed.

The cases of Toledo and Dayton demonstrate that having black members on the city council was not sufficient in itself to support mayoral initiatives, and they partially confirm Swain's conclusions. Swain argued that party trumped race in the representation of black interests, as white Democratic congressional members were found to advocate for black interests.[50] In the cases of Mayors Ford and McLin, however, it was not that black representation on the council did not matter but that it was insufficient. Hence the finding also confirms Tate's observation that black legislators play a significant role in promoting minority issues.[51]

*The Significance of the Findings*

The major conditions that determined whether Mayors Ford and McLin were successful in actively pursuing policies and programs to improve the quality of life of African Americans in non-majority-black cities were the following: the presence of a strong-mayor form of government, the presence of ideologically like-minded council members, the presence of effective business relationships, and a mayoral personality and style that enhanced community members' perceptions that the mayor was effective.

The importance of a strong-mayor form of government confirms previous research. The finding is significant in this case; it confirms the importance of mayoral structure in medium-sized cities, as well as the limitations of a weak-mayor system, under which most black mayors govern.[52] The finding also helps to explain the consequences of high expectations: the interview data demonstrate that blacks in both Toledo and Dayton regarded the mayor's efforts in respect to black interests less favorably than did whites. If a majority of black mayors govern within a system wherein the mayor is structurally unable to make noticeable strides to meet black expectations, blacks may continue to "grade" black mayors less favorably than their fellow white citizens.

The finding that ideology can trump race in respect to council members' support of mayoral agendas is significant because it demonstrates the usefulness of the political representation debate in the political science literature. As noted in chapter 1, one school argues that race trumps party, while the other argues that party trumps race. The research in Toledo and Dayton, however, shows that the presence of minority councilors matters but not as an end in itself. Rather mayors need the support of ideologically like-minded councilors of other racial groups to ensure enough votes to pass agenda items. Thus the finding in part confirms both of the opposing arguments within the political representation debate.

The finding that effective business relationships play a significant role confirms earlier scholarship that found that the business community was integral to a black mayor's success.[53] Additionally note-worthy is the finding that black mayors who are perceived as not having an understanding of business will be limited in their ability to finance desired city programs or an effective reelection campaign. The fact that the business community, including union leadership, is a large contributor to mayoral campaigns in medium-sized cities with union cultures like Toledo and Dayton is important. The union culture in such cities pinpoints the electoral and governing coalitions necessary for substantive change; both coalitions must have business members playing active roles.

Finally, the finding that Ford and McLin's personalities and per-ceived style and approach toward governing played a major role is important because it confirms previous scholarship on the roles and types of mayors given varying governmental power structures.[54] The finding also suggests that the extent to which Ford and McLin were able to advocate for black interests was largely within their own con-trol. While structural impediments are often insurmountable within a term or two, a mayor does have the ability to affect the way he or she is perceived by others. As in the case of Ford, however, if black mayors choose not to recognize the role of image or choose not to embrace the reality of its effects on implementing an agenda, they may be somewhat ineffective in establishing a lasting agenda of pol-icies that impact black quality of life.

*Lingering Effects*

One of the interview questions asked respondents, "In a city like X, where whites represent X percent of the population, how likely is it that Mayor X can actively pursue policies designed to improve the quality of life of black residents?" When probed further, respondents were asked to replace "Mayor X" with the name of the former white mayor. Whites and blacks reported that the black mayor could and would more actively pursue black-interest policies, with the former white mayor being considered on average 20 percent less likely to do so. This result indicates that Ford and McLin were perceived to be more likely to actively pursue policies designed to improve the quality of life of blacks than were their white predecessors. This finding is confirmed by previous research on black political representation.[55]

Generally the findings from the interviews and research observations confirm respondents' answers to this question, as Ford and McLin were both found to pursue black interests, though McLin did so less actively and Ford's efforts had short-term implications. This result also supports research that has found that black legislators are more likely than white legislators to make black-interest bills a high policy priority, given that black legislators are more likely to have a personal interest in black-interest policies than white members.[56]

Furthermore, the responses of black and white respondents that McLin and Ford more actively pursued black interests than their white predecessors confirm why it was reasonable to expect them as black mayors in non-majority-black cities to actively pursue black interests. Thereby the findings help to explain why black mayors are said to represent black issues better than white mayors, as well as why mayoral governing structure is a key determinant of black mayors' active pursuit of black interests.

Ford more actively pursued black interests than McLin, and the strong-mayor structure of government helped him in his effort. However, lessons can be learned from the Ford example. Ford arguably pushed an aggressive agenda for blacks for too long because as reelection approached, many residents could not identify other issues Ford promoted. Thus in order for black mayors to use Ford's example (while avoiding his mistakes and thereby actively pursue black interests in non-majority-black cities), they must have the active support of the business community, maintain super-majority support within the black community, cultivate positive relationships with ideologically congruent council members, and foster a personality and governing approach that is viewed favorably by the media, critics, and non-affluent whites. Moreover, they may secure reelection by cultivating comparable constituencies in their electoral and governing coalitions, as McLin's second-term bid successfully demonstrated. Without successful governing and electoral coalitions, as determined in part by community perceptions, the effort to substantively impact black quality of life is short-lived. Therefore, securing reelection is important to cement one's legacy and create stronger institutional structures that sustain the effort made to improve black quality of life. Regardless of the strength of the initiatives proposed or implemented, by serving only one term, it is unlikely that the efforts to improve black quality of life, in majority white cities, will have a long-term substantive and positive impact on the community.

# CHAPTER 8

# Racial Populism

## Ford's and McLin's Targeted Political Rhetoric

I believe in diversity. I teach it. I work it. I live it. A mayor should appoint
directors and commissioners who believe in diversity and hold them
accountable.

Jack Ford, campaign kickoff, June 10, 2001

I also want to recognize Mayor Smith and her colleagues in Kettering for
another joint effort between our two cities. Together we held a series of
meetings dealing with issues of race and reconciliation. The three-part
dialogues were an extension of the work initiated by the Dayton Dialogue
on Race Relations. . . . The discussions were instrumental in our on-going
efforts to break down stereotypes and create greater tolerance among
all peoples.

Rhine McLin, 2004 State of the City address

It has been documented that black mayors and other black politicians may seek to represent black interests in non-majority-black
contexts. Black members of the U.S. House of Representatives have
been found to represent black interests in non-majority-black districts. The rhetorical strategies of the nation's only reelected black
governor, Deval Patrick (D-MA), have been found to demonstrate an
effort to represent black interests in a state with a black population
of 7 percent.[1] Studies of black mayors of large and medium-sized
non-majority-black cities, such as Harold Washington of Chicago
and William Johnson Jr. of Rochester, have also acknowledged their

rhetorical strategies to represent black interests. However, Washington, Johnson, and most other black mayors of the twentieth century were elected under different circumstances than the black mayors of the twenty-first century.[2] Given the changing demographics of many cities in the twenty-first century, the question remains: how did Ford and McLin, in terms of their rhetorical strategies, represented black interests?

Some of the first major-city black mayors—Tom Bradley of Los Angeles, Harold Washington of Chicago, and Carl Stokes of Cleveland (and others)—were each first elected to cities that were majority Caucasian. Nonetheless, scholars have found that each sought to represent black interests. With the advent of Andrew Young to the Atlanta mayoralty and L. Douglas Wilder's election as governor of Virginia, scholars began to explore how these black politicians sought to represent black interests. Most of the findings frame the politicians' rhetorical strategies and governing approaches in the bifurcated racialization/deracialization dichotomy. For decades the conclusion has been that black politicians either explicitly referenced black interests in their electoral and/or governing coalitions or they did not. In fact scholars found that in order to win in majority-white jurisdictions, black politicians had to deemphasize race to increase their chances at victory.[3] In contrast, as chapters 5 and 6 demonstrate, Ford and McLin each maneuvered political outcomes in the interests of blacks without initially alienating many white constituents.

How Ford and McLin helped to establish political outcomes favorable to black interests remains unclear. In previous chapters I explained that Ford and McLin effectively maneuvered black interests with respect to specific issues, such as housing and contracting. In this chapter I will demonstrate that they were able to maneuver political outcomes through political rhetoric that sought to frame the proposed black interests in a universal context.

### The Salience of (Black) Political Rhetoric

Political rhetoric, as opposed to policy actions, is significant as rhetoric (specifically predictive appeals) affects constituents' policy opinions.[4] The finding implies that the rhetoric of a black politician may positively affect constituents' opinions on policy actions specific to black interests, thereby increasing the opportunities to implement policy outcomes that address black interests in majority-white areas. Thus how Ford and McLin may (or may not) have chosen to frame black interests affected constituents' opinions on black interests.

The literature on the impact of political rhetoric is well documented. For example, scholars have long described Aristotle and Hobbes as expert political rhetoricians.[5] Political rhetoric is said to function not simply as an episodic electoral contention that matters only as a campaign strategy to seek votes, but also as a utility function that evolves over time. While political rhetoric may have at one time been "expected and appropriate messages for the public" that were used solely to "win voters' support," it is now believed that political leaders support "a rhetoric that reacts to the problems and pressures of the office."[6]

Sonja K. Foss finds that in terms of political rhetoric in general, political leaders "seem destined to experience a rude awakening once they actually take office and tend to change their rhetoric accordingly to some extent."[7] Hence, a focus on political rhetoric is a key function of a political leader's tenure in office. For Foss political leaders must fight to keep their own worldviews alive while respecting the varied interests of their constituents. Foss's concept of political rhetoric as increasingly pessimistic is important as it frames the relevance of research on the earlier years of politicians' terms in office. Foss believes a politician's worldview is compromised over time as a result of increasing demands and as competing constituencies gain influence with an experienced representative.

Rhetoric is also a vital aspect of the American political process.[8] As Jeffrey W. Koch points out, "Through rhetoric, political elites attempt to draw attention to particular features of a policy proposal—while drawing attention away from others—thereby increasing the importance and accessibility of those considerations for citizens."[9] For many scholars rhetoric is a tool used in concert with framing, wherein a politician attempts to suggest what is at stake for a given issue or concern.[10] Framing takes many forms.[11] However, given that framing is centrally concerned with defining a public policy issue, how the defining occurs through rhetoric signals the importance of rhetoric in communicating a politician's worldview.

One of the key features of political rhetoric is the power of persuasion.[12] How African Americans and their allies have used political rhetoric to persuade has long been documented. From freed black slaves' pleas to their white owners for freedom, to white abolitionists' arguments on the morality of the "slavery question," to Reconstruction Era black elected officials' speeches, to 1960s black civil rights leaders' use of political rhetoric, blacks and their allies have used political rhetoric to persuade leaders within the power structure to be sympathetic to their cause for centuries.[13]

*Rhetoric in Black Mayoral Politics*

The variable of political rhetoric in black mayoral politics is significant. Famous black mayoral "firsts" Maynard Jackson, Tom Bradley, and Harold Washington used the power of their position and the black jeremiad roots of their shared African American experience to attract people to their worldview. For some scholars black mayoral political rhetoric takes the form of a mobilization effort, and such is vital to get elected: "The waging of emotionally stimulating campaigns is a key ingredient in the mobilization effort in the black community that must be made to elect a black man to the mayorship."[14] When Detroit's Coleman Young was first elected in 1973, for example, he campaigned largely on the issue of police-community relations, promising that if elected he would put more "Blacks into blue" and rein in a white-dominated police department that many black Detroiters viewed as an occupational army.[15] Young's campaign rhetoric was a mobilizing force for black Detroiters.

David Metz and Katherine Tate have observed of mayoral candidates in racially divisive urban campaigns that "black candidates . . . emphasize race in order to augment their chances of winning." They concluded: "Race is generally used by black candidates as a means of galvanizing and mobilizing the black voters in the city."[16] Paul

Kleppner saw this dynamic in the 1983 election of Harold Washington in Chicago, noting that Washington's original strategy to campaign as a candidate for everyone was reversed when his attempts at gaining white and Latino support were disappointing, in large part due to his racially polarizing campaign slogan. Washington told a largely black audience on the campaign trail: "We have given the white candidates our vote for years and years and years. Now, it's our turn. . . . It's our turn. . . . It's our turn." "It's our turn" became Washington's campaign slogan. As Washington himself noted of the slogan, "Every group, when it reaches a certain population percentage, automatically takes over. . . . They don't apologize. . . . They just move in and take over."[17] As a result, Washington "began to present himself as a symbol of black pride and progress."[18]

Atlanta's first black mayor, Maynard Jackson, campaigned on a similar message in his first bid for election in 1973. As Thompson notes of Jackson's campaign strategy, "His early image [was] as an advocate of Atlanta's predominantly poor black community."[19] Jackson made direct efforts to appeal to the black community, including his support of an aggressive affirmative action plan to result in a significant number of blacks receiving contracts to help expand the city's airport and establish businesses within it.

David R. Colburn observed that generally speaking, "Economic issues dominated campaign platforms of . . . black mayors. In nearly every campaign they called for programs to enhance economic development, recruit new businesses, and develop enterprise zones."[20] Such strategies were undoubtedly geared toward mobilizing black voters, who often lived in deteriorated economic conditions: "The stagflation of the 1970s followed by mounting unemployment in the 1970s and 1980s, stagnating personal incomes, the out-migration of the white and black middle class in the 1970s and 1980s and the transformation of the national economy from industry to service and high technology nearly devastated the old industrial inner cities. . . . Black residents felt these pressures more than most."[21] Colburn determined that "the rhetoric of campaigns in black neighborhoods was rooted initially in the civil rights movement and in an emerging black consciousness."[22] Coleman Young and Harold Washington are just two examples of black mayors who in their campaigns for mayor were successful in mobilizing black votes by rhetorically heightening expectations of their own performance if elected.

## MAYORAL SPEECH CODING

I utilize speeches of Ford and McLin to determine if they employed a targeted universalistic rhetorical approach in advocating for the interests of black constituents.[23] A study of the rhetorical strategies of the two mayors provides clues to interpret the behavior of black mayors of cities (particularly within Ohio and throughout the Midwest) with whom scholars and the general public are more familiar. Given the changing demographics in many cities, black mayors may be elected less often as majority-black cities disappear. Thus the study of Ford's and McLin's rhetorical strategies will contribute to implications of the national trends (see chapter 2).

In the speeches that follow, "race"-coded sentences were those that explicitly referenced race-specific programming or a particular racial group. "Universalized black interests"-coded sentences were those that mentioned policies and programs that were intended to target the black community or that were largely black issues introduced in a way to achieve broad appeal. Programs on community policing, housing, and economic development in black neighborhoods were among those included. "Other" comprised the remaining sentences in the text. At times the numerical coding of racial references in speeches is employed to efficiently capture the data; however, this procedure is utilized with caution, as it does not capture the substantive quality of the sentences' content.

### Universalizing the Interests of Blacks

To the extent that Ford and McLin were able to introduce policies and programs designed to improve the quality of life of black residents, they found the most success when they rhetorically framed their initiatives as affecting the lived conditions of, and common humanity shared among, all city residents. Embracing a targeted universalistic rhetorical strategy, some of their speeches directly noted the race variable, yet the mayors framed their black-interest policy actions and/or program developments as initiatives that benefited all citizens.

## FORD

Mayor Ford's first State of the City address in 2002, which focused on safety, infrastructure, technology, and education (SITE), included aggressive policy actions and program development proposals that were designed to have an impact on black quality of life. One of his initial agenda items was to focus city revenues on neighborhood improvements. Much of the increased attention went toward Toledo's inner-city neighborhoods, and Ford often drove through inner-city streets and alleys on Sunday afternoons to examine the progress of his initiative.[24] In the address Ford highlighted neighborhood improvements, noting the following: "Toledo is returning to basics. We will trim trees, remove the snow, fill the cracks, and maintain Toledo's infrastructure. No longer will citizens have to wait for a tree to fall or a car to be damaged by debris in our alleys."[25] Cornel West characterizes "the neglect of our public infrastructure" as a reflection of "not only our myopic economic policies . . . but also the low priority we place on our common life."[26] Thus Ford's focus on improving the infrastructure offered evidence of his interest in improving Toledo's common life, satisfying West's call for public leaders who emphasize common humanity and strive for better human relations. Ford's common humanity focus also included his stated desire to support community development agencies, including those with a targeted focus in Toledo's black community: "We will give them the tools they need to fix existing housing and make it attractive and affordable for working families."[27]

In respect to education and youth Ford aggressively emphasized the need to support the city's majority-minority school district: "We have over seventy thousand youngsters in Toledo. Each deserves nothing less than our best effort." As a consequence, he supported not only school reform but also several youth programs, including

Seeds of Success, which provided small loans to youth to encourage them to start businesses; Mayor's Time, which offered safe places and productive activities for youth between 3:30 and 6:30 p.m. and focused on reading, recreation, and remedial tutoring; and Fit for Kids, which used creative methods to encourage youth to lose weight, eat healthy, exercise regularly, and avoid alcohol and other drugs, as well as helping families with limited incomes to obtain affordable health care for their children through a state-subsidized program. Also in 2002 Ford proposed the creation of what would become CareNet: "Over 44,000 city residents are without health insurance ... and neither the state nor federal government is doing enough to help. Many of those forty-four thousand are adults who are sick. Others are hurt. None of them will seek care because they don't have insurance or can't afford to pay. This is unacceptable. We can do something about this, and we will."[28] As discussed in chapter 3, CareNet provides low-income, uninsured residents of Lucas County with improved access to primary and specialty medical and dental care, affordable prescriptions, and reliable transportation. The initiative has enrolled over fourteen thousand people since its inception in 2003 and has approximately five thousand active members.[29]

Finally, Ford spoke directly of race relations in 2002: "I believe we are at a high point. The recent election sent a strong message, not just here in Toledo, but to Ohio and the nation, that Toledoans voted for who they felt could best do the job—regardless of race and ethnicity."[30] In addition, as we see from the epigraph at the beginning of this chapter, in his campaign kickoff on June 10, 2001, Ford openly talked about diversity. Also, Ford made the following comment in his inaugural speech: "Some people believe that helping the disinherited is not the mayor's business—I disagree! I believe it is the mayor's business to help all—from corporate leaders to the homeless! We are going to do just that."[31] As his 2002 State of the City address attests, many of Ford's subsequent programs and policies were designed to put that understanding into action.

As in 2002, Ford's 2003 State of the City address focused in part on education and youth. In education he noted that "we raised funds to enhance the libraries at Nathan Hale and MLK schools," two elementary schools with black student enrollment surpassing 90 percent. On youth-related issues Ford spoke of his success with the city's "anti-drug, anti-delinquent" youth entrepreneur program, in which "14 or 15 year olds" earned "between six and seventeen hundred dollars."[32]

Ford's second State of the City address also mentioned broader diversity-related efforts, including the introduction of a summit on cleaning city neighborhoods that targeted many inner-city communities. He lauded the commencement of CareNet with five hundred enrollees and announced his support for a ban on smoking in public areas. Both programs had a significant impact on black quality of life: CareNet helped many low-income blacks obtain access to health care, and the smoking ban, while contributing to the city's overall health, significantly impacted blacks as well, as they are the second-largest group of smokers in the country and are more likely than other groups to work in occupations in which smoking is permitted.

In the same address Ford announced other programmatic developments that focused on human relations, common humanity, and the improved quality of life of blacks. He noted, for example, "Some have expressed disappointment in our fire recruitment process and the recent lack of African American hiring. We will strive to do better in recruitment but we will not drop standards for recruits." Moreover, Ford highlighted the opening of the Center for Capacity Building in conjunction with the University of Toledo, saying, "This center will create a new class of entrepreneurs and wealth in our community." Finally, near the conclusion of the speech, and similarly to the way in which he ended his 2002 address, Ford spoke directly of race-related issues: "Much has been made about my administration's commitment to diversity. Some say diversity is not important—that it doesn't mean anything in 2003. I disagree. To a society that is based in large part on the principles of fairness and equality—diversity with merit is big picture equality. It is of high value to my administration. It is our future and a key to the success of Toledo and Northwest Ohio."[33] For his first two years in office, then,

10. Mayor Jack Ford on the reelection campaign trail. Courtesy *Sojourner's Truth*.

Ford spoke directly and openly about race and diversity in his State of the City addresses in front of majority-white audiences.

In subsequent years (2004–2005), as reelection approached, Ford spoke less directly of race, of policies and programs that affected the black community, and of largely black issues in his State of the City addresses. He did highlight some programs that had an indirect im-

TABLE 10. Sentence content analysis of Mayor Ford's major speeches

| SPEECH | NUMBER OF SENTENCES | NUMBER "RACE"-CODED | NUMBER "UNIVERSALIZED BLACK INTERESTS"-CODED | OTHER |
|---|---|---|---|---|
| Campaign kickoff | 84 | 9 (10.7%) | 4 (4.7%) | 71 |
| Inaugural address | 71 | 1 (1.5%) | 8 (11.2%) | 62 |
| State of the City 2002 | 258 | 9 (3.5%) | 31 (12%) | 218 |
| State of the City 2003 | 203 | 10 (4.9%) | 37 (18.2%) | 156 |
| State of the City 2004 | 349 | 0 (0%) | 36 (10.3%) | 313 |
| State of the City 2005 | 219 | 0 (0%) | 16 (7.3%) | 201 |

pact on black quality of life, however. In 2004, for example, Ford spoke of increased funding for the Art Tatum Jazz Festival, named for the famous native Toledoan black pianist. He also announced mergers and collaborations within the city's Community Development Corporations (CDCs), where some inner-city-based CDCs that had been found to be inefficient were asked to merge with others to decrease costs. Finally, he chronicled an increased number of Block Watch groups in city neighborhoods.

In his 2005 State of the City address Ford asked HUD to advise him regarding Toledo's entitlement status as a designated urban county.[34] Such a designation is applicable only to counties that receive HUD (CDBG) funding through CDCs.[35] The request was significant, as "counties that do not have powers under state law to carry out community development and housing assistance activities may enter into cooperation agreements with local governments that do have such powers under state law essential to carry out the Urban County's CDBG program."[36] To qualify, counties have to demonstrate that they have met certain population requirements and that they have powers in community development and housing assistance for unincorporated areas within the county not associated with local governments, and they also have to produce a consolidated plan. The announcement demonstrated Ford's commitment to regionalism and his pursuit of additional funds to support the city's community development agencies. In 2005 he also announced the redevelopment of the inner city Hawley Street underpass with bright lights.

Hence it appears that Ford's rhetorical style incorporated mention of policy actions and program developments that benefitted blacks' quality of life. In his final years in office (2004–2005) Ford spoke less directly of race and issues that could be coded as universalizing the interests of blacks than in previous years.[37] A sentence content analysis of his major addresses in table 10 finds that the number of sentences that focused on race or on issues that could be counted as examples of universalizing the interests of blacks or mattering to blacks declined as he approached reelection. On average, of 1,184 sentences, 2.5 percent focused directly on race and 11 percent on issues that could be coded as universalizing the interests of blacks.

A numerical coding of Ford's racial references in speeches, while important, does not capture the substantive quality of the sentences' content. Arguably while his mentions of race and the universalizing of black interests were limited in extent when compared to the length of the speeches, the content of the sentences in which he mentioned race and universalized black interests was exceedingly strong.

MCLIN

Rhine McLin did not give a State of the City address in her first year in office, though she presented a First 100 Days Speech in April 2002. She began her annual State of the City addresses in 2003. Given the city's more polarizing (spatially and historically) racial context, I did not expect to find many explicit references to racial concerns in Mayor McLin's speeches. When McLin spoke of a new initiative—Strong Urban Neighborhoods or Project SUN, for instance—"urban" was not a coded term for black. Rather the examples McLin cited were in all segments of the city. Moreover, in her first State of the City address, there was no direct reference to the black community in Dayton.

It appears, however, that McLin did often indirectly speak of race. In her 2004 State of the City address McLin spoke of a development project in her predominantly black neighborhood, Wright-Dunbar. She highlighted the success of the Citirama Wright-Dunbar event as

11. Mayor Rhine McLin with Mayor Marilou Smith of Kettering, Ohio. Courtesy Rhine McLin.

"an ambitious marriage of both historic preservation and new construction." The event showcased the redevelopment underway in the city's historically black neighborhood and business district. In 2004 McLin also directly recognized the prevalence of the racial issue in the community, when, as seen in the epigraph above, she referred to discussions with her colleagues from Kettering and their joint efforts in dealing with issues of race relations.[38] In directly mentioning race in her 2004 address, McLin displayed her race sensitivity while framing her words in such a way as to remain racially inclusive. She did not, for example, specifically reference the topics discussed or the primary racial groups involved in the discussions.

In her 2005 State of the City address McLin made no specific references to race. While she did discuss some policies and projects that may have been of interest to blacks, she did so far less than she had in the year prior. In her 2006 State of the City address the strongest reference McLin made to race was limited to a discussion of the 2005 mayoral race, in which she noted that her opponent wrote in the local newspaper "about the underlying nature of race in the mayor's campaign." She said: "It was there not because either one of us put it in the campaign. But because it is an underlying sore in our community."[39] This is an example of McLin's fairly consistent, though indirect, conscious notation of the problem of race that existed in Dayton.

In her 2007 State of the City address McLin again made no direct reference to race. Whereas she announced the hiring of the new city manager, Rashad Young, the first black male in that position, she did not comment on his race in the speech, saying only, "I would like to recognize City Manager Rashad Young and his fine team for the excellent work they do in managing our city and providing first-rate services to the citizens of Dayton."[40] As an example of a reference to issues that mattered to blacks and could be coded as universalizing the interests of blacks, McLin also noted the inception of the ORION Solution and the city's support of laws opposing predatory lending. Again in her 2008 State of the City address she made no direct reference to race, and she focused less than in the prior year on issues that could be coded as universalizing the interests of blacks.

Given that McLin governed in a more polarized racial climate than Ford in Toledo, it is no surprise that McLin's references to race and her universalizing of black interests ebbed and flowed in her major addresses. As she mentioned in our interview, she preferred to deemphasize the prevalence of racial divisions. She expressly noted that she was mayor "of everyone" and that for her all of Dayton's citizens, from the east and the west, were her constituents.[41]

A sentence content analysis of McLin's major addresses in table 11 finds that the number of sentences that focused on race or on issues that could be counted as examples of universalizing the interests of blacks or mattering to blacks declined as McLin approached reelection. According to this analysis, McLin spoke more often of race and issues that could be coded as universalizing the interests of blacks than did Ford. Like Ford, in her later years in office (2007–2008), she also spoke less directly of race and issues that could be

TABLE 11. Sentence content analysis of Mayor McLin's major speeches

| SPEECH | NUMBER OF SENTENCES | NUMBER "RACE"- CODED | NUMBER "UNIVERSALIZED BLACK INTERESTS"- CODED | OTHER |
|---|---|---|---|---|
| First 100 Days speech | 63 | 9 (14.2%) | 5 (7.9%) | 50 |
| State of the City 2003 | 123 | 5 (4%) | 13 (10.5%) | 105 |
| State of the City 2004 | 189 | 5 (2.6%) | 46 (24.3%) | 138 |
| State of the City 2005 | 190 | 0 (0%) | 25 (13.1%) | 165 |
| State of the City 2006 | 178 | 17 (9.5%) | 34 (19.1%) | 127 |
| State of the City 2007 | 184 | 0 (0%) | 25 (13.5%) | 159 |
| State of the City 2008 | 174 | 0 (0%) | 20 (11.5%) | 154 |

coded as universalizing the interests of blacks than she had in previous years. On average, of 1,101 sentences, 3.2 percent focused directly on race and 15 percent on issues that could be coded as universalizing the interests of blacks.

FORD AND MCLIN SPEECH CONTENT COMPARISON

McLin spoke more often of race and related issues than did Ford. This finding may appear to contradict the earlier findings that Ford more actively pursed black interests than did McLin. That is not the case, however. This analysis demonstrates that McLin used the informal powers of her position in a weak-mayor form of government to introduce the variable of race and related content when she had the forum to do so. In this analysis consideration must be given to the historic racial climate in Dayton and to the mayor's oratorical style. Finally, the frequency of racial references does not highlight substantive content or implemented results.

It can be noted from this analysis that McLin seemed to view her role as mayor in less historically racial terms than Ford. (She was the city's third black mayor, whereas Ford was Toledo's first black mayor.) Given her limited mayoral powers, she was unable to take individual credit for city initiatives, such as improvements in neighborhoods that were predominantly black. In her speeches as mayor she spoke for the entire commission and the city manager while highlighting each of their collective administrative and management successes. As a result, more explicit references to race were expected to be limited, as she could not knowingly speak for everyone's racial views. She had the additional responsibility of noting city efforts that involved other officials with power largely equal to her own.

The nature and purpose of the State of the City address in Dayton was different from that in Toledo as a result of the cities' differing government structures. While Ford made fewer explicit references to race, those that he did make were largely generated from the individual leadership afforded the strong mayor in Toledo. In contrast, McLin's seemingly more frequent references to race, even given their ebbs and flows, could not be framed as individual mayoral efforts. Hence, though McLin spoke more often of race, her level of involvement in the issues discussed was more limited than Ford's. Thus when the two mayors' speeches and addresses are compared, it can still be said that Ford more actively pursued black interests than did McLin.[42]

### Black Interest Rhetoric Policy Outcomes

The case studies in Toledo and Dayton show that Mayor McLin and Mayor Ford rhetorically advanced black interests. Both mayors made limited direct references to black interests, suggesting that black politicians of majority Caucasian areas must tread lightly even when such issues are framed in the targeted universalism context. Table 12 indicates the number of policy-based outcomes that developed out of the mayors' rhetoric. While the number of policies and programs is important, their substantive impact is of more value, such as Ford's development of the Center for Capacity Building or McLin's support for the Wright-Dunbar housing initiative (see chapters 5 and 6). These data are useful in that they indicate the number of policy and program efforts pursued by the mayors. Moreover, they are instructive as they provide clues concerning the time the mayors spent actively pursuing black interests.

In table 12 introduced or implemented policies are coded as "policy actions." Introduced or developed city programs are coded as "pro-

TABLE 12. Efforts by McLin and Ford to improve black quality of life

| POLICY OR PROGRAM | MAYOR FORD 2002–2005 | MAYOR MCLIN 2002–2008 |
|---|---|---|
| Number of policy actions | 28 | 48 |
| Number of program developments | 20 | 48 |
| Annual average of policies and programs | 12 | 12 |
| Total number of policies and programs | 48 | 96 |

gram developments." Policy actions and program developments were determined using various sources, including printed campaign leaflets, city budgets, proposed mayoral budgets, administration press releases, State of the City speeches, council/commission meeting minutes and agendas, and newspaper articles. Despite the argument presented by Foss,[43] the data show that during the course of their years in office the rhetoric used by Mayor Ford and Mayor McLin resulted in policy introductions and outcomes in the interests of blacks. The findings reveal that Mayors Ford and McLin annually introduced and/or implemented an average of twelve policy actions and program developments—or roughly one initiative per month—that impacted the quality of life of blacks in Toledo and Dayton.

IMPLICATIONS

Many black leaders have long framed matters concerning the quality of black life by pointing out what is "right" and by invoking the notion of common humanity.[44] Similarly the advocacy of black interests by Mayors Ford and McLin was framed as simply the right thing to do. The analysis of the mayors' efforts at effectively advancing black interests in majority-white contexts demonstrate these mayors accomplished something unique to race-conscious public service delivery. Mayors Ford and McLin were able to advance black interests not solely as issues that affected black residents, but also as interests in which everyone was positively affected and ultimately played a role in shaping. They framed their appeals in the language of citizenship. For them it was "right" to support such policies and programs because their black beneficiaries were citizens of the city as well. Thus they might have argued, "If we help them, we help all of the city's citizens and strengthen the broader foundation of the city's structure." As a result of their universal approach and their effective rhetoric, Mayors Ford and McLin were able to secure whites' support of black policy initiatives. This is significant because prior research has suggested deracialization is the variable in the urban governing context by which minority mayors can influence white opinion and support.[45] However, as Ford and McLin's governing outcomes in the black community demonstrate, their ability to se-cure white support was not a function of the racialization/deracial-ization dichotomy.

## LINKED BY SHARED RACIAL EXPERIENCE

Congressional literature explains that shared racial experience is the linchpin that holds together black politicians' efforts to represent black interests within majority-white districts. As mentioned above, Gamble has noted that many black congressional members nation-wide carry a heavy burden as they are often expected to represent not only their districts, but also "black America."[46] In addition, Richard F. Fenno found that black members of Congress often perceived their black constituency as extending beyond their districts, to include blacks nationwide.[47] Finally, Melissa Williams has found that despite an increasingly diverse black community, black members of Con-gress share the experience of being members of a historically mar-ginalized group and that blacks generally have a shared memory of oppression.[47] It seems, then, that the rhetorical strategies of Ford and McLin to represent black interests were determined in part by shared racial experience, regardless of the composition of their constituen-cies. The inclination to universalize the interests of blacks was de-pendent upon Ford's and McLin's feeling connected to other blacks.[48]

The example of Mayors Ford and McLin represents a continued trend whereby blacks are increasingly elected to political offices where the majority of their constituents is not black. While research on this question tends to characterize black politicians' efforts to rep-resent black interests in two frames (deracialized or racialized), Ford and McLin are examples of black politicians who no longer find either explicit racial appeals or universal, deracialized appeals appropriate for their electoral goals.[49]

As the rhetoric of McLin and Ford shows, these black mayors have begun to universalize the interests of their black constituents. The results demonstrate that black mayors' campaign and governing approaches in majority-white areas have changed as a new generation of black leaders has emerged.[50] As a result, targeted universalism—the universalizing of black interests *as interests that matter to all constituents*—is of particular interest and utility to black candidates and elected officials.

The concept of targeted universalism is different from deracialization in that with universalizing the interests of blacks, elected officials and candidates reference racial disparities given the issue(s) they support. When critics found that Ford's appointment of an African American chief of staff was insignificant, Ford disagreed, and his reply—beginning with "Diversity with merit is big picture equality"—is an example of targeted universalism. By exercising executive authority to diversify city personnel and hiring the first-ever black chief of staff and Ford showed how diversity was beneficial to all; Ford targeted a universal appeal to all that the appointment mattered. This targeted universalistic approach was key for both McLin and Ford.

Deracialization suggests that race-specific issues are polarizing in campaign rhetoric and governance and that race-specific rhetoric must be defused and avoided by political actors.[51] That deracialization highlights a transcendence of race-specific policies suggests that it places any direct attention to racial disparities out of bounds. Meanwhile, Ford and McLin were able to utilize rhetoric to produce substantive policy actions and program developments on behalf of black interests. In addition, they were able to introduce policies and programs aimed at improving black quality of life while maintaining significant white support for their efforts. Their rhetorical strategy in advancing black interests resulted in black-friendly policy outcomes. Thus it is expected that other black politicians may seek to produce similar black-friendly urban policy outcomes. This expectation is reasonable given that McLin and Ford initially retained significant white support, an outcome that suggests others may be able to do the same should they utilize similar rhetorical strategy centered on targeted universalism. That strategy includes taking up the interests of black constituents and popularizing them by rhetorically advocating for these interests in a way that does not deemphasize race or alienate all whites—that is, universalizing black interests. This concept demonstrates that in the twenty-first century, black elected officials of majority-white areas can (and will) pursue black interests. By universalizing black interests as interests that matter to everyone, Mayors Ford and McLin popularized black interests, maintained white governing and/or electoral support for some time, and substantively impacted the lived conditions of blacks in Dayton and Toledo.

# CHAPTER 9

# Target Practice

## Universalizing the Interests of Blacks for All

The role of black leadership [in the twenty-first century] should begin with the acknowledgement of its limitations. The limitations include the leadership's inability to solve every conceivable problem facing the [black] community. It should recognize that the black community's problems are American problems that require an American solution.

Donald Cunnigen

Toledo Mayor Jack Ford and Dayton Mayor Rhine McLin's support of black interests extended beyond their State of the City speeches and related addresses. For example, in an interview, Ford once asked, "Why run for mayor, if you're not going to help black people? That was the point."[1] As noted, in his inaugural address Ford framed the policies and programs that were designed to have an impact on the quality of life of blacks by appealing to his constituents with the message found in Isaiah 58: helping the most needy was helping everyone. Ford's efforts with minority contracting, described in chapter 5, are another indication of his approach to universalizing the interests of blacks. In those efforts Ford managed to effectively secure major political, construction industry, and university support from white leaders to improve the quality of life of blacks in Toledo. He was able to persuade all these leaders that the interests of blacks in minority contracting were relevant to all of them.

McLin's efforts with housing and related initiatives critically involved maintaining supportive working relationships with white county and city leaders, including members of the city and county commission, the business community, and organizations like the DMHA (see chapter 6). While her role was largely supportive in each context, she effectively facilitated white leadership support for policies and programs that were in the interests of blacks. I have labeled this approach toward securing policy gains for a particular racial constituency as a third tier in the study of race politics, one that applies the understanding of targeted universalism to the existing scholarship on racialized and deracialized mayoral political actions.

Jack Ford and Rhine McLin are examples of mayors who did not explicitly advocate for race policies. However, neither did they seek the fulfillment of race-specific policies by deemphasizing race (for example, by replacing a racial label with the "urban" label) through deracialization.[2] Rather Ford and McLin are examples of twenty-first-century black mayors of non-majority-black cities who were successful in their active pursuit of policies and programs designed to improve the quality of life of blacks because they noted the racial significance of policies and programs where appropriate. They are examples of black mayors using targeted universalism in rhetoric and policy introductions. Their strategy recognized and identified the interests of African Americans in Dayton and Toledo as black interests. But many sympathetic whites who were willing to support the mayors' efforts on behalf of all city residents also supported the strategy.

In some instances the mayors' advocacy of the interests of blacks was framed as simply the "right" thing to do. As Ford indicated in his 2004 State of the City address regarding the city's smoking ban, "It is the right thing to do, period!"[3] McLin, though indirectly, invoked a similar argument as she spoke of her city's long-standing Third and Main Streets dilemma in her 2005 State of the City address. Many African Americans (including students) who utilize public transportation transfer at this intersection, and it was the subject of contention, as white constituents in the downtown area allegedly often accosted transitioning blacks whom they viewed as deterrents to their pursuit of customers. In response, McLin commented: "We

12. Mayor Rhine McLin and Mayor Jack Ford. Courtesy Rhine McLin.

[the commission] have also directed our focus at the human element as well—our own civility. . . . We believe it was important to remind people about the value of personal interaction as we go about our daily lives. The Civility Resolution encourages all of us to remember the basics of courtesy and respect."[4] Hence both Ford and McLin in their own way addressed the quality of life of blacks in their cities by responding to concerns with programmatic infusions and policy introductions that were framed in speeches as the "right" thing to do and as important for lived and shared human experience, not solely as issues that affected black residents.

While many other leaders, black and white, have long framed matters concerning the quality of black life by pointing out what is "right" and by invoking the notion of common humanity, such efforts have been largely unsuccessful. Some leaders of the civil rights movement or the NAACP, for example, attempted to push the civil rights mission to focus more broadly on human rights, though with little success. In his 1963 "Letter from a Birmingham Jail," Rev. Dr. Martin Luther King Jr. noted that his organization, the Southern Christian Leadership Conference, had assistance from other groups:

"We have some eighty five affiliated organizations across the South, and one of them is the Alabama Christian Movement for Human Rights. Frequently we share staff, educational and financial resources with our affiliates."[5] Thus King (and others) in part viewed the civil rights efforts in Birmingham in the context of human rights: "To put it in the terms of St. Thomas Aquinas: An unjust law is a human law that is not rooted in eternal law and natural law. Any law that uplifts human personality is just. Any law that degrades human personality is unjust. All segregation statutes are unjust because segregation distorts the soul and damages the personality. It gives the segregator a false sense of superiority and the segregated a false sense of inferiority."[6] However, the attempts of some civil rights activists to frame black civil rights issues as human rights issues are usually considered to have failed as scholars have long considered the civil rights movement as distinct from other rights-based movements.[7]

Perhaps recognizing how the language of "rights" can detract from attempts to build a coalition of support, Ford and McLin did not invoke the "universalized black interest" approach in their appeal to garner support for black-friendly public policies by framing their statements in the language of rights. Rather, as I noted in chapter 8, they framed their appeals in the language of citizenship.[8] For them it was "right" to support such policies and programs because their black beneficiaries were citizens of the city as well.

*Alternative Approaches*

The alternative approaches to universalizing the interests of blacks are racialization and deracialization. As the content analysis of the mayors' speeches and addresses in chapter 8 showed, however, and as their policy and program development actions demonstrated, the "universalized black interests" approach is the most effective of these three options. The racialization approach is largely ineffective not because it fails to produce substantive results, but due to a cultural and demographic shift that has occurred since the 1970s; explicit appeals to one racial group's problems are likely to be ineffective as increasing numbers of minority groups compete for representation.[9] While Harold Cruse suggests that given the nature of the African American experience, race-specific policies are needed to mitigate the impact of racism on both the black middle class and the disadvantaged, in a climate where race is decreasingly bifurcated and increasingly multicultural, the successful implementation of such policies becomes more complex.[10] Thus while scholars like Cruse suggest that racialization will have the most direct impact on the quality of life of blacks, the political and social climate of the twenty-first century has limited the utility of that option.

The deracialization, or race-neutral, universal perspective suggests that race-specific issues are polarizing in campaign rhetoric and governance and that race-specific rhetoric must be defused and avoided by political actors. This approach is increasingly exhausted as well. However, it has likely been the most popular approach taken by black elected officials in the late twentieth and early twenty-first centuries. The fact that this approach attempts to transcend race-specific policies in favor of mobilizing a diverse coalition of electoral and governing support suggests that it places any direct attention to racial disparities and municipal problems that may disproportionately affect one race more than another out of bounds. Yet deracialized policies often manage to help the black community only to a limited extent. For example, the approach, to which is famously attributed the rise of the black middle class and black political governance in Atlanta, has noticeably had little positive impact on the city's poorer black community.[11]

McCormick and Jones address the dilemma of black elected officials of predominately white jurisdictions and ask if they should pursue an openly racial public policy agenda after winning office. They find "no ready answers to this difficult question." They suggest, however, that such politicians should find a balance, as white voters and elected officials will be needed to support "any race-specific policy option . . . considered by an African-American elected official." They go so far as to say that "white support is necessary to make such options become reality." The authors suggest that the racial balance of political power may determine the extent to which black politicians in predominately white areas can pursue an aggressive race agenda. While they argue that it is risky for a black elected official with a majority-black power structure to introduce race-specific policies in a white jurisdiction, they also find that such an official's failure to introduce such policies carries its own risks: "While we consider it politically improbable for these politicians in predominately white jurisdictions to be constantly at the vanguard on race-specific policy issues, their failure to address such issues periodically and send appropriate signals to the black community could undoubtedly cost them crucial support within that community that could prove to be damaging when reelection is sought."[12]

While McCormick and Jones note that white support is necessary to implement a black elected official's race-specific policies, they don't discuss in detail political ideology. In the case of Ford and McLin the racial balance of power on city council or commission impacted legislative support for their mayoral agenda, but it was not the only factor determining such support. Indeed it often was liberal white support that helped Ford and McLin achieve their black-friendly policy goals. As a result, the deracialization premise that black elected officials should defuse racial issues is in part problematic because it is based on the idea that whites in general will be against a race-specific agenda. Shared ideology between a black politician and a white politician may in fact trump whites' supposed race-based opposition to black-friendly policies. Ford's and McLin's ability to court white support for their efforts on minority contracting and housing again stand out as examples of white support for programs and policies that had the effect of improving black quality of life. Browning, Marshall, and Tabb have noted how liberal and white dominant coalitions in some of the cities they studied developed policies and programs that directly benefitted blacks:

> In Richmond, San Francisco, and Berkeley federal social programs did not become the focus for minority electoral mobilization efforts. But the programs did contribute directly to some increases

in policy responsiveness because they permitted the dominant coalition to expand services to minorities and produced some institutionalization of minority interests. The clearest example is Richmond. . . . A liberal administrative coalition was led by the city manager, a white, and his top staff, with acquiescence from a liberal-to-moderate majority on the council. . . . They used Model Cities to promote modestly redistributive programs, which were responsive to blacks but which also served to avoid disruptive conflict.[13]

Hence while Donald R. Kinder and Lynn M. Sanders, Stanley Feldman and Leonie Huddy, and others have noted whites' "racial resentment" of race-specific policies, some whites who can be defined as ideologically liberal have in fact supported race-specific policies and programming.[14]

Other scholars have noted how whites may find themselves supporting black programs. S. Steele and Richard D. Harvey and Debra L. Oswald, for example, found that whites' guilt could lead to their support of programs, policies, and laws that support blacks.[15] Feldman and Huddy have more recently noted a connection between racial resentment and ideology, finding that "conservatives are more likely than liberals to hold highly individualistic beliefs" and that "there are fundamental differences in the character of racial resentment for liberals and conservatives."[16] In the final analysis, however, they maintain, "It is difficult to conclude that resentment constitutes a clear measure of ideology among conservatives."[17] That finding is based on the fact that the authors found no evidence that "resentment was more closely tied to values like individualism and limited government for conservatives than for liberals." Yet the authors did find that conservative ideology "apparently [had] ideological effects on opposition [to a college scholarship program that is targeted at specific racial groups]."[18] Consequently while the correlation between racial resentment and prejudice is undetermined, it remains the case that conservatives oppose race-specific policies and programs more than do liberals.[19]

*The Genesis of the "Universalized Black Interests" Approach*

As the introduction underscored, Cornel West arguably began the "universalized black interests" theoretical reasoning for public policy in *Race Matters*. In his introduction West argued that a new framework was needed in order to effectively engage in a serious discussion of race in America. He noted, "We must begin not with the problems of black people, but with the flaws of American society."[20] To that end West suggested that the new framework must include reference to our common humanity: "To establish a new framework, we need to begin with a frank acknowledgment of the basic humanness and Americanness of each of us. And we must acknowledge that as a people—E Pluribus Unum—we are on a slippery slope toward economic strife, social turmoil, and cultural chaos. If we go down, we go down together."[21] Hence West concluded that any serious discussion of race in America must not be limited to the black experience.

West implicitly suggested that to ignore race would be perilous, but he also seemed to understand that explicit racial appeals had exhausted themselves in favor of a process that would invoke the shared human experience: "We must focus our attention on . . . the common good that undergirds our national and global identities. The vitality of any public square ultimately depends on how much we care about the quality of our lives together. The neglect of our public infrastructure, for example . . . reflects not only our myopic economic policies, which impede productivity, but also the low priority we place on our common life."[22] Perhaps without knowing it, West wrote the handbook for twenty-first-century black mayors in non-majority-black cities in respect to how they might use the power of their positions to impact the substantive quality of life of blacks.

*Mayoral Leadership Models and the Active Pursuit of Black Interests*

The "universalized black interests" approach that Mayors Ford and McLin employed to actively pursue black interests can be framed in terms of preexisting scholarship that focuses on different mayoral leadership and governing styles. In fact some scholars argue that it is necessary for mayors to cast their leadership approach as a governing process in order to be effective. Bowers and Rich write that "constructing a leadership infrastructure and coaligning processes, structures, and forces that might otherwise constrain [mayoral] leadership efforts is necessary for mayors if they hope to remain relevant to and participate in defining the long-term sustainability of their cities."[23] They maintain that good mayoral leadership is a necessity for small and medium-sized cities. Their emphasis on leadership confirms earlier scholarship that found leadership to be important in mayoral governance and black communities and speaks in concert with later research.[24] All of these studies note that strong leadership is required to force change and action in cities and in black communities.

As the case studies in the preceding chapters highlighted, how a mayor defines leadership and executes his or her agenda is critical to the active pursuit of black interests in non-majority-black cities. The case studies underscored that such leadership determines the number and level of substantive policy actions and program developments actively pursued by the mayors. While mayoral leadership may be affected by structural constraints, such as the weak-mayor system of government in Dayton, shared racial experience and ideological views can also circumvent these constraints.

Despite findings that suggest "across a range of measures of taxing, spending, and hiring, [there are] few differences between black mayors and their white counterparts," to varying degrees the case studies of Toledo and Dayton demonstrate that black mayoral leadership in non-majority-black cities can bring about substantive change for black residents.[25] Toledo mayor Jack Ford engaged in a type of substantive leadership by merging the city's Affirmative Action and Contract Compliance office with the Division of Purchasing. Ford also aggressively advocated for the capacity of black and minority contractors to bid for and ultimately receive public contracts. Dayton mayor Rhine McLin actively supported the redevelopment of mixed-community and black neighborhoods, such as Wright-Dunbar Village. McLin also moved into Wright-Dunbar—a substantive and symbolically significant step. These actions by Ford and McLin are evidence of what Clarence Stone labels change-producing leadership.[26]

As the variance in substantive policy actions and program developments underscored in chapter 8 suggests, however, not all of the mayors' pursuits were so active that they produced the substantive changes Stone's criteria describe. Both Ford and McLin engaged in the pursuit of black interests that were purely symbolic. The prevalence of such symbolic actions was a function of their cities' political governing environments. As Bowers and Rich note, "a city's political-governing environment affects the likelihood that successful change-producing mayoral leadership will occur."[27] They continue:

> This environment includes the structure of city government, particularly the formal powers of the mayor. It also includes such important contextual variables as the city's history, ethnicity, economy, and political traditions. Collectively, these political-governing variables define the extent to which mayors are at the center of their city's leadership environment. More often than not, mayors, particularly elected ones, come to recognize that although they may be at the political centers of their cities, they are not necessarily at the centers of those cities' political and economic power. . . . Thus the successful managing of the political governing environment in which they act becomes crucial to their ability to lead and bring about desired change.[28]

This nexus of political and governing variables and how mayors respond through their political and governing coalitions was evident in the case studies of Toledo and Dayton. For example, both McLin and Ford found that their political power was in part a function of relationships with the city's business community, arguably the source of the city's power structure.[29]

In addition, the case studies of Ford and McLin confirm the importance of personality. For instance, Mayor Ford was labeled "lackluster" by the city's media and was generally perceived by residents to be dull and boring. His approach was viewed in contrast to the city's first strong mayor, Carleton Finkbeiner. The perception of Ford's lack of enthusiasm and dull personality led to the prevalent notion that Ford did not do enough in his term as mayor to merit reelection. Mayor McLin's personality was viewed as an asset on the campaign trail against a Republican opponent in 2001, though some residents, particularly business leaders, found her "wacky and capricious" once she assumed office. Thus Ford's and McLin's ability to actively pursue black interests was in part a function of their personalities and their development over time.[30]

Closely related to the recognition of the importance of personality is the centrality of mayoral leadership style or governing approach to the active pursuit of black interests. Ford's efforts in Toledo reinforce Rich's assertion that a risk-taking leadership style is relevant to achieving change-producing actions: "Risk-taking is an unusual use of power, which is rooted in the belief that power cannot be depleted—that there is an endless supply. The joy of exercising power is thus triggered by its value as a risk and as an endless resource in a game of change."[31] Political actors who are risk-takers "love to experiment . . . and endorse grandiose plans. The more resistance they receive, the more convinced they are that their course is right. They are prone to action that upsets other politicians and attracts audiences."[32] While Ford likely fits this description, his efforts as mayor were also coupled with the public perception that he was dull—a variable Rich did not consider. To be a risk-taker and dull seemingly did not attract audiences for Ford for the long term.

The strong-handed, powerful approach to the active pursuit of black interests, moreover, likely contributed to Ford's failure to be reelected. An example of the substantive limitations of targeted universalism in urban politics, Ford was too aggressive for too long in his first several years in office. Ford noted in an interview that he "probably should have introduced the smoking ban in a second term," but he chose instead to take the risk in his first term.[33] Hence Ford's risk-taking, reform-oriented approach was beneficial to blacks in Toledo while it lasted, but given that it contributed to Ford's failure to be reelected, the approach may also have limited any long-term effects of Ford's mayoralty on black quality of life.

Mayor McLin's behavior in office was different. Her largely symbolic efforts to impact black quality of life in Dayton are best described as the result of her adoption of a "public entrepreneurial" style of leadership.[34] Kotter and Lawrence describe this type of leadership as an approach that "entails originality, initiative, energy, openness, organizational ability, and promotional ingenuity."[35] The public entrepreneur approach requires that a mayor be a bold problem solver, very active, and possess a mild willingness to take risks. McLin fit this description; as mayor, she was interested in taking risks, but she did not have an aggressive, active, or reform-minded approach. McLin's perceived openness to residents, as well as her energetic and quirky demeanor, was evident in her promotion of a charitable fund and of various symbolic programs for Dayton youth. In addition, her enthusiastic move into Wright-Dunbar demonstrated her willingness to be associated with the project, yet the action cannot be described as a substantive pursuit of black interests.

One of the most important observations that can be made about the case studies of Toledo and Dayton utilizes Stone's emphasis on the importance of mayors' controlling the existing governing and political infrastructure or building new structures they control.[36] Mayor Ford had the benefit of neither. Mayor McLin had the luxury of both. Ford admitted that he had little political power.[37] Though Ford had little control over the existing political and governing infrastructure, he actively pursued more substantive policy actions and program developments than did McLin. As a result of his lack of political and governing control and his seeming disinterest in building his own coalition while mayor, however, he failed to be reelected, effectively nullifying many of the gains.[38]

The structure in which McLin governed, meanwhile, limited the number of substantive actions she could pursue, yet her success at maintaining control over the Montgomery County Democratic political and governing infrastructure may imply that her more symbolic efforts could have a greater impact on black quality of life over a longer period of time than did Ford's more substantive ones.

When mayors do not have effective relationships with the business community, support on the city council, positively perceived personalities and governing approaches, or the formal powers of a strong-mayor system, they are handicapped in their ability to *actively* pursue black interests in non-majority-black cities. As the case studies of Ford and McLin attest, mayors who lack any of the necessary four components may be limited in their ability to actively pursue black interests either substantively (McLin) or over time (Ford).

That McLin's ability to substantively improve black quality of life from her position in a weak-mayor system perhaps reinforces Floyd Hunter's business and power structure model, which argues that we should pay attention not to a mayor's ability so much as to the power structure within which that mayor operates.[39] The occasional inability of mayors, like Ford, who govern in a strong-mayor system to have a sustained impact on black quality of life, on the other hand, perhaps reinforces Stone's emphasis on the importance of mayors controlling more than just the mayoral office.[40] Without the support of an electoral coalition that allows a mayor to sustain power throughout a second term, his or her ability to substantively affect black quality of life is either transferred or forfeited to other political and economic elites. As a result, the black mayoralty, and the black residents who benefit from it in non-majority-black cities, may be denied the benefits of municipal leadership based on shared racial experience.

For Ford and McLin the act of representing black interests in majority-white cities was a racial balancing act. The specter of race had to be balanced between their electoral and governing coalitions. McLin did so successfully to win a second term and a narrow defeat for a third term. Ford was not successful. However, the racial content of black interests must also be balanced so as to invite whites to envision black interests as interests that should matter to everyone. McLin was successful in her use of racial rhetoric, albeit with fewer substantive results. Ford was initially successful early in his term, but the success waned as his early black-interest rhetoric was remembered as too aggressive by whites and of little consequence by blacks in an economy perceived to be declining.

Despite differences in effectiveness Ford and McLin both utilized the theory of targeted universalism and the application of the "universalized black interests" approach to represent black interests in their majority-white cities. In both cases whites supported such initiatives for a period. This window of opportunity suggests it is possible to actively represent black interests without deemphasizing race or being racially specific. In framing black interests as universal interests, Ford and McLin found electoral and governing success. Their example is good "target practice" for others.

# EPILOGUE

In *No Name in the Street*, from which this book's introductory epigraph is borrowed, James Baldwin chronicles America's immediate post–civil rights racial status. In it Baldwin talks about the race problem: "It has been vivid to me for many years that what we call a race problem here is not a race problem at all: to keep calling it that is a way of avoiding the problem. The problem is rooted in the question of how one treats one's flesh and blood, especially one's children."[1] Baldwin's comment is significant because the mayors studied in this book, in their efforts to advance black interests in majority-white cities, often spoke of the city's young people and how to prepare a better environment for them. This approach worked. Whereas they might have faced political battles, friends and foes alike would often join them at various events throughout their communities as they sought to lift up the city's youth. Their ability to connect with largely non-black audiences in this way to fight the rust-belt "brain-drain" problem led to their ability to convince many whites that what was in the interests of the city's black residents was in the interests of the city as well and thereby important to all.

In cities where relations between whites and blacks continue to be the major racial story line, these mayors sought to weave a path for improvement that was targeted at blacks, inclusive of everyone, and framed as critical to moving their cities forward. As Baldwin continues in *No Name in the Street*, such a path is vital for American progress: "The black and white confrontation, whether it be hostile, as in the cities and the labor unions, or with the intention of forming a common front and creating the foundations of a new society, as with the students and the radicals, is obviously crucial, containing the shape of the American future and the only potential of a truly valid American identity."² Apparently for Baldwin these mayors are either radicals or students as they represent an effort to form a "common front." As I write, both mayors, students of politics and professors on college campuses, seek to reenter the political climate to serve again.

Both McLin and Ford have successfully pursued post-mayoral careers in politics. McLin, after losing a bid for a third term (in large part due to her support of a city ordinance that extended the city's anti-discrimination policies to include sexual orientation) considered entering the 2013 race for a seat on the Dayton City Commission. While she has since indicated she did not wish to join the 2013 race for a seat on the commission she once led, she's been vindicated perhaps in other ways. While her support for lesbian, gay, bisexual, and transgender (LGBT) rights was an enigma to her campaign in 2010, social scientists and the nation have since learned, for example, that Americans, including African Americans, increasingly support municipal and corporate non-discrimination policies. Hence while McLin was ahead of her time in 2010, the nation and various constituencies within it have increasingly come to share her view. Meanwhile, she remains very active in Ohio Democratic Party politics, hosting fundraisers and events for major candidates and advising others' efforts to serve the Dayton community as vice-chairwoman of the Ohio Democratic Party. I fully expect she will serve the public again someday.

Jack Ford, upon leaving office in 2006, has served as a member of the Toledo School Board and was a candidate for an at-large city council seat in Toledo's November 2013 election. At his announcement for the council seat, his long-time political foe and friend Carty Finkbeiner, who kept Ford from a second term, actively supported his bid. By the time this book is published, I'd guess Ford will be back in Toledo's government again, serving the public, advocating for the area's youth.

With a new lease on political life, McLin and Ford remain active Ohio political figures whose political philosophies and inclusive orthodoxy continue to inspire the many constituents they seem to never tire of serving.

# Statistics on McLin and Ford Mayoral Victories

**TABLE A1:** Dayton Wards, Selected Census Data, and McLin Margin of Victory in 2001 Mayoral Election *(Range; Mean)*

| DAYTON WARD | CENSUS TRACT COUNT[a] | TOTAL POPULATION[b] | PERCENT NON–HISPANIC BLACK PERSONS[b] |
|---|---|---|---|
| 1 | 4 | 2,156–8,595; 4,996 | 3–51; 18 |
| 2 | 6 | 2,476–6,077; 4,156 | 3–14; 5.3 |
| 3 | 9 | 1,358–8,189; 4,663.9 | 0–49; 14.2 |
| 4 | 4 | 467–4,223; 2,562.25 | 21–71; 47.75 |
| 5 | 5 | 1,191–4,230; 2,714.6 | 64–95; 79.4 |
| 6 | 3 | 3,346–4,334; 3,721 | 68–97; 87 |
| 7 | 4 | 1,126–4,334; 2,748.5 | 94–97; 96 |
| 8 | 4 | 3,046–8,595; 5,222 | 4–5; 4.5 |
| 9 | 4 | 2,871–4,208; 3,454.3 | 1–5; 3 |
| 10 | 5 | 2,024–6,158; 4,688.4 | 1–7; 3.2 |
| 11 | 6 | 2,024–5,496; 3,618 | 1–7; 3.3 |
| 12 | 5 | 2,476–6,158; 4,256.4 | 3–4; 3.4 |
| 13 | 4 | 1,126–5,403; 2,437.3 | 94–98; 96.3 |
| 14 | 7 | 1,170–4,184; 2,613.6 | 41–98; 83.1 |
| 15 | 8 | 1,170–5,203; 3,170.4 | 54–97; 77.8 |
| 16 | 6 | 3,094–6,337; 4,360.7 | 50–91; 77.7 |
| 17 | 3 | 3,711–5,102; 4,540.7 | 41–71; 57 |
| 18 | 4 | 2,089–5,102; 4,267 | 39–70; 52.3 |
| 19 | 6 | 1,311–3,403; 2,561.5 | 93–98; 95.8 |
| 20 | 4 | 2,282–4,208; 3,078.5 | 1–5; 2.25 |
| 21 | 3 | 3,094; 4,796; 3,769 | 85–91; 89 |
| 22 | 5 | 1,931–5,073; 3,605 | 70–95; 85.8 |

*Source:* Author's results conducted with ArcGIS (Geographic Information Systems), ArcMap 9.1. Layer One: Re-Drawn Dayton wards; Layer Two: Selected U.S. Census data, 2000.

| PERCENT OF PEOPLE BELOW POVERTY[b] | PERCENT OF PEOPLE UNEMPLOYED[b] | PERCENT COLLEGE EDUCATED[b] | MCLIN VOTE % |
|---|---|---|---|
| 28–54; 41 | 6–17; 11.25 | 12–41; 23.25 | 39.3 |
| 4–29; 21.6 | 5–13; 8.3 | 6–12; 9.7 | 23 |
| 1–47; 16.3 | 1–17; 6.7 | 2–38; 14 | 22.7 |
| 21–34; 28.5 | 7–12; 8.75 | 15–36; 21.25 | 47.8 |
| 9–39; 26.4 | 8–14; 10.8 | 7–30; 19 | 74.5 |
| 25–29; 26.7 | 12–16; 14 | 2–7; 5.3 | 86.4 |
| 25–44; 34 | 12–23; 18 | 2–7; 5.75 | 85 |
| 9–54; 22.5 | 4–17; 7.75 | 13–41; 25.6 | 21.1 |
| 7–12; 9.75 | 2–5; 3.5 | 14–35; 20.75 | 17.1 |
| 7–15; 11.2 | 3–9; 5.6 | 13–21; 15.6 | 15.7 |
| 9–29; 16 | 3–13; 7.83 | 6–21; 12.5 | 21.4 |
| 9–37; 23.2 | 5–13; 10 | 6–16; 10.2 | 20.5 |
| 30–44; 39 | 14–23; 20.3 | 2–7; 5.5 | 87.7 |
| 6–50; 32.4 | 4–25; 15.6 | 6–20; 11.4 | 84.5 |
| 8–35; 22.5 | 4–18; 12.75 | 2–20; 10.3 | 84 |
| 14–31; 20 | 3–13; 7.5 | 3–29; 14.3 | 79.4 |
| 11–21; 15 | 5–12; 7.3 | 12–18; 15 | 55.8 |
| 7–16; 11.75 | 3–4; 4.25 | 12–29; 21.5 | 44.6 |
| 30–50; 39.17 | 2–25; 18.83 | 2–13; 7 | 88.8 |
| 7–9; 8.25 | 3–5; 3.5 | 9–14; 12 | 17 |
| 21–31; 25.3 | 9–13; 11 | 3–15; 8.3 | 82.6 |
| 9–39; 23.8 | 4–14; 9.8 | 7–30; 19.2 | 76.2 |

a. Census tract count is the total number of census tracts that intersected the ward.

b. To generate the range and mean of the census data for each variable within the wards, I included all the census tracts that intersected each ward. The range is the minimum value for all census tracts that intersected the ward. The mean is the average for all census tracts that intersect the ward.

**TABLE A2:** Toledo Wards, Selected Census Data, and Ford Margin of Victory in 2001 Mayoral Election *(Range; Mean)*

| TOLEDO WARD | CENSUS TRACT COUNT[a] | TOTAL POPULATION[b] | PERCENT NON-HISPANIC BLACK PERSONS[b] |
|---|---|---|---|
| 1 | 18 | 2,287–5,801; 3,342 | 0–59; 5.88 |
| 2 | 18 | 2,025–3,575; 2,068 | 10–71; 36.38 |
| 3 | 15 | 3,653–5,801; 4,818 | 3–11; 5.33 |
| 4 | 19 | 2,025–5,261; 3,344 | 6–71; 47.78 |
| 5 | 12 | 4,502–5,089; 4,777 | 11–32; 17.16 |
| 6 | 15 | 1,797–6,124; 4,100 | 32–75; 54.6 |
| 7 | 10 | 2,665–4,113; 3,632 | 2–35; 7.9 |
| 8 | 16 | 530–2,510; 1,784 | 44–96; 86.3 |
| 9 | 16 | 3,708–5,748; 4,974 | 4–39; 9.93 |
| 10 | 11 | 2,003–4,299; 3,304 | 46–84; 72.5 |
| 11 | 14 | 2,432–5,434; 4,039 | 1–46; 8.07 |
| 12 | 15 | 2,419–5,748; 3,149 | 3–39; 15.3 |
| 13 | 17 | 1,797–3,708; 2,701 | 39–96; 72.5 |
| 14 | 14 | 1,451–2,275; 1,899 | 54–95; 86.28 |
| 15 | 19 | 222–5,624; 3,971 | 3–85; 23.1 |
| 16 | 16 | 2,087–4,480; 3,347 | 1–12; 3.87 |
| 17 | 17 | 900–4,480; 3,065 | 8–93; 24 |
| 18 | 12 | 2,400–5,146; 3,751 | 3–21; 10.08 |
| 19 | 15 | 2,240–5,146; 4,048 | 4–54; 14 |
| 20 | 19 | 1,913–4,063; 2,967 | 1–45; 14.15 |
| 21 | 15 | 2,419–3,258; 2,849 | 2–15; 4.2 |
| 22 | 11 | 1,588–5,453; 3,792 | 2–6; 4.72 |
| 23 | 16 | 2,189–5,913; 4,228 | 1–4; 2.81 |
| 24 | 11 | 3,738–4,952; 4,516 | 7–48; 20.9 |

*Source:* Author's results conducted with ArcGIS (Geographic Information Systems), ArcMap 9.1. Layer One: Re-Drawn Toledo wards; Layer Two: Selected U.S. Census data, 2000.

| PERCENT OF PEOPLE BELOW POVERTY[b] | PERCENT UNEMPLOYED | PERCENT COLLEGE EDUCATED | FORD VOTE PERCENT |
|---|---|---|---|
| 3–20; 8.1667 | –9; 5.83 | 5–16; 10.38 | 46.3 |
| 29–55; 35.4 | 7–29; 16.16 | 1–6; 4.1 | 59.5 |
| 7–15; 9.3 | 3–7; 4.8 | 11–17; 13.4667 | 50.7 |
| 9–31; 22.947 | 3–18; 10.57 | 4–13; 5.31 | 67.8 |
| 6–18; 12.1667 | 2–7; 4.667 | 17–30; 22.08 | 59.9 |
| 15–27; 18.5 | 6–11; 6 | 11–30; 15.26 | 83.1 |
| 1–27; 6.4 | 2–11; 3.3 | 20–36; 29.2 | 50.7 |
| 29–70; 39.18 | 9–21; 13.56 | 2–20; 7.25 | 88.8 |
| 6–15; 9.93 | 3–7; 5.56 | 11–31; 15.37 | 56.4 |
| 25–36; 29.45 | 11–26; 17.27 | 4–26; 12.72 | 85.8 |
| 6–28; 8.7 | 3–18; 5.21 | 4–18; 11.85 | 52.7 |
| 3–34; 13.8 | 1–23; 4.6 | 14–67; 43.6 | 66.4 |
| 9–36; 24.35 | 4–18; 11.11 | 5–31; 15.05 | 87.9 |
| 21–46; 32.71 | 11–19; 15 | 3–12; 7.5 | 89.5 |
| 6–39; 19.26 | 0–19; 8.42 | 2–22; 15.15 | 54.6 |
| 2–35; 10.75 | 14–81; 5.06 | 3–41; 24.75 | 52.3 |
| 17–43; 31 | 7–15; 11.7 | 2–13; 5.05 | 60 |
| 17–35; 25.83 | 8–16; 11 | 3–6; 4.08 | 54.9 |
| 17–55; 31.06 | 7–25; 12.26 | 5–13; 6.3 | 55 |
| 7–38; 23.26 | 4–29; 12.05 | 1–13; 5.84 | 54.6 |
| 3–19; 6.6 | 2–5; 3.53 | 18–43; 28.7 | 52.8 |
| 1–11; 9.18 | 2–13; 6.9 | 19–54; 33.6 | 52.5 |
| 2–8; 6.81 | 3–6; 4.87 | 9–39; 16.06 | 52 |
| 4–27; 12.09 | 1–11; 5.18 | 13–34; 27 | 58.9 |

a. Census tract count is the total number of census tracts that intersected the ward.

b. To generate the range and mean of the census data for each variable within the wards, I included all the census tracts that intersected each ward. The range is the minimum value for all census tracts that intersected the ward. The mean is the average for all census tracts that intersect the ward.

# Appendix B

## Research Methodologies

*Process for Newspaper Coverage Analysis*

The following question was considered in the conducting of content analysis of newspaper articles to gauge coverage of the black mayors as candidates: "Does the major local newspaper coverage focus on McLin's and Ford's actual election potential, or are they viewed as underdogs?" In addition to that question, three methods of comparative analysis were used to analyze the print media coverage. One measured the frequency of articles about McLin and Ford as candidates for mayor and as first-term mayors. The selected articles were not random. A second method focused on the placement of those articles, which primarily discussed McLin and Ford yet were not centrally located in the local newspapers and therefore were less likely to be read. Such positioning of articles was also a significant aspect of the analysis and was termed "article placement."[1] It was categorized in this manner because the position of articles determines to what extent articles are read. A third method consisted of analytical commentary on the articles' content as defined by the criteria established below. The methods of analysis were useful in seeking, for example, the number of times "race" was simply mentioned in the articles and the number of times the issue of race in the campaign or administration was mentioned and how.

It is the third analysis method that merits further explication. Searching for a way to demonstrate how the various local newspaper articles on McLin and Ford accomplished a particular purpose; wanting to objectify the analysis of content; and needing to identify, categorize, measure, and tabulate differentials, I devised a five-label rubric.[2] This instrument served to offer a systematic analysis of the newspaper coverage. Specifically the categories were: policy/race (positive); policy/race (positive-neutral); neutral; policy/race (negative-neutral), and policy/race (negative). The following is an explanation of the terms.

> *Policy/race (positive)* referred to articles that fairly represented McLin and Ford and did not include potentially stereotypical or politically or racially damaging language. *Positive* indicated that the article's placement in the local newspaper was good and that the article content was primarily factual and predominantly based on political issues and campaign policies. *Positive* did not suggest formal support for a particular candidate, although the article may have done so.
>
> *Policy/race (positive-neutral)* referred to articles that appeared to be positive and seemingly shared the characteristics mentioned above, yet often because of article placement, subject, and/or language, they no longer could be labeled as such. Often an article in this category lacked the necessary information to be labeled as positive, yet it included substantial information about the candidate.
>
> *Neutral* referred to articles that were not negative or positive. Frequently these articles were unbiased, but lacked detail. Occasionally they may have had subject-related inconsistencies and outliers or may not have included enough information about the candidates for a label to be affixed to them. Articles included were considered generally negative because of a lack of information to the reader about a candidate or elected official, from which perhaps possible voter apathy or uninformed voters could be inferred.
>
> *Policy/race (negative-neutral)* referred to articles that appeared to be negative and seemingly shared the characteristics of the preceding category yet included factual information or bias equally in terms of the candidates and/or elected officials discussed

and lacked seemingly deliberate racialized or potentially damaging language.

*Policy/race (negative)* referred to articles that unfairly represented McLin and Ford and included potentially racially stereotypical, unnecessary, and/or politically damaging language. *Negative* also indicated that an article's placement in the newspapers and its content were likely in a position not to be read. Also, the negative article content may not have been related to campaign issues or factual information, although the article's title suggested that it would be. For example, if the article posed personal or campaign issues as opposed to policies and initiatives, it was labeled negatively.

*Interview Questions*

QUESTIONS FOR MAYORS

1. While mayor, what do/did you see as the major problems facing City X?
2. How were/have these issues been addressed by your office? A. Very Well; B. Somewhat Well; C. Not Very Well; D. Poorly
3. From your perspective, what do you see as the major problems facing African Americans in City X?
4. How were/have these issues been addressed by your office? A. Very Well; B. Somewhat Well; C. Not Very Well; D. Poorly
5. Are/were there important new policy ideas from your office that have been generated?
6. Are/were there important new policy ideas directly affecting the African American community implemented by your office?
7. What policies failed? Why did they fail?
8. As Mayor, what policy initiatives or programs were/are you especially concerned with?
9. How do things get done in City X?
10. Describe the nature of the political process in City X. Is it partisan? Does true party competition exist?

11. How have changes in business in City X over the last 8–10 years led to changes in the community?
12. What has been the impact of a changing business climate on the African American community?
13. How did African American leadership communicate and interact with the city's leadership during your term(s)?
14. Are/were these issues a priority to your administration and the city's (then) political leaders?
15. What are the names of the important and active organizations within the African American community?
16. To what extent do these organizations work together to pursue their own set of issues?
    A. Well; B. Somewhat Well; C. Just about Right; D. Poorly
17. Who are the leaders in each of these organizations?
18. Are there individuals in the African American community who are not necessarily leaders but are well informed about the community?
19. Are there individuals in City X who are not necessarily elected officials but have significant political influence?
20. Did the major newspaper/networks endorse you in either of your campaigns for office? From your perspective, why do you think they did or did not? If not, why do you think they did not?
21. How would you characterize your relationship with White and black leaders throughout City X?
22. What, if anything, do you recall doing on behalf of African American issues? Statements—public or private—press conferences, personal requests.
23. Do you recall approaching specific businesses or organizations directly or indirectly to assist with efforts related to the African American community?
24. How would you characterize your commitment to African American issues?
    Did you initiate any "firsts" when it came to producing substantive benefits for African Americans?

25. If so, do you think you suffered any negative backlash as a result?
26. Did you make any key personnel changes within your appointment powers that benefited African Americans?
27. Do you know of any African Americans whose lives have positively changed in some substantive way as a result of a direct action by you while in office?
28. In a city like X, where whites represent X % of the population, how likely is it that you can actively pursue policies designed to improve the quality of life of black residents?
    A. Very Likely; B. Somewhat Likely; C. Not Very Likely; Not Likely at All
29. How important is it to have fellow African Americans on city council/commission—whether or not they support your every initiative?
30. (Mayor Ford) What do you attribute to your failed re-election bid?
31. (Mayor Ford) What role do you think the Nazi march/race riot two weeks prior had in affecting your standing as a *black* mayor and your chances at re-election?
32. (Mayor McLin) What do you attribute to your successful re-election?

QUESTIONS FOR GENERAL INFLUENTIALS

("General influentials" include newspaper editorial board members and publishers, mayors' campaign and administration officials and appointees, business leaders, union leaders, and former political officials.)

1. From your perspective, what do you see as the major problems facing City X?
2. How were/have these issues been addressed by Mayor X?
   A. Very Well; B. Somewhat Well; C. Not Very Well; D. Poorly
3. From your perspective, what do you see as the major problems facing African Americans in City X?

4. How were/have these issues been addressed by Mayor X?
   A. Very Well; B. Somewhat Well; C. Not Very Well; D. Poorly
5. Are/were there important new policy ideas from Mayor X's administration that have been generated?
6. Are/were there important new policy ideas directly affecting the African American community implemented by Mayor X's administration?
7. As a community leader, what policy initiatives or programs are you especially concerned with currently? During Mayor X's administration?
8. How do things get done in City X?
9. Describe the nature of the political process in City X. Is it partisan? Does true party competition exist?
10. How have changes in business in City X over the last 8–10 years led to changes in the community?
11. What has been the impact of a changing business climate on the African American community?
12. How did African American leadership communicate and interact with the city's leadership during Mayor X's term(s)?
13. Are/were these issues a priority to Mayor X's administration and the city's (then) political leaders?
14. What arc the names of the important and active organizations within the African American community?
15. To what extent do these organizations work together to pursue their own set of issues?
    A. Well; B. Somewhat Well; C. Just about Right; D. Poorly
16. Who are the leaders in each of these communities?
17. Are there individuals in the African American community who are not necessarily leaders but are well informed about the community?
18. Are there individuals in City X who are not necessarily elected officials but have significant political influence?
19. Did the major newspaper/networks endorse Mayor X in either of his/her campaigns for office? From your perspective, why

do you think they did or did not? If not, why do you think they did not?

20. How would you characterize Mayor X's relationship with white and black leaders throughout City X?

21. How would you characterize Mayor X's efforts at pursuing programs designed to improve the quality of life of black residents?
A. Doing a Lot; B. Not Enough; C. Just about Right; D. Not Nearly Enough

22. [If applicable] Do you recall Mayor X or his/her staff approaching your business/organization directly or indirectly to assist with efforts related to the African American community?

23. How would you characterize Mayor X's commitment to African American issues?
Did Mayor X initiate any "firsts" when it came to producing substantive benefits for African Americans?

24. If so, do you think Mayor X suffered any negative backlash as a result?

25. Did Mayor X make any key personnel changes within his/her appointment powers that benefited African Americans?

26. Do you know of any African Americans whose lives have positively changed in some substantive way as a result of a direct action by Mayor X while in office?

27. In a city like X, where whites represent X % of the population, how likely is it that Mayor X can actively pursue policies designed to improve the quality of life of black residents?
A. Very Likely; B. Somewhat Likely; C. Not Very Likely; Not Likely at All

28. How much interaction have you had with Mayor X?
A. Daily/Frequent; B. Somewhat Frequent/Weekly; C. Not That Frequent; D. Rarely Ever

29. Demographic Information collected on each respondent:
Gender: ____Male ____Female
Ethnicity/Race:
____Hispanic
____African American

_____White

_____Asian American

_____Native American

_____Other (Specify:_____)

30. How long have you lived in City X? _____# of Years

QUESTIONS FOR PUBLIC OFFICIALS

("Public officials" include any elected members of the political community currently holding office.)

1. From your perspective, what do you see as the major problems facing City X?
2. How were/have these issues been addressed by Mayor X?
   A. Very Well; B. Somewhat Well; C. Not Very Well; D. Poorly
3. From your perspective, what do you see as the major problems facing African Americans in City X?
4. How were/have these issues been addressed by Mayor X?
   A. Very Well; B. Somewhat Well; C. Not Very Well; D. Poorly
5. Are/were there important new policy ideas from Mayor X's administration that have been generated?
6. Are/were there important new policy ideas directly affecting the African American community implemented by Mayor X's administration?
7. As a community leader, what policy initiatives or programs are you especially concerned with currently? During Mayor X's administration?
8. How do things get done in City X?
9. Describe the nature of the political process in City X. Is it partisan? Does true party competition exist?
10. How have changes in business in City X over the last 8–10 years led to changes in the community?
11. What has been the impact of a changing business climate on the African American community?
12. How did African American leadership communicate and interact with the city's leadership during Mayor X's term(s)?

13. Are/were these issues a priority to Mayor X's administration and the city's (then) political leaders?
14. What are the names of the important and active organizations within the African American community?
15. To what extent do these organizations work together to pursue their own set of issues?
    A. Well; B. Somewhat Well; C. Just about Right; D. Poorly
16. Who are the leaders in each of these communities?
17. Are there individuals in the African American community who are not necessarily leaders but are well informed about the community?
18. Are there individuals in City X who are not necessarily elected officials but have significant political influence?
19. Did the major newspaper/networks endorse Mayor X in either of his/her campaigns for office? From your perspective, why do you think they did or did not? If not, why do you think they did not?
20. How influential is it for a Mayor in City X to have a county party endorsement in their campaign(s)? What effect do (did) the local, county political parties have on Mayor X's efforts to pursue programs designed to improve the quality of life of black residents?
21. How would you characterize Mayor X's relationship with white and black leaders throughout City X?
22. What, if anything do you recall Mayor X doing on behalf of African American issues? Statements—public or private—press conferences, personal requests [if applicable to your office]?
23. [If applicable] Do you recall Mayor X or his/her staff approaching your business/organization directly or indirectly to assist with efforts related to the African American community?
24. How would you characterize Mayor X's commitment to African American issues? Did Mayor X initiate any "firsts" when it came to producing substantive benefits for African Americans?
25. If so, do you think Mayor X suffered any negative backlash as a result?

26. Did Mayor X make any key personnel changes within his/her appointment powers that benefited African Americans?
27. Do you know of any African Americans whose lives have positively changed in some substantive way as a result of a direct action by Mayor X while in office?
28. In a city like X, where whites represent X % of the population, how likely is it that Mayor X can actively pursue policies designed to improve the quality of life of black residents?
A. Very Likely; B. Somewhat Likely; C. Not Very Likely; Not Likely at All
[Where applicable, for city council/commission members]
29. [For those in districts] Is your main purpose to voice the concerns of those in your districts or the citizens of City X in general?
30. Who or what groups constitute your core constituency?
31. While he/she was Mayor, how much interaction have you had/did you have with Mayor X?
A. Daily/Frequent; B. Somewhat Frequent/Weekly; C. Not That Frequent; D. Rarely Ever
32. Demographic Information collected on each respondent:
Gender: ____Male____Female
Ethnicity/Race:
____Hispanic
____African American
____White
____Asian American
____Native American
____Other (Specify:_____)
33. How long have you lived in city X? ____# of Years

QUESTIONS FOR COMMUNITY ACTIVISTS/ADVOCACY GROUPS

("Community activists/advocacy groups" include black community religious leaders, the black press, neighborhood activists, and other leaders.)

1. From your perspective, what do you see as the major problems facing City X?
2. How were/have these issues been addressed by Mayor X?
   A. Very Well; B. Somewhat Well; C. Not Very Well; D. Poorly
3. From your perspective, what do you see as the major problems facing African Americans in City X?
4. How were/have these issues been addressed by Mayor X?
   A. Very Well; B. Somewhat Well; C. Not Very Well; D. Poorly
5. Are/were there important new policy ideas directly affecting the African American community implemented by Mayor X's administration?
6. As a community leader, what policy initiatives or programs are you especially concerned with currently? During Mayor X's administration?
7. How do things get done in City X?
8. What has been the impact of a changing business climate on the African American community?
9. How did African American leadership communicate and interact with the city's leadership during Mayor X's term(s)?
10. Are/were these issues a priority to Mayor X's administration and the city's (then) political leaders?
11. What are the names of the important and active organizations within the African American community?
12. To what extent do these organizations work together to pursue their own set of issues?
    A. Well; B. Somewhat Well; C. Just about Right; D. Poorly
13. Who are the leaders in the African American community?
14. Are there individuals in the African American community who are not necessarily leaders but are well informed about the community?
15. Did the African American newspaper(s)/networks endorse Mayor X in either of his/her campaigns for office? From your perspective, why do you think they did or did not? If not, why do you think they did not?

16. Can white political leaders represent African American constituencies or do African Americans need African Americans in office in order to be represented? Why or why not?
17. Can a mayor survive in City X if he or she ignores African Americans?
18. If no, when was the last time that African Americans could be ignored?
19. Why can African Americans no longer be ignored?
20. How would you characterize Mayor X's relationship with white and black leaders throughout City X?
21. What, if anything, do you recall Mayor X doing on behalf of African American issues? Statements—public or private—press conferences, personal requests [if applicable, to your office]?
22. [If applicable] Do you recall Mayor X or his/her staff approaching your business/organization directly or indirectly to assist with efforts related to the African American community?
23. How would you characterize Mayor X's efforts at pursuing programs designed to improve the quality of life of black residents? A. Doing a Lot; B. Not Enough; C. Just about Right; D. Not Nearly Enough? ——— Mayor Finkbeiner's/Turner's
24. Did Mayor X initiate any "firsts" when it came to producing substantive benefits for African Americans?
25. Did Mayor X make any key personnel changes within his/her appointment powers that benefited African Americans?
26. Do you know of any African Americans whose lives have positively changed in some substantive way as a result of a direct action by Mayor X while in office?
27. In a city like X, where whites represent X % of the population, how likely is it that Mayor X can actively pursue policies designed to improve the quality of life of black residents?
A. Very Likely; B. Somewhat Likely; C. Not Very Likely; Not Likely at All
28. How much interaction have you had with Mayor X while in office or while campaigning for office?

A. Daily/Frequent; B. Somewhat Frequent/Weekly; C. Not That Frequent; D. Rarely Ever

29. Demographic Information collected on each respondent:

Gender: ____Male ____Female

Ethnicity/Race:

____Hispanic

____African American

____White

____Asian American

____Native American

____Other (Specify:_____)

30. How long have you lived in city X? ____# of Years

*Issue-Area Categories*

A respondent's perspective on the mayor's active pursuit of policies and programs designed to improve the quality of life of blacks is somewhat determined by his or her perception of the problems the mayor needs to address. Therefore of the dozens of questions asked respondents, one was of particular significance: "What do you see as the major problems facing African Americans in City X?" Respondents provided a variety of answers to this open-ended question. I then grouped these answers into larger categories. For example, various respondents said that lack of jobs, the poor economy, the loss of the automotive industry, or job creation was a major problem facing their respective city. I concluded that white and African American interviewees were giving the same response if one said "economic development" and the other said "loss of the manufacturing base"; both responses were thus grouped in a "jobs and economy" category. If a respondent's answer was not direct, even after significant probing, I inferred a response and affixed a label to the respondent's reply. The following is a list of issue categories and a selected sample of respondents' statements. It will show how open-ended responses were coded as "positive" or "negative" concerning the major problems facing African Americans in the city and the mayors' efforts to address them.

**Jobs and Economy**
Jobs
Limited employment opportunity
Economics
Businesses can't get viable customer base
Too few jobs
Minority contracting
Lack of jobs
Unemployment
Lack of wealth
Getting share of resources
Lending institutions
Small black business
High-paying factory jobs without education

**Public Safety**
Criminal justice
High incarceration rate
Higher drug arrests
Concentrated black population
Safe streets

**Education**
Schools
Schools need better resources
Schools not financed, structured, or staffed as they should be
Public school system deficient
Inner city schools not supported
High dropout rate
Lack of educational attainment
No solid education

**Housing**
Severely segregated housing patterns

## Opportunity and Access
Personal belief in ability to access community resources
Belief that the system will serve (me)
Belief in the public trust
Getting beyond the red tape to survive
Lack of leadership
Second-tier leadership
Lack of influence even in diversity-related matters

## Intra-Community Concerns
Togetherness
Separate class of people
Media portrayal of blacks
Perception that Toledo hasn't moved far in race relations
No one "standout" leader
Racism
Lack of cohesiveness and trust
Lack of willingness to sacrifice
Skepticism
Knowing the right people
'50s and '60s mentality
Confluence of race and poverty
Behind the starting line in opportunities
Tendency to be stuck in the past
Reluctance of leaders to step back in their roles
No long-term strategic opportunities for leadership
Inclusion
African Americans (we are the problem)
Self-appointed leaders
Lack of pro-activity
Lack of real role model
blacks themselves
A lot of naysayers

**Healthcare**
Lack of available health care
Lack of health insurance
Mental health

**Youth**
Young children in programming
Divorced families/single-family homes

*Interview Statistics*

Number of interviewees in Toledo: 53
Number of interviewees in Dayton: 30
Total: 83

|                                    | Dayton | Toledo |
| ---------------------------------- | ------ | ------ |
| General influentials               | 12     | 32     |
| Public officials                   | 10     | 11     |
| (Elected, current office holders;  |        |        |
| Dayton's city manager included)    |        |        |
| Mayors                             | 1      | 2      |
| Community Activists                | 7      | 8      |
| TOTAL                              | 30*    | 53     |

*One of the interviews in Dayton was a joint meeting with three city officials in the Department of Planning and Community Development. I counted that meeting as though it were with one individual.

*Interviewees*

TOLEDO

1. Michael Ashford
   City council president during Finkbeiner's second term in 2007; current member of the Ohio House of Representatives
   July 1, 2008

2. Alan Bannister
   Former mayoral assistant
   June 28, 2008

3. Michael Beazley
   Former clerk of council and chair of Democratic Party
   June 19, 2008

4. Bob Bell
   President and CEO, Toledo
   Symphony; friend of Mayor
   Ford
   July 2008
5. Michael Bell
   Former fire chief for City of
   Toledo; former State of Ohio
   fire marshal; current mayor
   of Toledo
   July 21, 2008
6. Jay Black Jr.
   Former chief of staff
   June 10, 2008
7. John Block
   Publisher of *Toledo Blade*
   July 15, 2008
8. Bill Brennan
   President of Associated
   General Contractors of
   Northwest Ohio
   August 4, 2008
9. Wilma Brown
   District councilwoman
   June 17, 2008
10. Phillip Copeland
    At-large member of city
    council
    July 15, 2008
11. Thomas Crothers
    Former chief of staff
    June 18, 2008
12. George Davis Jr.
    Community activist; former
    first vice-president of NAACP
    July 1, 2008

13. Kelli Daniels
    Ford campaign staffer
    September 19, 2008
14. Louis Escobar
    Former president of Tole-
    do City Council
    August 12, 2008
15. Teresa Fedor
    Former state representa-
    tive; current state senator;
    former teacher in Toledo
    Public Schools
    July 14, 2008
16. Carleton Finkbeiner
    Mayor (Mayor Ford's pre-
    decessor and successor)
    July 16, 2008
17. Jack Ford
    Former mayor of Toledo;
    former member of Toledo
    school board
    June 24, 2008 (initial inter-
    view)
18. Pete Gerken
    Current member of Lucas
    County Board of Commis-
    sioners
    August 21, 2008
19. Ellen Gracheck
    Former district council-
    woman
    July 1, 2008

20. Juanita Greene
    Executive director of the
    City of Toledo Board of
    Community Relations
    June 19, 2008
21. Barbara Herring
    Former law director
    July 4, 2008
22. George Hilliard
    Community activist; Dem-
    ocratic Party ward chair and
    precinct committeeman
    July 10, 2008
23. Dr. Dan Johnson
    Former president of the
    University of Toledo
    August 4, 2008
24. Joslyn Jones
    Engineer for City of Toledo
    August 19, 2008
25. Wade Kapszukiewicz
    Former city councilman;
    current Lucas County trea-
    surer
    June 10, 2008
26. Ben Konop
    Member, Lucas County
    Board of Commissioners
    July 18, 2008
27. Anita Lopez
    Former head of Office of
    Affirmative Action and
    Contract Compliance; cur-
    rent Lucas County auditor
    June 19–20, 2008

28. Lloyd Mahaffey
    Director of Region 2B of
    the United Auto Workers
29. Ted Mastroianni
    Consultant to Ford cam-
    paign; executive director of
    transition committee
    July 1, 2008
30. Yulanda McCarty-Harris
    Former director of Office
    of Affirmative Action and
    Contract Compliance
    July 2008
31. Doni Miller
    Executive director, Neigh-
    borhood Health Associa-
    tion; former president of
    Toledo-Lucas County Port
    Authority
    August 4, 2008
32. James Murray
    President of Ohio Opera-
    tions of FirstEnergy Corp.
    (based in Toledo)
    July 2, 2008
33. Michael Navarre
    Chief of police
    July 8, 2008
34. Willie Perryman Jr.
    Mayoral assistant and pas-
    tor of Jerusalem Baptist
    Church
    July 3, 2008

35. Susan Reams
    Former Arts Consultant for
    Ford Administration
    July 10, 2008
36. Paula Ross
    Former chair of Lucas
    County Democratic Party
    June 23, 2008
37. Jan Ruma
    Executive director of
    CareNet
    August 21, 2008
38. James Ruvolo
    Consultant
    June 19, 2008
39. George Sarantou
    At-large city councilman
    June 20, 2008
40. Robert Savage
    Transition team co-chair;
    friend of Ford
41. Peter Silverman
    Former president of Tole-
    do school board
    June 15, 2008
42. Tina Skeldon-Wozniak
    President, Lucas County
    Board of Commissioners
    July 2, 2008
43. Robert Smith
    Founder of African Ameri-
    can Legacy Project of
    Northwest Ohio
    July 19, 2008

44. Larry Sykes
    Former president of Tole-
    do school board
    July 5, 2008
45. Francis Szollosi
    At-large city councilman
    June 25, 2008
46. James Telb, PhD
    Sheriff, Lucas County
    July 9, 2008
47. Duane Tisdale
    Pastor of Friendship Bap-
    tist Church
    July 23, 2008
48. Megan Vahey
    Former campaign manag-
    er, public information offi-
    cer, and executive assistant
    June 28, 2008
49. Robert Vasquez
    Friend of Ford and former
    member of Toledo school
    board
    June 18, 2008
50. Joe Walter
    Former safety director
    June 17, 2008
51. Charles Welch
    Owner of WJUC-The
    Juice–107.3 FM
    August 4, 2008
52. Linnie Willis
    Executive director of Lucas
    County Metropolitan
    Housing Authority
    July 17, 2008

53. Fletcher Word
    Editor and publisher of
    weekly black newspaper,
    *Sojourner's Truth*
    June 18, 2008

DAYTON

1. Ronald F. Budzik
   Member, Dayton Business
   Committee
   August 7, 2008
2. Philip L. Parker
   CEO, Dayton Chamber of
   Commerce
   Telephone interview, August 6, 2008
3. Ginny Strausburg
   Executive director, Dayton
   Power and Light Company
   Foundation
   August 5, 2008
4. Rev. Dr. P. E. Henderson Jr.
   Pastor, Corinthian Baptist
   Church
   August 5, 2008
5. City officials with Dayton
   priority boards
   Department of Planning
   and Community Development
   July 3, 2008
6. Claude Bell Sr.
   President, Innerwest Priority Board
   August 5, 2008

7. Annie C. Bonaparte
   First vice-president, Innerwest Priority Board
   August 5, 2008
8. Carole L. Grimes
   Member, Dayton Metropolitan Housing Authority
   Board
   August 5, 2008
9. Idotha Bootsie-Neal
   President, Wright-Dunbar,
   Inc., and former city commissioner
   Telephone Interview
10. Rhine McLin
    Mayor, City of Dayton
    June 26, 2008
11. Ken Sulfridge
    President of AFSCME Local
    101
    August 5, 2008
12. Harry Delaney
    WIIIO-TV vice-president
    and general manager
    August 7, 2008
13. B. Cato Mayberry
    Director, Office of Alumni
    Relations, Central State
    University
    August 6, 2008
14. Marsha Greer
    Director of educational
    programs, Parity, Inc.
    August 7, 2008

15. James Cummings
    *Dayton Daily News* reporter
    Telephone interview, June
    26, 2008
16. Karl L. Keith
    Montgomery County audi-
    tor
    August 7, 2008
17. Judy Dodge
    Montgomery County com-
    missioner
    August 5, 2008
18. Matt Joseph
    Dayton city commissioner
    July 3, 2008
19. Nan Whaley
    Dayton city commissioner
    June 26, 2008
20. Kurt Stanic
    Superintendent, Dayton
    Public Schools
    August 5, 2008
21. Daniel G. Gehres
    Judge, Dayton municipal
    court
    August 7, 2008
22. Martin Gottlieb
    Editorial columnist, *Dayton
    Daily News*
    July 22, 2008
23. Rashad Young
    City manager, City of Day-
    ton
    July 16, 2008

24. Don G. Black
    Editor and publisher, *Day-
    ton Weekly News*
    July 23, 2008
25. Alvin Freeman
    Founding member, Con-
    cerned Christian Men
    August 7, 2008
26. Debbie Lieberman
    Montgomery County com-
    missioner
    August 14, 2008
27. Mark E. Owens
    Chair, Montgomery Coun-
    ty Democratic Party
    July 22, 2008
28. Richard S. Biehl
    Chief of police, City of
    Dayton
    July 22, 2008
29. Willis E. Blackshear
    Montgomery County re-
    corder
    July 22, 2008
30. Daniel K. Foley
    Montgomery County com-
    missioner
    August 5, 2008

*Roster of Significant Activities of Mayors McLin and Ford*

MAYOR MCLIN

1. Housing and neighborhood redevelopment (Project SUN; HOPE VI; 2003 Citirama in Wright-Dunbar Village and Paul Laurence Dunbar Event; ORION Solution)
2. "Hiring" of police chief and city manager
3. Support of school system
4. Symbolic gestures (e.g., Mayor's Valentine's Day Jam, Showcase of Talent)

MAYOR FORD

1. Center for Capacity Building
2. Merger of the Office of Affirmative Action and Contract Compliance with Division of Purchasing
3. CareNet
4. 2003 smoking ban passage
5. Hiring of blacks/promotion in key positions in city government

*Research Process*

COUNCIL/COMMISSION MINUTES CONTENT
ANALYSIS METHODOLOGY

Step 1: Examination of minutes and an agenda for one meeting[3]
Step 2: Identification of content that impacted African Americans

> Example for Dayton:
> Meeting of the Dayton City Commission, Wednesday, August 31, 2005:
> McLin support of Informal Resolution No. 650-05—Authorizing Support of the Proposed Triangle Project Sponsored by Improved Solutions for Urban Systems (ISUS). Voting in the affirmative were Mayor McLin, Commissioners Lovelace, Williams, Zimmer, and Joseph. A roll call vote was taken resulting in a 5-0 vote. The Informal Resolution was adopted.

Step 3: Coding of examples as policy action or program development

Step 4: Coding by year

Step 5: Consultation of interview data; coding into 1–5 typology

*African Americans Appointed by Mayor Ford*

IN MAYOR'S OFFICE

Jay Black Jr., chief of staff[4]

Cynthia Savage, secretary

Cynthia Wilkes, secretary

Cecelia Burton, secretary

Alan Bannister, mayoral assistant

Tracy Hopkins, mayoral assistant, administrative specialist, and member of Youth Commission

Art Jones, member of Constituent Affairs

DIRECTORS OF DEPARTMENTS

Joyce Chappele, director of human resources

Yulanda McCarty-Harris, director of Department of Affirmative Action, Contract Compliance and Purchasing

Michael Bell, chief of fire department

Juanita Greene, member, Board of Community Relations

Kattie Bond, member, Parks and Recreation

Jimmy Gaines, consultant on public service

BLACK COMMISSIONERS OF OR WITHIN DEPARTMENTS

Julian Highsmith, Fleet and Facilities

Robert Gilchrist, Economic Development

Jerry Jones, Utilities Administration and Environmental Services

John Walthal, commissioner of Environmental Services and water treatment plant

Todd Mitchell, commissioner of special projects in Department of Parks and Recreation

Willie Perryman, commissioner of development under Department of Neighborhoods

Jeannette Ball, Environmental Services

Michelle Hughes-Tucker, manager of the landfill in solid waste, Department of Public Services

Angela Lynn Stewart, manager of special projects/benefits in Department of Human Resources

Art Jones, manager of special projects in Department of Public Utilities

John Walthal, Water Treatment Plant

Rose Ellis, manager of benefits in Department of Human Resources

## OTHER PROFESSIONAL POSITIONS

George Robinson, Environmental Services

Patekka Bannister, Environmental Services

Adea Boston, attorney in Office of Affirmative Action and Contract Compliance (worked under consent decree project)

Marcy Cannon, attorney in Office of Affirmative Action and Contract Compliance (worked under consent decree project; later moved to Law Department as attorney)

Josyln Sumers-Jones, engineer

Veronica Cottingham, engineer

*Itemized Mayoral Activities*

FORD'S BLACK QUALITY OF LIFE ACTIVITIES IN 2002

*POLICY ACTIONS*

- Balanced $15 million budget shortfall (did not lay off any police or firefighters)
- Reviewed the role of Community Development Corporations as they impacted all citizens
- Formed an economic development staff that visited five hundred businesses (to determine how government could meet business needs)
- Raised funds for two predominantly black elementary schools' libraries

- Settled an eleven-year-old U.S. EPA lawsuit (the longest-running lawsuit of its kind in the country aimed at developing cleaner water

## PROGRAM DEVELOPMENT

- Introduced a "no broken windows" approach toward crime (focused on neighborhood blight, rehabilitation and/or demolition of abandoned buildings and broken streetlights)
- Pursued establishment of a police substation in a working-class neighborhood
- Appointed black female police sergeant to revitalize Toledo's Block Watch Program
- Initiated "Make the Grade," a program of adult tutors to children in need of help with core subjects
- Initiated Seed of Success, an entrepreneurial program to provide small loans to youth to start their own businesses
- Initiated "Mayor's Time," a program that focuses on organized productive activities at locations available to youth between the hours of 3:30 and 6:30 p.m.
- Initiated Fit for Kids program, an initiative focused on youth weight, healthy eating, exercise, and alcohol/drugs
- Initiated CareNet, a network of coordinated health care for adults without health insurance

## FORD'S BLACK QUALITY OF LIFE ACTIVITIES IN 2003
## POLICY ACTIONS

- Merger of Office of Affirmative Action and Contract Compliance and Division of Purchasing
- Collaborated with fire department to provide more homes with smoke detectors
- Collaborated with police department to reinstate a gun buyback program through the use of drug forfeiture funds
- Created city's first written ethics policy
- Balanced budget (without safety layoffs)

- Reduced sick-time abuse and city vehicle take-home and cell-phone use
- Reformed CDBG funding process
- Tore down vacant or abandoned units
- Appointed full-time safety director
- Supported resurfacing of roads program

*PROGRAM DEVELOPMENT*

- Initiated Mayor's Coalition on Prostate Cancer Awareness and Education
- Created Center for Capacity Building Built a skateboard complex
- Established a disability-accessible park
- Created an alley-clean strike team (for the purpose of monitoring illegal dumping, nuisance abatement, litter, and blight)
- Created a department of information services
- Hired a director to fix city hall's technology infrastructure
- Increased the number of Block Watch groups

FORD'S BLACK QUALITY OF LIFE ACTIVITIES IN 2004
*POLICY ACTIONS*

- Began renovation of crime lab
- Authorized installation of video cameras at high-risk carry-outs
- Supported Local Initiatives Support Corporation (a program to fund projects to change the image of neighborhoods)
- Reported the building of new housing units, rehabilitations, and demolition of blighted or abandoned units
- Issued eight thousand tickets for property nuisance violations
- Held four city-wide cleanups (debris in largely inner-city neighborhoods)
- Filled nearly fifty-nine thousand potholes and paving of twenty-two miles of streets, including brick crosswalks downtown
- Repaired two bridges with significance to blacks—one downtown named after Martin Luther King Jr. and another in inner-city black neighborhood

- Repaired an underpass and installation of bright lights in a predominantly low-income black neighborhood
- Upgraded tennis courts in predominantly black neighborhood
- Approved request for a new basketball court in a predominantly black neighborhood
- Requested that HUD advise the city on status as an Urban County designation

PROGRAM DEVELOPMENT

- Secured funding for Art Tatum Jazz Festival
- Increased the number of Block Watch groups
- Completed the process to reform the CDGB grant process (eliminated poor performing agencies and rewarded well-performing ones)
- Reported seventy-three youths started their own businesses in youth entrepreneur program

MCLIN'S BLACK QUALITY OF LIFE ACTIVITIES IN 2002
POLICY ACTIONS

- Initiated city's first-ever racial profiling policy
- Evaluated the effectiveness of the Human Rehabilitation Center for incarcerated criminals
- Supported the plan to end school busing
- Supported diversification in police and fire departments
- Initiated mayoral meetings with school board and administration
- Organized economic meetings with selected business leaders
- Initiated home rule provision suit against State of Ohio
- Supported school levy
- Supported development of former Frigidaire plant into Tech Town

PROGRAM DEVELOPMENT

- Initiated Mayor's Nights (a program to talk one-on-one with Dayton citizens)

- Initiated annual program to read to children (summers, in all city libraries)
- Initiated Mayor's Walks (in a dozen selected communities annually to identify problems within neighborhoods)
- Visited and encouraged economic development staff to make 370 contacts with local businesses
- Supported creation of Dayton Technology Task Force (to attract technologically based companies)
- Influenced the Department of Economic Development to devote business assistance resources for suppliers to expand markets

MCLIN'S BLACK QUALITY OF LIFE ACTIVITIES IN 2003
*POLICY ACTIONS*

- Initiated Project SUN
- Initiated TeamGov (a regional effort to develop collaboration across government jurisdictions)
- Made joint application with City of Kettering for $100,000 U.S. Conference of Mayors/DuPoint Corp. grant (to remove lead-based paint from neighborhood housing units)
- Supported Phoenix Project (comprehensive neighborhood redevelopment project in northwest Dayton)
- Provided support of rewrite of city's zoning code
- Provided support for Building Services' enforcement of illegal dumping
- Provided support for Greater Dayton Regional Transit Authority (RTA) (a new Park-N-Ride facility in Wright-Dunbar Village)
- Worked to balance the budget (without layoffs)
- Supported Commission Retreat to provide direction for monthly financial and budgetary issues
- Supported creation of Strategic Financial Plan Study Commission (a collaboration of public and private sectors to study impact of the economy on Dayton region)

- Supported Genesis Project (a community rebuilding partnership)
- Supported redevelopment of the Arcade and the Biltmore (downtown) into affordable housing
- Provided support for the Inventing Flight Festival
- Collaborated with City of Kettering on a dialogue on race and reconciliation
- Issued permits for 276 new homes
- Supported Citirama event in Wright-Dunbar Village
- Provided support for City's Forest and Ecumenical Homes housing project
- Provided support for HOPE VI project (a collaboration of HUD and DMHA)
- Provided support for $627 million School Facilities Master Planning Process in building new schools

MCLIN'S BLACK QUALITY OF LIFE ACTIVITIES IN 2004
*POLICY ACTIONS*

- Helped city government achieve a bond rating by Moody's Investors Service from A1 to A2
- Pursued more resources from the state's Local Government Fund
- Provided support to encourage residents to take advantage of federal Earned Income Tax Credit and Child Tax Credit
- Provided support for free financial education training program (sponsored by the Division of Citizen Participation and the Southwest Priority Board)
- Provided support for collaborative regional partnership to reduce chronic homelessness
- Supported passage of Civility Resolution to encourage citizens' basic and mutual respect

- Provided support for new downtown housing development
- Created teen council to address youth concerns
- Initiated road repavement program
- Provided support for Building Services' demolition of nuisance structures
- Supported community policing efforts, which led to a 17 percent decrease in major crime since 2001
- Provided support for police department's Park and Patrol program (designed to get officers out of their cars and onto neighborhood streets)
- Provided support for Department of Parks, Recreation and Culture's Safe Haven program (to provide designated safe locations for youth between the hours of 2 and 8 p.m. Monday through Friday)
- Provided support for housing development team's processing of 208 single-family home permits
- Provided support for mortgage credit counseling program

MCLIN'S BLACK QUALITY OF LIFE ACTIVITIES IN 2005

POLICY ACTIONS

- Proposed Mayor's Heritage Program (an initiative to encourage citizens to put forth twenty hours of community service)
- Collaborated with Miami Township to complete first joint economic development district agreement
- Provided endorsement for city's $100,000 contribution to Community Blood Center's expansion and renovation project
- Provided support for a tax-sharing agreement with Montgomery County (Kettering, Vandalia, and Moraine)
- Reported that overall crime decreased by 25 percent over last five years
- Provided support for community-based policing (resulting in a purported reduction in major crime)

- Provided support for the Shaming Sign program (designed to pressure owners of neglected property)
- Helped develop ORION Solution (a program that provides city and quality of life resources for neighborhoods)
- Provided support for predatory lending legislation

*PROGRAM DEVELOPMENT*

- As mayor and member of city commission, voted for purchase of new police vehicles
- As mayor and member of city commission, voted for purchase of new ladder truck for fire department
- As mayor and member of city commission, voted for purchase of new waste collection truck
- Advocated for development of brownfields (Nibco property, McCalls printing plant site, and old HG and R foundry)
- Provided support for new class of police officer recruits
- Provided support for development of regional crime-fighting effort (designed to equip police officers with central database access to track suspects)
- Provided support for housing and neighborhood task force initiative to demolish nuisance structures
- Provided support for development of market rate houses
- Provided support for Youth Anti-Violence Seminar
- Provided support for creation of Dayton Commission on Youth
- Initiated mayor's program to showcase talented young people's positive activities
- As mayor and member of city commission, supported DPS by allotting $552,000 (funds collected as a result of the economic development tax-sharing program)

MCLIN'S BLACK QUALITY OF LIFE ACTIVITIES IN 2006
*POLICY ACTIONS*

- As mayor and member of city commission, "hired" first black male city manager

- Provided support for passage of city's .5 percent renewable portion of 2.25 percent earnings tax
- Completed update of zoning code
- As mayor and member of city commission, authorized hiring of firefighters and police officers
- Provided support for Operation Safe Summer (a regional initiative to focus on troubled locations)
- Provided support for adoption of regulations to reduce persons' illegal stripping of metals and other materials from buildings and construction sites
- Provided support along with Commission on Youth for hiring of youth development coordinator
- As mayor and member of city commission, enacted disclosure ordinance for residential properties to help get existing code violations resolved before property changed hands
- Provided support for regional comprehensive two-year plan to reduce chronic homelessness

*PROGRAM DEVELOPMENT*

- Reinitiated Mayor's Reading Challenge
- Encouraged implementation of recommendations from Strategic Financial Plan Study Committee
- Provided support for Youth and Young Adult Trade and Skills Fair (designed to offer advice to youth on career planning and education)
- Provided support for city's collaboration with DPS Construction Technologies program (designed to provide students with technical skills to rehabilitate a property in Wright-Dunbar village)
- Supported development of Ball Park Village (a comprehensive downtown riverfront development project)

MCLIN'S BLACK QUALITY OF LIFE ACTIVITIES IN 2007
*POLICY ACTIONS*

- Reported all major crime categories, including homicide and vehicle theft, decreased 25 percent or more

- As mayor and member of city commission, appointed chief of police (who had experience in community policing)
- As mayor and member of city commission, doubled the financial resources directed toward demolition of nuisance, abandoned properties
- Reported increase in volunteers and projects registered for the Mayor's Heritage Community Service program
- Provided support of city manager's implementation of key recommendations from an independent study of Dayton's economic development programs

PROGRAM DEVELOPMENT

- As mayor and member of city commission, scheduled demolition of deteriorating housing complex
- Provided support for investment in Salvation Army Community Center
- Provided support and attended dedication of new bridge connecting West Dayton with downtown
- Created and implemented City Life Sculpture exhibit downtown
- Provided support for Urban Nights, a free event showcasing downtown's dining, nightlife, art, music, retail, and urban living options (twice a year on a Friday night—an all-inclusive street party)
- Provided support for city internship program to acquaint youth with city hall
- Provided support for creation and development of Homeless Solutions Taskforce

## NOTES

### Preface

1. R. Perry, "Introduction."
2. Moore, *Carl B. Stokes and the Rise of Black Political Power*, 5.
3. Thompson, *Double Trouble*, 132.
4. Quoted in H. Perry, *Race, Politics and Governance in the United States*, 6.
5. Quoted in Foeman, "An Interracial Comparative Analysis of the Impact of Central-City Mayors during the Urban Transition of the 1980s," 86.

### Introduction

1. Haynie, *African Americans Legislators*.
2. See DeLeon,"Research Methods."
3. King, Keohane, and Verba, *Designing Social Inquiry*, 44.
4. I define "black interests" as issues of relevance to the black communi-ty. I recognize the growing diversity among blacks, and it is therefore difficult to define "black interests." Yet at the same time I make some important assumptions because there are certain policies and pro-grams politicians may pursue that are in the interest of blacks. There-fore, I have taken into account objective measures of social and economic disparities between blacks and whites to define black inter-ests. Some issues that blacks deem relevant are also of interest to oth-er communities. However, for blacks these issues are of special relevance, given the intensity of black preferences. See Gamble, "Black Political Representation." Also see Cohen, *The Boundaries of Blackness*; Reed, *Class Notes*; and Young, *Inclusion and Democracy*.
5. See, for example, Gamble, "Black Political Representation," and Haynie, *African American Legislators*.
6. See, for example, Russ Bynum, "Nation's 478 Black Mayors Hail Prog-ress: More Minority Leaders in Mostly White Cities," Associated Press, March 10, 2001.

7. See, for example, Gillespie, *The New Black Politician.*
8. Orey, "Deracialization or Racialization."
9. Gillespie, *Whose Black Politics?*
10. Gillespie: "Meet the New Class," and *The New Black Politician.*
11. McCormick and Jones, "The Conceptualization of Deracialization," 76.
12. See R. Perry, *21st Century Urban Race Politics.* Also see Burnside and Rodriquez, "Like Father, Like Son?" and A. King, Shaw, and Spence, "Hype, Hip-Hop, and Heartbreak."
13. Franklin, "Situational Deracialization."
14. Hajnal, *Changing White Attitudes.*
15. McCormick and Jones, "The Conceptualization of Deracialization," 76.
16. McCormick and Jones, "The Conceptualization of Deracialization," 72.
17. J. Wilson, *Negro Politics.*
18. Cunnigen, "Black Leadership in the Twenty-First Century"; Nelson, "Black Mayoral Leadership in the Twenty-First Century"; and Franklin, "Situational Deracialization."
19. Hajnal, *Changing White Attitudes,* 160.
20. It is important to acknowledge that "active pursuit" does not equal influence or necessarily tell us about outcomes. Nevertheless, evidence of active pursuit provides insight into how active black mayors are in the governing process inside their administrations and on which issues. Furthermore, an examination of differences in mayors' actions in terms of levels of active pursuit, given unique governmental structures, provides new evidence about black mayors' policy and program priorities on issues relevant to their black residents and helps to provide a more thorough understanding of mayoral constraints and how black interests are represented in non-majority-black urban contexts.
21. Moore, *Carl B. Stokes and the Rise of Black Political Power,* 191.
22. Lane, "Black Political Power and Its Limits," 61.
23. Curvin, "Black Power in City Hall," 56.
24. Biles, "Mayor David Dinkins and the Politics of Race in New York City," 141.
25. Biles, "Mayor David Dinkins and the Politics of Race in New York City," 141.
26. Reed, "The Black Urban Regime."
27. Nelson, "Black Mayoral Leadership in the Twenty-First Century," 3.
28. Preston, "Big City Black Mayors," 131.
29. Quoted in Bayor, "African-American Mayors and Governance in Atlanta," 181.
30. Nelson and Meranto, *Electing Black Mayors,* 339.

31. See Frey: "A Pivotal Decade," "Melting Pot Cities and Suburbs," "America's Diverse Future," and "Diversity Spreads Out"; and Frasure, "Beyond the Myth of the White Middle Class."

32. See, for example, Sabrina Tavernise, "A Population Change, Uneasily," *New York Times*, July 17, 2011; Judy Keen, "Blacks' Exodus Reshapes Cities, *USA Today*, May 19, 2011; "Gentrification Changing Face of New Atlanta," *New York Times*, March 11, 2006; "New York City Losing Blacks, Census Shows," *New York Times*, April 3, 2006; "Blacks Say Life in Los Angeles Is Losing Allure, *New York Times*, January 8, 1995; "The Census Shows Growth in Atlanta's Population," *New York Times*, March 21, 2001; "Atlanta Mayor: Shrinking Black Population Could Hurt Social Policies," *Cox News Service*, June 2, 2007; "D.C. May Be Losing Status as a Majority-Black City," *Washington Post*, May 17, 2007; "San Francisco Hopes to Reverse Black Flight," *USA Today*, August 26, 2007; "Central District: Change Is Inevitable, but Forsaking Past Is Regrettable," *Seattle Times*, November 6, 2002; "Study: New Orleans Could Lose 80 Percent of Black Population," *Associated Press*, January 26, 2006; "Major Cities Rapidly Losing Black Population: Could Have Major Negative Impact on Black Political Power," *Taylor Media Services*, September 25, 2007.

33. Sabrina Tavernise, "A Population Change, Uneasily," *New York Times*, July 17, 2011.

34. Sabrina Tavernise, "A Population Change, Uneasily," *New York Times*, July 17, 2011, and Judy Keen, "Blacks' Exodus Reshapes Cities," *USA Today*, May 19, 2011.

35. R. Hall, *Participation in Congress*.

36. M. Williams, *Voice, Trust, and Democracy*, 192.

37. Dawson, *Behind the Mule*, 75.

38. See Dawson, *Behind the Mule*, and Tate, *From Protest to Politics*, 21-29.

39. Gamble, "Black Political Representation"; see also Clay, *Just Permanent Interests*, and Guinier, *Tyranny of the Majority*, 47.

40. Fenno, *Going Home*, 7.

41. Gamble, "Black Political Representation," 425.

42. See Nelson, "Black Mayoral Leadership in the Twenty-First Century."

43. Exceptions include Karnig and Welch, *Black Representation and Urban Policy*, and Bowers and Rich, *Governing Middle-Sized Cities*.

44. See Svara: *Facilitative Leadership in Local Government, Official Leadership in the City*, and "Mayoral Leadership in Council-Manager Cities."

45. See Button, *Blacks and Social Change*.

46. See Bowers and Rich, *Governing Middle-Sized Cities*.

47. United Nations, *World Urbanization Prospects*, 2005 revision, 5.

48. See Vey and Forman, "Demographic Change in Medium-Sized Cities."
49. "State of the World's Cities 2010/2011—Cities for All: Bridging the Urban Divide." Retrieved from http://www.unchs.org/pmss/listItem Details.aspx?publicationID=2917; accessed April 2, 2013.
50. Hajnal, *Changing White Attitudes*, xxi.
51. Hajnal, *Changing White Attitudes*, 3.
52. Hajnal, *Changing White Attitudes*, 3.
53. I do not examine the psychological reasons behind the mayors' active pursuit of policies designed in the interests of blacks; however, I do examine the presence (or not) of such a pursuit and theorize the role that shared racial experiences play in the actions pursued. See chapters 8 and 9.
54. Bostitis, *2008 National Opinion Poll*, 2. See also Saad, "Economy Reigns Supreme for Voters." The use of national polling data to identify shared white and black interests is applied given the paucity of medium-sized city polling data generally and particularly as it concerns black interest issues.
55. The consequence is that a "black threat" is not the primary reason why, after the election of the nation's first black mayors in cities with similar contexts in the 1960s and 1970s, the representation of black mayors in non-majority-black cities continues to be significant. Rather, reasons like changing demographics might be more salient. See chapter 2 for an expansion on the relevance of the demographic variable.
56. West, *Race Matters*, 11.
57. West, *Race Matters*, 11–13.
58. West, *Race Matters*, 6.
59. West, *Race Matters*, 6.
60. West, *Race Matters*, 8.
61. Cunnigen, "Black Leadership in the Twenty-First Century," 28.
62. W. Wilson, "Race-Neutral Policies and the Democratic Coalition."
63. See Gillespie, "Meet the New Class."

### 1. A Way Out of No Way

1. Friesema, "Black Control of Central Cities."
2. Keller, "The Impact of Black Mayors on Urban Policy."
3. Keller, "The Impact of Black Mayors on Urban Policy," 49–50.
4. Karnig and Welch, *Black Representation and Urban Policy*, 152.
5. Eisinger, "Black Employment in Municipal Jobs," 391.
6. Eisinger, "Black Mayors and the Politics of Racial Economic Advancement."
7. Browning, Marshall, and Tabb, *Protest Is Not Enough*, 168.

8. Saltzstein, "Black Mayors and Police Policies," 539.

9. Brown, "Race and Politics Matter," 26.

10. Brown, "Race and Politics Matter," 38.

11. Bobo and Gilliam, "Race, Sociopolitical Participation, and Black Empowerment," 387.

12. Marschall and Ruhil, "Substantive Symbols."

13. For example, see Bobo and Gilliam, "Race, Sociopolitical Participation, and Black Empowerment"; Fagan and Howell, "Race and Trust in Government"; and Abney and Hutcheson, "Race, Representation and Trust."

14. Keller, "The Impact of Black Mayors on Urban Policy."

15. Reed, "The Black Urban Regime," 97.

16. Stokes, *Promises of Power*.

17. Woody, *Managing Crisis Cities*, 101–2.

18. Preston, "Limitations on Black Urban Power."

19. Preston, "Limitations on Black Urban Power," 125.

20. Nelson, "Black Mayors as Urban Managers," 53–67.

21. Nelson, "Black Mayors as Urban Managers," 61.

22. Judd and Swanstrom, *City Politics*, 385.

23. Thompson, *Double Trouble*, 193–94.

24. Reed, "The Black Urban Regime," 89.

25. Kraus and Swanstrom, "Minority Mayors and the Hollow Prize Problem," 103.

26. See Reed, "The Black Urban Regime"; Keller, "The Impact of Black Mayors on Urban Policy"; Nelson: "Black Mayoral Leadership: A Twenty Year Perspective" and "Black Mayoral Leadership in the Twenty-First Century"; Nelson and Meranto, *Electing Black Mayors*; and Preston, "Limitations on Black Urban Power."

27. Pressman introduced a model, which he called the "preconditions of mayoral leadership," that focused on the financial, political, and personal resources available to a mayor. He found, however, that there were significant informal attributes or resources at a mayor's disposal, which, when used effectively, could make up for the limited formal authority of some mayors. The model lists seven preconditions: (1) sufficient city government financial and staff resources; (2) city jurisdiction to enact social welfare programming; (3) mayoral jurisdiction within such programming; (4) a full-time salary; (5) sufficient staff support; (6) favorable avenues of publicity; and (7) supportive political groups. See Pressman, "Preconditions of Mayoral Leadership."

28. Judd and Swanstrom, *City Politics*, 384.

29. Mier and Moe, "Decentralized Development," 77.

30. M. Jones, "Black Political Empowerment in Atlanta," 116.
31. M. Jones, "Black Political Empowerment in Atlanta," 116.
32. M. Jones, "Black Political Empowerment in Atlanta," 99.
33. Nelson, "Cleveland."
34. Nelson, "Cleveland," 191.
35. Karnig and Welch, *Black Representation and Urban Policy*, 152.
36. See, for example, Orr: *Black Social Capital* and *Transforming the City*.
37. The predominance of attention is devoted to electoral politics, leadership styles, and a public official's responsiveness to a particular issue, often lacking a thorough analysis of mayoral governance. See Burns, *Electoral Politics Is Not Enough*.
38. Browning, Marshall, and Tabb, *Protest Is Not Enough*, 168.
39. Button, *Blacks and Social Change*.
40. Swain, *Black Faces, Black Interests*, and Pitkin, *The Concept of Representation*.
41. Swain, *Black Faces, Black Interests*, 19.
42. Tate, *Black Faces in the Mirror*, 122.
43. Swain, *Black Faces, Black Interests*, 189.
44. Swain, *Black Faces, Black Interests*, 217.
45. This observation reflects Pitkin's definition of descriptive representation as "standing for" and not "acting for" representation. Since descriptive representation is primarily inferred as benefiting minority groups, it seems implied that the "acting for" representation is like unto the theme of white male representation common during the era in which Pitkin was originally writing. Yet the "standing for" descriptive representation, which she deems not representation at all, is counterproductive. Swain's discussion in *Black Faces, Black Interests* is limited to people of color.
46. Tate, *Black Faces in the Mirror*, 6.
47. Runciman, "The Paradox of Political Representation."
48. Tate, *Black Faces in the Mirror*, 85.
49. However, Swain (*Black Faces, Black Interests*) was studying a different Congress and notes her findings should be limited to that of the one hundredth session. For Tate (*Black Faces in the Mirror*) race matters in that it fosters better deliberation and leads to the promotion of more black-interest policies. Both Swain and Tate identified partisanship as a key variable in studies of representation and implementation of black interests. For example, the partisanship identification of the city, the state, the mayor, or council members is likely to have an effect on a black mayor's promotion of black interests.
50. See Elazar, *American Federalism*.

51. Key, *Southern Politics.*

52. See Engstrom and McDonald, "The Effect of At-Large versus District Elections"; Karnig, "Black Representation on City Councils"; Karnig and Welch, *Black Representation and Urban Policy*; and Latimer, "Black Political Representation in Southern Cities."

53. Ferman, *Governing the Ungovernable City.*

54. See Peterson, *City Limits*, and B. Jones and Bachelor, *The Sustaining Hand.*

55. Such studies of unconventional channels of black political influence are not without their critics. In some cases governments have chosen to appease these groups through financial resource allocation. See Orr, *Transforming the City.* Also, some scholars suggest those who comprise neighborhood groups tend to be of a higher socioeconomic status or that these groups exist to maintain forms of residential segregation. Putnam, *Bowling Alone*, 57.

56. Powell, "Race, Place, and Opportunity."

57. See, for example, Grogan and Patashnik, "Universalism within Targeting"; Anttonen, "Universalism and Social Policy"; Manza, "Race and the Underdevelopment of the American Welfare State"; Mkandawire, "Targeting and Universalism in Poverty Reduction"; Barnett, Brown, and Shore, "The Universal vs. Targeted Debate"; Baker and Feldman, "Revealed Preferences for Car Tax Cuts"; Dynarski, "The Consequences of Merit Aid"; Roberts, "Welfare and the Problem of Black Citizenship"; Skocpol: "Targeting within Universalism," *Social Policy in the United States*, and "Sustainable Social Policy"; W. Wilson: "Public Policy Research and the Truly Disadvantaged," *The Truly Disadvantaged*, and *When Work Disappears*; Greenstein, "Universal and Targeted Approaches to Relieving Poverty"; Roger Wilkins, "The Black Poor Are Different," *New York Times*, August 22, 1989, A23; Massey and Denton: "The Dimensions of Residential Segregation," "Hypersegregation in U.S. Metropolitan Areas," and *American Apartheid*; Massey and Eggers, "The Ecology of Inequality"; Boger, "The Eclipse of Anti-Racist Public Policy"; Hasenfeld, *We the Poor People*; Midgley, Tracy, and Livermore, *The Handbook of Social Policy*; and Rosanvallon and Harshav, *The New Social Question.*

58. See Midgley, Tracy, and Livermore, *The Handbook of Social Policy*, and Greenstein, "Universal and Targeted Approaches to Relieving Poverty."

59. W. Wilson, *The Truly Disadvantaged*, 119.

60. W. Wilson, *The Truly Disadvantaged*, 119.

61. W. Wilson, *The Truly Disadvantaged*, 120.

62. W. Wilson, *The Truly Disadvantaged*, 146.

63. In the urban context Stone's regime theory in *Regime Politics* is comparable. Regime theory assumes a political economy perspective and maintains that class is the leading variable to consider in urban politics. It follows, then, that proponents of regime theory often favor a class-based approach to address urban social problems, including those that disproportionately plague black urban constituencies. Other scholars, such as Nelson, *Black Atlantic Politics*, find that the approach does not adequately address the racial variable prevalent in the urban context and are perhaps most comparable with scholars like Greenstein, who finds that universal policies to address national social problems through public policy are limited. Also see Kraus, "The Significance of Race in Urban Politics."
64. See Skocpol: "Targeting within Universalism," and *Social Policy in the United States*.
65. Skocpol, *Social Policy in the United States*, 267.
66. For example, see Roger Wilkins, "The Black Poor Are Different," *New York Times*, August 22, 1989, A23; Massey and Denton, *American Apartheid*, 8; and Massey and Eggers, "The Ecology of Inequality."
67. Greenstein, "Universal and Targeted Approaches to Relieving Poverty," 443. Greenstein also argues that Skocpol overstates the success of universal programs by "using programs for the elderly as her primary example." He describes how Skocpol compares programs that provide entitlements for the elderly with programs that are not focused on the elderly and "are not considered earned benefits." Hence, Greenstein argues, "It would be better to compare a universal program for the elderly such as social security with a means-tested program for the elderly such as supplemental security income.
68. Sawhill, "Comments on 'Targeting within Universalism,'" 3.
69. Massey and Eggers, "The Ecology of Inequality."
70. Historically scholars have disagreed with the universalist approach. For more information concerning why protecting minority rights (the particular) within the context of the majority (the universal) is significant, see Madison's *Federalist* no. 10 or Kymlicka, *Multicultural Citizenship*.
71. Young, *Justice and the Politics of Difference*, 110.
72. Young, *Justice and the Politics of Difference*, 105.
73. Young, *Justice and the Politics of Difference*, 227.
74. Moreover, Gunnar Myrdal found that poor blacks and poor whites were not similarly situated as blacks suffered from cumulative causation or mutual restraint. See Myrdal, *An American Dilemma*, 75–76, and Powell, "Post-Racialism or Targeted Universalism?" Roger

Wilkins also noted how the experiences of the black poor were unique to them in "The Black Poor Are Different," *New York Times*, August 22, 1989, A23.

75. Young, *Justice and the Politics of Difference*, 236.

76. Young, *Justice and the Politics of Difference*, 255.

77. The inverse of "targeting within universalism" is "universalism within targeting," "a pattern that can arise whenever a targeted program's threshold of means-tested income is set high enough that a significant number of people from mainstream backgrounds qualify." See Grogan and Patashnik, "Universalism within Targeting," and Gilbert, *Targeting Social Benefits*. An example of such a program, cited by Grogan and Patashnik, is the reliance of senior citizens in nursing homes on Medicaid. Also see Skocpol, "Targeting within Universalism," 414, and Midgley, Tracy, and Livermore, *The Handbook of Social Policy*.

78. Skocpol, "Targeting within Universalism," 429.

79. Powell, "Race, Place, and Opportunity."

80. Cose, "Revisiting 'The Rage of a Privileged Class.'"

81. See Jaynes and McKinney, "Do Blacks Lose When Diversity Replaces Affirmative Action?"

82. Powell, "Race, Place, and Opportunity."

83. Powell and Menendian, "Race vis-a-vis Class in the U.S.?" Harold Washington's neighborhood improvement program in Chicago and William A. Johnson Jr.'s similar program in Rochester, New York, appear to be examples of universal programs that benefitted all city neighborhoods but provided resources to black neighborhoods as well. For more information of Washington's neighborhood efforts, see Clavel and Wiewel, *Harold Washington and the Neighborhoods*. For more information on Johnson's neighborhood efforts, see Clavel, "Rochester." In both texts the authors cite how the universal neighborhood programming, like Johnson's creation of Neighbors Building Neighborhoods, improved the quality of life in the city's minority neighborhoods. Dayton mayor McLin's ORION solution, then, may also be an example (see chapter 6).

84. McCormick and Jones, "The Conceptualization of Deracialization," 78.

85. See Gilen, *Why Americans Hate Welfare*.

86. See Lieberman, *Shifting the Color Line*.

87. See Roediger, *How Race Survived U.S. History*.

88. Powell, "Post-Racialism or Targeted Universalism?"

89. Hamilton and Hamilton, *The Dual Agenda*.

90. Powell, *Racing to Justice*.

## 2. The Model of Ohio

1. See G. Porter, *Ohio Politics during the Civil War Period*, and Flinn, "Continuity and Change in Ohio Politics."
2. See Gold, *Democracy in Session*; Cayton, *Ohio*; Welsh-Huggins, *No Winners Here Tonight*; and Faber, *The Toledo War*.
3. As noted, much of the scholarship on the governing of black mayors focuses on the mayors' responses to single issues. For example, see Nelson, "Cleveland"; Woody, *Managing Crisis Cities*; Piliawsky, "The Impact of Black Mayors on the Black Community"; Stone, *Regime Politics*; Orr, *Black Social Capital*; Reed, "The Black Urban Regime"; Rich, *Coleman Young and Detroit Politics*; Moore, *Carl B. Stokes and the Rise of Black Political Power*; Bowers and Baker, "William A. Johnson Jr. and Education Politics in Rochester, New York"; H. Perry, *Race, Politics and Governance in the United States*; Grenell and Gabris, "Charles Box and Regime Politics"; and Thompson, *Double Trouble*.
4. For more rich detail regarding Coleman, see Stefanie Chambers et al.'s chapter in R. Perry, *21st Century Urban Race Politics*.
5. For more information on the Public Accommodations Law, see Van Alstyne, "Civil Rights."
6. Rich, "Foreword," and Kraus and Swanstrom, "The Continuing Significance of Race."
7. Rogers, "Black Like Who?"
8. See Sabrina Tavernise, "A Population Change, Uneasily," *New York Times*, July 17, 2011.
9. "Atlanta Mayor: Shrinking Black Population Could Hurt Social Policies," *Cox News Service*, June 2, 2007.
10. Frey, "America's Young Adults."
11. See Frasure, "Beyond the Myth of the White Middle Class."
12. Adam Nossiter, "New Orleans Population Is Reduced Nearly 60%," *New York Times*, October 7, 2006, 9.
13. Campbell Robertson, "Smaller New Orleans after Katrina, Census Shows," *New York Times*, February 4, 2011, 11.
14. Bowers and Rich, *Governing Middle-Sized Cities*, 2–3.
15. Nelson, "Black Mayoral Leadership in the Twenty-First Century," 125–26.
16. Nelson, "Black Mayoral Leadership in the Twenty-First Century," 138.
17. Nelson, "Black Mayoral Leadership in the Twenty-First Century," 122.
18. See chapter 8.
19. Nelson, "Black Mayoral Leadership in the Twenty-First Century," 123.
20. See Thompson, *Double Trouble*, 219.

21. Thompson, *Double Trouble*, 258.
22. Cunnigen, "Black Leadership in the Twenty-First Century."
23. Cunnigen, "Black Leadership in the Twenty-First Century," 28.
24. Bowers and Rich, *Governing Middle-Sized Cities*, introduction.
25. Bowers and Baker, "William A. Johnson Jr. and Education Politics in Rochester, New York."
26. H. Perry, "Richard Arrington Jr. and Police-Community Relations in Birmingham, Alabama."
27. Grenell and Gabris, "Charles Box and Regime Politics."
28. Bowers and Rich, *Governing Middle-Sized Cities*, 3.
29. "Toledo City Planning Commission."
30. Ford's political biography is explored in more detail in later chapters but is introduced here to emphasize how Toledo's white and black communities came to elect a black mayor. Toledoans had long been introduced to successful and prominent Toledo black community leadership.
31. See McLin with Howard and Rickman, *Dad, I Served*, 74.
32. Amid the Dayton Urban League's closure, then CEO Kimberly Carter filed a lawsuit against the organization, claiming the non-profit had committed fraud and failed to pay her $25,000 in severance as a result of the office's closing. The city of Dayton also cited evidence of fraud by the Dayton Urban League in its handling of a housing assistance program, funded through a $454,000 grant by the Department of Housing and Urban Development in Washington DC. In addition to the Dayton Urban League's fiscal mismanagement problems, Dayton's black community has suffered other recent setbacks as well. In 2008 a lawsuit filed by the U.S. Department of Justice found the city of Dayton's hiring practices discriminatory, investigating area such as job experience requirements and discrimination against minorities. For more information, see Department of Justice, "Justice Department Settles Lawsuit Against the City of Dayton, Ohio."

    The Miami Valley Housing Opportunities (MVHO) purchased the former Dayton Urban League building in downtown Dayton, where, according to reports, MVHO planned to relocate its headquarters and lease space to community services providers. MVHO planned to rename the building "The Opportunity Center." For more information, see Englehart, "MVHO Buys Former Urban League Building." For more information on the closure of the Dayton Urban League, see Amelia Robinson and Lucas Sullivan, "National Urban League Accuses Local Affiliate of Fiscal Mismanagement, Lack of Leadership," *Dayton Daily News*, February 13, 2011.

### 3. An Ebb and Flow System

1. *All Things Considered*, National Public Radio, March 18, 2007. The epigraph is from the author's interview with Michael Navarre, July 8, 2008.
2. T. Porter, *Toledo Profile*, 27.
3. Faber, *The Toledo War*.
4. "Toledo War."
5. T. Porter, *Toledo Profile*, 28.
6. *Detroit News*, May 21, 2000.
7. T. Porter, *Toledo Profile*, 23.
8. Elazar, *American Federalism*. Hero (*Faces of Inequality*, 9) tackles Elazar's political culture typology, arguing that it is limiting because it is based on Elazar's research of people mostly of European background. Hero prefers instead a social diversity perspective, which contends that much of state politics and policy can be understood in terms of racial and ethnic diversity.
9. For additional information on early black Toledo, see Hinehart, "The Negro in a Congested Toledo Area"; Johnson, "A Study of Negro Families," 243–45; Toledo Chapter of the NAACP, "Containment of Minority Groups through Housing"; B. F. Williams, "Interracial Activities in Toledo"; and Wheaton, "The Social Status of the Negro in Toledo, Ohio."
10. L. Williams, "Newcomers to the City," 5.
11. L. Williams, "Newcomers to the City," 10.
12. See Levstik, "The Toledo Riot of 1962."
13. See Ohio History Central Encyclopedia Archive, 89:10. Quotation located at http://www.ohiohistory.org/search/index.html; accessed March 9, 2009. Not all Toledoans were anti-black, however. In a speech commemorating the ninety-ninth anniversary of the NAACP, U.S. senator Sherrod Brown noted that white Toledo mayor Brand Whitlock had helped to organize the 1909 conference that produced the NAACP.
14. L. Williams, "Newcomers to the City," 22.
15. See "History."
16. See Kaptur, Rep. Floor Statement.
17. "Trailblazers Topple Local Racial Barriers: Black Leaders Reflect on Their Journeys," *Toledo Blade*, February 1, 2009.
18. John Herbers, "Black Poverty Spreads in 50 Biggest U.S. Cities," *New York Times*, January 26, 1987, 27.
19. "Toledo Police Officer Killed in 1970 Shooting," *Toledo Blade*, February 21, 2007.
20. Churchill, "To Disrupt, Discredit, and Destroy," 66.

21. George Davis Jr., interview with author, July 1, 2008.
22. "Democrats Back Ford for Furney Seat on Council," *Toledo Blade*, December 19, 1986.
23. "Ford Withdraws Name for Vacant Council Seat," *Toledo Blade*, January 12, 1987.
24. Quoted in "Step Up Drug Fight, Council Hopeful Urges," *Toledo Blade*, October 1, 1987.
25. "5 Toledo Ministers Go on Trial over Bias Protest," *New York Times*, December 20, 1988.
26. *City Paper*, November 19, 2008.
27. "5 Toledo Ministers Go on Trial over Bias Protest," *New York Times*, December 20, 1988.
28. "Mr. Ford Has a Point," *Toledo Blade*, August 8, 1988.
29. Norris P. West, "Affirmative-Action Plan Drafted, Held," *Toledo Blade*, July 19, 1989.
30. U.S. Commission on Civil Rights, "Race Relations in Toledo."
31. Norris P. West, "Affirmative-Action Plan Drafted, Held," *Toledo Blade*, July 19, 1989.
32. U.S. Commission on Civil Rights, "Race Relations in Toledo."
33. "King Bridge: A Symbolic Span," *Toledo Blade*, January 15, 1988.
34. Quoted in "King Bridge: A Symbolic Span," *Toledo Blade*, January 15, 1988.
35. Quoted in Mark Zaborney, "Strong-Mayor Plan Draws Skepticism," *Toledo Blade*, October 27, 1988.
36. The Lucas County Board of Elections could not provide data on how black districts voted on the strong-mayor ballot initiatives. See Jeff Harrington, "Strong-Mayor Issue Is 'Dead Duck' If Voters Don't Pass It, Ford Says," *Toledo Blade*, October 5, 1988.
37. Quoted in Jim Saunders, "Leadership Called Key in Black Community," *Toledo Blade*, October 14, 1988.
38. "Ford Wants to End Bias against AIDS Victims," *Toledo Blade*, October 17, 1988.
39. "Hawkey Blamed for Failure to Hire Minorities," *Toledo Blade*, March 18, 1988.
40. "Toledo Almost Had Black Candidate," *Toledo Blade*, March 5, 1989.
41. "Inexpensive Housing Is Goal of Ford Effort," *Toledo Blade*, April 15, 1989.
42. Quoted in Norris P. West, "Mayor Chastises Ford, Says He Should Back Tax," *Toledo Blade*, May 31, 1989.
43. Mark Rollenhagen, "Activist Ford Not Camera-Shy," *Toledo Blade*, August 19, 1989.

44. "'Questions for Candidates' Survey," *Toledo Blade* library; accessed July 2008.

45. *Toledo Blade*, March 15, 1990.

46. James Drew, "Ford, as TV Host, Takes Viewers behind Scenes," *Toledo Blade*, April 20, 1992.

47. James Drew, "$350,000 Campaign Is Proposed to Rid Homes of Lead-Paint Hazard," *Toledo Blade*, January 13, 1993.

48. James Drew: "8 Democrats on Council Support Ford for Top Post," *Toledo Blade*, December 1, 1993, and "Ford Elected Council Chief; Mayor's Revamp under Study," *Toledo Blade*, January 4, 1994.

49. James Drew, "Mayor Eyes Draft-Ford Campaign," *Toledo Blade*, February 4, 1994; William Brower, "Carty's Motives Pretty Clear Cut," *Toledo Blade, February 8, 1994.*

50. Tom Troy, "Ford Captures Seat in Ohio House," *Toledo Blade, November 9, 1994.*

51. Quoted in Bob Stiegel, "Toledo to Get King Street Next Year," *Toledo Journal, March 29, 2000.*

52. Bob Stiegel, "Cherry St. May Become King-Kennedy Pkwy.: Committee Given Street Name Change Recommendations to Consider," *Toledo Journal*, January 3, 2001.

53. Bob Stiegel, "Cherry St. May Become King-Kennedy Pkwy.: Committee Given Street Name Change Recommendations to Consider," *Toledo Journal*, January 3, 2001.

54. Quoted in Bob Stiegel, "Make It King—and King Alone: Rev. Floyd Rose Says Designated Street Should Bear Only Civil Rights Leader's Name," *Toledo Journal*, January 24, 2001.

55. Bob Stiegel, "Put King's Name on Train Station, Mayor Says," *Toledo Journal*, July 4, 2001.

56. Bob Stiegel, "Objections Raised to King Boulevard Proposal: Old West End Area Residents Vow to Stop Renaming Committee's Efforts," *Toledo Journal*, March 14, 2001.

57. Bob Stiegel, "Objections Raised to King Boulevard Proposal: Old West End Area Residents Vow to Stop Renaming Committee's Efforts," *Toledo Journal*, March 14, 2001.

58. Bob Stiegel, "Objections Raised to King Boulevard Proposal: Old West End Area Residents Vow to Stop Renaming Committee's Efforts," *Toledo Journal*, March 14, 2001.

59. Bob Stiegel, "Airport Top Candidate for Renaming for Dr. King," *Toledo Journal*, May 2, 2001.

60. Bob Stiegel, "Black Leaders Show Conciliation in King Tribute Saga: 'Lukewarmish' Acceptance of Train Station Given," *Toledo Journal*, August 1, 2001.

61. Dresser, *Multicultural Manners*, 169.

62. Dresser, *Multicultural Manners*, 169.

63. Ford campaign announcement address, undated text of speech, *Toledo Blade* library; accessed July 2008.

64. "Ford Backs Affirmative Action Office," *Toledo Blade*, June 28, 2001.

65. Interview respondents suggested that the *Toledo Journal* supported Ray Kest because as county treasurer, he had regularly paid for large advertisements with the paper.

66. That Toledo has two black newspapers when blacks comprise approximately 25 percent of the city's population may be a sign of the factions within the black community.

67. "A Ford in Our Future," *Toledo Blade*, November 8, 2001.

68. The large percentage of black support may also serve as an indicator for why Ford may actively have pursued the interests of African Americans, even in a non-black context.

69. Speech given February 21, 2002; accessed on the Internet while Ford was mayor in November 2005.

70. The correlation between percent black and percent vote is statistically significant at $p < .001$. In a linear regression, this relationship holds when controlling for poverty, unemployment, and percentage of college-educated individuals in each ward.

71. Bob Stiegel, "Sylvania Council Told to Drop Fight for Lathrop House: Others Speak Up for Preservation of Underground Railroad Station," *Toledo Journal*, May 14, 2003.

72. "Ford Heralds Commitment to City Business Community," *Toledo Blade*, November 27, 2001.

73. Roberta De Boer, "For Some, Ford Has a Better Idea," *Toledo Blade*, January 12, 2002.

74. *Toledo Blade*, January 3, 2002.

75. Quoted in Tom Troy, "Mayor Castigates Toledo Schools for Poor Showing," *Toledo Blade*, January 8, 2002.

76. Chapter 7 examines Ford's entire term of administrative actions as they relate to his active pursuit of black interests.

77. Author's interviews with Paula Ross, June 23, 2008, and Jack Ford, June 24, 2008.

78. Many saw the A-Team/B-Team rift as due in part to race and to some conservative Democrats' discontent with having a black mayor.

79. These conclusions are drawn from multiple interviews conducted in the summer of 2008. Chapter 7 explores in detail the content of those opinions.
80. "Neighbors Defend Protest over Neo-Nazi March," *Associated Press*, October 16, 2005.
81. "Neighbors Defend Protest over Neo-Nazi March," *Associated Press*, October 16, 2005.
82. Tom Troy, "State Panel Faults Toledo in Discipline of 3 Black Employees," Toledo Blade, February 1, 2008.
83. J. C. Reindl, "Toledo's Blacks Told to Vote Down .75% Tax Renewal," *Toledo Blade*, January 30, 2008.
84. Workforce analysis data were not available for 1993–2001, the two terms of Ford's predecessor. However, appendix 2 includes a roster of middle-level and upper-level management positions that were filled by blacks after Mayor Ford took office. According to my interviews with administration members, blacks had not occupied these positions previously.
85. Browning, Marshall, and Tabb, *Protest Is Not Enough*, and Orr, "The Struggle for Black Empowerment in Baltimore." The data in table 7 are for full-time employees only. The lack of corresponding labels between the 2002–2005 and 2007–2009 data is yet another example of data problems in medium-sized cities. From 2002 to 2005, while Ford was mayor, the city kept more detailed records, as evidenced by service and protective worker subcategories. Comparable data for Dayton were not made available upon request. Given that McLin did not have the power to make such appointments, the absence of the data is not significant.

    The "Finkbeiner years" data reflect the administration of Ford's predecessor, who also succeeded him as mayor. The data are as of June 30, 2008.
86. See Saltzstein, "Black Mayors and Police Policies."
87. While I cannot compare with previous administrations given the problems of gathering data in medium-sized cities, see appendix 2 for a roster of black city of Toledo employees promoted or hired during Mayor Ford's tenure.
88. Nye, Rainer, and Stratmann, "Do Black Mayors Improve Black Employment Outcomes?," 2.
89. Lucas County residents are eligible for CareNet if they have no other health insurance and their total household income is at or below 200 percent of the federal poverty level, or $46,100 for a family of four. For more information on the Ford-initiated innovative public-private

partnership to ensure that low-income Lucas County residents received health insurance, visit http://www.toledocarenet.org/about
_carenet/.

90. The quotations here and in the paragraphs below are from my interviews with Ashford on July 1, 2008.

91. Author's interview with Wilma D. Brown, June 17, 2008.

92. Author's telephone interview with Yulanda McCarty-Harris, July 7,
2008.

93. Author's interview with Jay Black, June 10, 2008.

94. Author's interview with Fletcher Word, June 18, 2008.

95. *Omaha World Herald*, November 4, 2007.

96. "Toledo Leads State Again in Unemployment," *Toledo Blade*, January
27, 2009.

97. See table 4.

*4. Are We "to Be" or Not?*

1. Rhine McLin's grandfather, a two-time unsuccessful candidate for
Dayton city commission, had been an active member of Dayton's
black political establishment in the 1930s and 1940s; he formed the
Democratic Voters League in West Dayton, once the political epicen-
ter of Dayton's black residents.

2. See Loyacano, *A History of Race Relations in the Miami Valley*, 31.

3. Elazar, *American Federalism*.

4. Myers, *Ninety-Five Years after Lincoln*, 22.

5. Myers, *Ninety-Five Years after Lincoln*, 25. Myers's observation is confirmed by statistical evidence. Dayton has been and remains one of
the largest cities with a large Appalachian white population. See
Pulera, *Sharing the Dream*.

6. Levine, *Resolving Racial Conflict*, 174.

7. Myers, *Ninety-Five Years after Lincoln*, 38.

8. Drury, *History of the City of Dayton and Montgomery County, OH*, 166.

9. Drury, *History of the City of Dayton and Montgomery County, OH*, 254.

10. Drury, *History of the City of Dayton and Montgomery County, OH*, 166.

11. Peters, *Dayton's African American Heritage*.

12. Peters, *Dayton's African American Heritage*, 15.

13. Peters, *Dayton's African American Heritage*, 25.

14. Myers, *Ninety-Five Years after Lincoln*, 25–26.

15. Loyacano, *A History of Race Relations in the Miami Valley*, 26.

16. Peters, *Dayton's African American Heritage*, 85.

17. Peters, *Dayton's African American Heritage*, 91.

18. Myers, *Ninety-Five Years after Lincoln*, 26–27.

19. Peters, *Dayton's African American Heritage*, 94.
20. Peters, *Dayton's African American Heritage*, 145.
21. Loyacano, *A History of Race Relations in the Miami Valley*, 26.
22. Marable, *Beyond Black and White*, 1.
23. Marable, *Beyond Black and White*, 2.
24. Marable, *Beyond Black and White*, 2.
25. Marable, *Beyond Black and White*, 3. The racial divide in Dayton in the 1950s was further enforced when U.S. Expressway 25, later Interstate 75, was built along the east bank of the Great Miami River near the center of the city, serving as a structural indicator of the east/west racial divide. See Loyacano *A History of Race Relations in the Miami Valley*, 26.
26. Peters, Dayton's African American Heritage, 165.
27. Loyacano, *A History of Race Relations in the Miami Valley*, 27.
28. Quoted in *Dayton Daily News*, September 1, 1990.
29. Quoted in *Dayton Daily News*, July 22, 2007.
30. Loyacano, *A History of Race Relations in the Miami Valley*, 31.
31. Levine, *Resolving Racial Conflict*, 174.
32. Levine, *Resolving Racial Conflict*, 174.
33. See U.S. Supreme Court, Dayton Board of Education v. Brinkman, *443 U.S. 526, 530*.
34. Watras, *Politics, Race and Schools*, 166.
35. Levine, *Resolving Racial Conflict*, 174.
36. Watras, *Politics, Race and Schools*, 187.
37. See U.S. Supreme Court, Dayton Board of Education v. Brinkman, 433 U.S. 406.
38. See U.S. Supreme Court, Dayton Board of Education v. Brinkman, 433 U.S. 406.
39. Scott Elliott, "Desegregation Busing Ends," *Dayton Daily News*, April 16, 2002.
40. City of Dayton, *City of Dayton, Ohio Community Involvement Strategy*.
41. Peters, *Dayton's African American Heritage*, 173.
42. "Black Police Chief in Dayton Quits with $100,000 Payment," *New York Times*, December 7, 1987.
43. *Dayton Daily News*, December 7, 1987.
44. Peters, *Dayton's African American Heritage*, 166.
45. Loyacano, *A History of Race Relations in the Miami Valley*, 33.
46. Loyacano, *A History of Race Relations in the Miami Valley*, 35.
47. *Dayton Daily News*, March 1, 1990.
48. "McLin, Roberts Move on for Better, Worse," *Dayton Daily News*, September 11, 1999.

49. Quoted in Jim Bebbington, "McLin to Run for Mayor," *Dayton Daily News*, December 30, 1999.
50. Quoted in Jim Bebbington, "McLin, Zimmer, Williams Win Nods," *Dayton Daily News*, January 26, 2001.
51. Jim Bebbington, "McLin, Turner Make It Official," *Dayton Daily News*, March 9, 2001.
52. Jim Bebbington, "McLin, Turner Make It Official," *Dayton Daily News*, March 9, 2001.
53. Jim Bebbington, "McLin, Turner Courting Voters," *Dayton Daily News*, August 12, 2001.
54. Quoted in Jim Bebbington, "McLin Criticizes Mayor on Loss of Jobs," *Dayton Daily News*, September 6, 2001.
55. Jim DeBrosse, "Rhine McLin Faces Tough Race to Continue Family Tradition," *Dayton Daily News*, September 23, 2001.
56. Jim DeBrosse, "Rhine McLin Faces Tough Race to Continue Family Tradition," *Dayton Daily News*, September 23, 2001.
57. Quoted in Jim DeBrosse, "Rhine McLin Faces Tough Race to Continue Family Tradition," *Dayton Daily News*, September 23, 2001.
58. Quoted in Jim DeBrosse, "Rhine McLin Faces Tough Race to Continue Family Tradition," *Dayton Daily News*, September 23, 2001.
59. Quoted in Jim DeBrosse, "Rhine McLin Faces Tough Race to Continue Family Tradition," *Dayton Daily News*, September 23, 2001.
60. Quoted in Jim DeBrosse, "Rhine McLin Faces Tough Race to Continue Family Tradition," *Dayton Daily News*, September 23, 2001.
61. Jim Bebbington, "McLin Tops Turner in Mayor's Race," *Dayton Daily News*, November 7, 2001.
62. "Mayor Turner Still the Right Choice," *Dayton Daily News*, October 28, 2001.
63. "McLin Found Turner's Weakness," *Dayton Daily News*, November 7, 2001.
64. Ken McCall, "McLin Digs into Turner Strongholds," *Dayton Daily News*, November 7, 2001.
65. Attempts to gather turnout percentages from the Montgomery County Board of Election to compare with previous elections were unsuccessful.
66. Quoted in Ken McCall, "Base of Support Critical in McLin's Victory," *Dayton Daily News*, November 18, 2001.
67. The correlation between percent black and percent vote is statistically significant at $p < .001$. In a linear regression this relationship holds when controlling for poverty, unemployment, and percentage of college educated individuals in each ward.

68. Ken McCall, "Base of Support Critical in McLin's Victory," *Dayton Daily News*, November 18, 2001.

69. Mary McCarty, "McLin Making 'Her'-Story," *Dayton Daily News*, November 9, 2001.

70. See table 5, chapter 3.

71. McLin's election was part of a wave of elections of Democratic mayors, mostly black, in the six major cities of Ohio. The November 2001 elections signaled the first time in Ohio history that so many black mayors—or so many Democrats—served simultaneously.

72. Quoted in Jim Bebbington, "Ex-Officer Interim Dayton Manager," *Dayton Daily News*, February 14, 2002.

73. Quoted in Jim Bebbington, "Commission Balks at, but Approves, Budget," *Dayton Daily News*, March 21, 2002.

74. Ken McCall, "Diversity Plan to Be Changed," *Dayton Daily News*, March 29, 2002.

75. *Dayton Daily News*, January 20, 2002.

76. Ken McCall, "City Moves to Shutter Workhouse," *Dayton Daily News*, May 16, 2002.

77. Personal communication from Rhine McLin, August 2008.

78. Jim Bebbington, "Officer's Promotion Protested," *Dayton Daily News*, June 6, 2002.

79. Quoted in Jim Bebbington, "Officer's Promotion Protested," *Dayton Daily News*, June 6, 2002.

80. Quoted in Jim Bebbington, "Mayoral Contest Focuses on Budget, Resources," *Dayton Daily News*, April 3, 2005.

81. Quoted in Jim Bebbington, "Mayor, Challenger Disagree on City Safety," *Dayton Daily News*, September 16, 2005.

82. Jim Bebbington, "Future Mayor Faces Big Changes," *Dayton Daily News*, September 18, 2005.

83. "McLin Has Been Making the Tough Calls," *Dayton Daily News*, November 1, 2005.

84. "McLin Didn't Coast to Her Re-election," *Dayton Daily News*, November 9, 2005.

85. Loyacano, *A History of Race Relations in the Miami Valley*, 34. The NCCJ was formerly the National Conference of Christians and Jews.

86. U.S. Commission on Civil Rights (from NCCJ data), *Employment Opportunities for Minorities in Montgomery County, Ohio*, chapter 2: "Racial Attitudes in Montgomery County, Ohio," 1.

87. U.S. Commission on Civil Rights (from NCCJ data), *Employment Opportunities for Minorities in Montgomery County, Ohio*, chapter 2: "Racial Attitudes in Montgomery County, Ohio," 3–4.

88. Reported in Charlise Lyles, "Apology? A Few Opinions," *Dayton Daily News*, June 20, 1997.

89. Briand, *Practical Politics*, 165.

90. "Vineyard Project Hopes to Bridge Gaps," *Dayton Daily News*, October 27, 1990.

91. Briand, *Practical Politics*, 165.

92. Amelia Robinson, "Dayton Race Dialogue to Mark First Year," *Dayton Daily News*, October 22, 2001.

93. "Black Leaders Not Backing McLin," WDTN News, March 5, 2009.

94. *Dayton Daily News*, March 7, 2009.

95. *Advocate*, November 6, 2009.

### 5. *"Lowest and Best" Bids*

1. Ford inaugural speech, January 2, 2002; accessed while Ford was mayor at the official website of the City of Toledo.

2. *Michigan Daily*, March 14, 2002. The epigraph at the beginning of this chapter is from this source as well.

3. Friesema, "Black Control of Central Cities."

4. Author's interview with Jack Ford, June 24, 2008.

5. Text from Judge James Graham's ruling in Associated General Contractors of Northwest Ohio, Inc. v. Sandra A. Drabik.

6. Data retention regarding the awarding of MBE contracts in the Toledo area is severely limited. The current director of the MBCAP office for the Toledo Regional Chamber of Commerce and the current commissioner for affirmative action at the city of Toledo both cite the lack of such information. While it is possible to cite the number of enrollees and graduates from the Capacity Building Program, the number of minorities who subsequently bid for and were awarded contracts is unavailable.

7. Quoted in *Toledo Journal*, June 21, 2000.

8. Bob Stiegel, "School's in Session for Innovative Center for Capacity Building," *Toledo Journal*, January 22, 2003.

9. Bob Stiegel, "First Class of 'Capacity' Graduates Better Prepared to Go after 'Serious Money,'" *Toledo Journal*, March 3, 2004.

10. Quoted in Bob Stiegel, "School's in Session for Innovative Center for Capacity Building," *Toledo Journal*, January 22, 2003.

11. Http://www.eopa.org/.

12. Author's telephone interview with Weldon Douthitt, project manager, EOPA, January 17, 2008.

13. Author's interview with George Robinson, February 11, 2009.

14. Quoted in Bob Stiegel, "City, University and Industry Team Up to Assist Minority Contractors: Officials Promise Results at Announcement
for Center for Capacity Building," *Toledo Journal*, September 4, 2002.

15. Quoted in Bob Stiegel, "School's in Session for Innovative Center for
Capacity Building," *Toledo Journal*, January 22, 2003.

16. Quoted in Bob Stiegel, "City, University and Industry Team Up to Assist Minority Contractors: Officials Promise Results at Announcement
for Center for Capacity Building," *Toledo Journal*, September 4, 2002.

17. Bob Stiegel, "First Class of 'Capacity' Graduates Better Prepared to
Go after 'Serious Money.'" *Toledo Journal*, March 3, 2004.

18. Bob Stiegel, "School's in Session for Innovative Center for Capacity
Building," *Toledo Journal*, January 22, 2003.

19. Quoted in Bob Stiegel, "First Class of 'Capacity' Graduates Better
Prepared to Go after 'Serious Money.'" *Toledo Journal*, March 3, 2004.

20. Quoted in Bob Stiegel, "Center for Capacity Building Participants
Point to Networking Opportunities," *Toledo Journal*, June 25, 2003.

21. Author's interview with George Robinson, February 11, 2009.

22. Bob Stiegel, "Center for Capacity Building Participants Point to Networking Opportunities," *Toledo Journal*, June 25, 2003.

23. Author's interview with George Robinson, February 11, 2009.

24. Bob Stiegel, "Center for Capacity Building Participants Point to Networking Opportunities," *Toledo Journal*, June 25, 2003; author's interview with Jack Ford, June 24, 2008.

25. Author's interview with Dan Johnson, August 4, 2008.

26. According to George Robinson, the program's shift in focus had led to
an increase in black contractors without capacity skills. Given the limited focus on the environment, many black contractors saw little utility in the program to serve their immediate needs.

27. Author's interview with Jack Ford, June 24, 2008.

28. See "The Ford Plan 2002," http://uac.utoledo.edu/Publications/appendix
-2-Ford-Plan.pdf. Materials discussed below are from this document.

29. Text of the Toledo Municipal Code was provided by Adam Loukx, the
acting director of the Department of Law at the City of Toledo, following a public records request.

30. I could not determine why the ordinance sat in committee. Mayor
Ford and the members of the council at the time who were interviewed could not specifically recall why the ordinance was not formally approved for an entire year. Interview respondents suggested that
Ford's administration operated as if the ordinance would be approved
prior to its final approval, suggesting perhaps that members of the
council did not find it imperative to formally approve the ordinance.

31. Transcript, meeting of Toledo City Council, Committee of the Whole, November 25, 2003.
32. Text of the Toledo Municipal Code, provided by Adam Loukx.
33. Audio transcript, Committee of the Whole meeting, December 9, 2003.
34. Audio transcript, Committee of the Whole meeting, December 9, 2003.
35. Author's interview with Yulanda McCarty-Harris, July 2008.
36. Audio transcript, Committee of the Whole meeting, December 9, 2003.
37. Audio transcript, Committee of the Whole meeting, December 9, 2003.
38. Audio transcript, Committee of the Whole meeting, December 9, 2003.
39. Author's interview with Jack Ford, January 2009.
40. Author's interview with Jack Ford, January 2009.
41. Author's interviews with Anita Lopez, June 19–20, 2008; Jack Ford, June 24, 2008; Yulanda McCarty-Harris, July 2008; George Robinson, February 11, 2008; and telephone interview with Weldon Douthitt, January 17, 2008.
42. Author's interview with Anita Lopez, June 19–20, 2008.
43. Author's interview with Yulanda McCarty-Harris, July 2008.
44. Tom Troy, "State Panel Faults Toledo in Discipline of 3 Black Employees," *Toledo Blade*, February 1, 2008.
45. Fletcher Word, "Mayor Jack Ford: Focusing on Fiscal Responsibility and Helping People," *Sojourner's Truth*, September 7, 2005.
46. Author's telephone interview with Jack Ford, January 14, 2009.

*6. Strong Housing and a Weak Mayor*

1. Quoted in Jim Bebbington, "Artists Paint Picture of Friendship," *Dayton Daily News*, August 29, 2003.
2. City of Dayton City Charter.
3. Mayor McLin made limited appointments to the following boards: Enterprise Zone Tax Incentive Review Council, Dayton Foundation Governing Board, Parade Permit Board, Compensation Board, Dayton Metropolitan Housing Authority, Mayor's Forum For Real Estate Development, and the Dayton-Montgomery County Port Authority. While she could make most appointments without commission approval, the port authority required the advice and consent of the commission.
4. Scott Elliott, "Ohio's Grad Rate 13th in Nation, but the Report Says the State's Gap between Blacks and Whites is among Country's Worst," *Dayton Daily News*, June 21, 2006, A4.
5. State of the Cities Data Systems Census.
6. *USA Today*, February 2, 2009.
7. U.S. Census Bureau, *American Community Survey 2006 Summary File*.

8. Scott Elliott, "How Dayton Spends Its Money," *Dayton Daily News*, April 29, 2007.
9. "CitiPlan Dayton: The 20/20 Vision Report" is a comprehensive strategy and development plan for Dayton originally adopted in 1999 by the City Plan Board and the Dayton City Commission. The report includes an analysis of business and economic conditions, proposals, and recommendations to address significant challenges. The implementation of the plan was the responsibility of the city commission, according to the report. Six working committees were established: Downtown; Community Development and Neighborhoods; Youth, Education and Human Services; Economic Development; Open Space and Quality of Life; and City Services. Recommendations and outcome goals were reported by 2003, including a future land-use plan and development patterns in the region.
10. Cunningham, Furdell, and McKinney, *Tapping the Power of City Hall to Build Equitable Communities*, 143.
11. "Dayton City Manager Job Just Got Harder," *Dayton Daily News*, February 19, 2006.
12. In an Ohio Democratic Party campaign leaflet supporting McLin, provided by the Montgomery County Democratic Party.
13. McLin seems to have advocated for the housing concerns of black residents in Dayton similarly to the way in which some black mayors, like W. W. Herenton of Memphis, Tennessee, made down-payment assistance for first-time homebuyers a priority. Such a priority can be beneficial for black residents seeking to purchase a house in inner-city neighborhoods. See Wright, *Race, Power, and Political Emergence in Memphis*.
14. Rothstein and Mehta, "Foreclosure Growth in Ohio 2009." Figure is from the following website: http://www.policymattersohio.org/ foreclosure-filings-in-ohio-1995-2008-tables/montgomery-county -foreclosure-filings-1995-2008.
15. In November 2008 Dayton compiled an NSP to compete for federal HUD-awarded grants from the Housing and Economic Recovery Act of 2008, which contained $3.92 billion in NSP funding. On September 29, 2008, the City of Dayton had been awarded a special allocation of $5,582,902 in Community Development Block Grant funds to be used as part of the NSP for foreclosed and abandoned properties in the city. NSP funds are to be used primarily for the acquisition and rehabilitation of abandoned and foreclosed properties, including the establishment of temporary land banks of abandoned or foreclosed properties to facilitate redevelopment; the demolition of blighted

structures; the purchase of foreclosed or abandoned parcels; the re-development of vacant, abandoned, or foreclosed properties; and the purchase and redevelopment assistance to income-eligible buyers of foreclosed or abandoned properties. In addition to applying for the federal grant, the City of Dayton applied to the State of Ohio for $2.2 million of additional funding through the Ohio Neighborhood Stabilization Program.

16. McLin, interview with MayorTV, a project of *The Nation* and the Drum Major Institute, which interviewed select mayors nationwide. See http://mayortv.com/rhine_l_mclin/.

17. Morgan and Morgan, *City Crime Rankings*.

18. U.S. Federal Bureau of Investigation, *Crime in the United States*. Parker is quoted in Elena Temple, "U.S. Conference of Mayors Denounces Crime Rankings as Bogus, Damaging to Cities," press release, November 21.

19. The unemployment rates in Dayton and the country have all increased since March 2009. National unemployment data were retrieved from http://www.nidataplus.com/lfeus1.htm; Ohio unemployment data from http://jfs.ohio.gov/releases/; Dayton crime data reported by Harry Moroz at the Drum Major Institute Blog and retrieved from http://mayortv.com/rhine_l_mclin/. Dayton unemployment rate data reported by the Ohio Department of Job and Family Services Historical Civilian Labor Force Estimates; http://lmi.state.oh.us/asp/laus/vbLaus.htm.

20. U.S. Census Bureau, *2005-2007 American Community Survey*.

21. Horton, "Race and Wealth."

22. Belsky and Retsinas, "New Paths to Building Assets for the Poor."

23. Preservation Dayton Inc., "The Historic Arcade"; http://preservationdayton.com/historic-arcade.cfm.

24. McLin, interview with MayorTV, http://mayortv.com/rhine_l_mclin/.

25. It appears McLin's definition of affordable housing was not entirely congruent with the city's utilization of the federally defined term. The city's NSP Substantial Action Plan Amendment of November 2008 noted the following: "The City adheres to HUD's generally accepted definition of affordability. A household is to pay no more than 30 percent of its annual income on housing. Families who pay more than 30 percent of their income for housing are considered cost burdened and may have difficulty affording necessities such as food, clothing, transportation and medical care" (p. 16).

26. "McLin Struck Strange Note in City Speech," *Dayton Business Journal*, February 21, 2003.

27. 2000 Census of Population and Housing Summary File 3—Downtown Priority Board. Retrieved from http://www.cityofdayton.org/depart ments/pcd/Documents/2000%20CensusPDFs/Downtown/SF3DT PB.pdf; accessed July 24, 2008.

28. For more information on the spatial mismatch hypothesis, blacks' barriers to public transportation access, and their effects on employment, see Holzer, "The Spatial Mismatch Hypothesis"; Kain, "Housing Segregation"; Gordon, Kumar, and Richardson, "The Spatial Mismatch Hypothesis"; Johnston-Anumonwo: "Race, Gender," "Commuting Constraints of African American Women," and "Persistent Racial Differences in the Commutes of Kansas City Workers"; McLafferty and Preston: "Spatial Mismatch" and "Gender, Race and Determinants of Commuting"; Chung et al., "Racial Differences in Transportation Access to Employment"; Kasarda, "Urban Change and Minority Opportunity"; and Goering and Kalachek, "Public Transportation and Black Unemployment."

29. See, for example, "City of Dayton 2008 Action Plan," 16.

30. Census 2000 Summary File 1 (machine-readable data file); prepared by the U.S. Census Bureau, 2001 (www.census.gov); produced by Northern Ohio Data and Information Service, Levin College of Urban Affairs, Cleveland State University (nodis.csuohio.edu).

31. ProjDel Corporation was competitively hired to provide project and construction management, public relations, and marketing services for Wright-Dunbar. It compiled a report of its services entitled "Wright-Dunbar Redevelopment, Dayton, Ohio: A Case Study." See "Wright-Dunbar Redevelopment. Dayton, Ohio: A Case Study." Retrieved from http://www.projdel.com/Wright-Dunbar.pdf; accessed July 2008.

32. Census 2000 Summary File 1 (machine-readable data file); prepared by the U.S. Census Bureau, 2001 (www.census.gov); produced by Northern Ohio Data and Information Service, Levin College of Urban Affairs, Cleveland State University (nodis.csuohio.edu).

33. Anonymous personal communication with the author.

34. "Wright-Dunbar Redevelopment. Dayton, Ohio: A Case Study." Retrieved from http://www.projdel.com/Wright-Dunbar.pdf; accessed July 2008.

35. In addition, with the help of Congress, in 1992 the project also included the development of the Dayton Aviation Heritage National Historical Park. The park was slated to be developed by 2003. As of 2008 the park included the Wright Cycle Company Complex, the Wright-Dunbar Interpretive Center, the Aviation Trail Visitors' Center and

Museum, the Paul Laurence Dunbar House, Dayton History at Carillon Park, and the Huffman Prairie Flying Field.

36. "Wright-Dunbar Redevelopment. Dayton, Ohio: A Case Study." Retrieved from http://www.projdel.com/Wright-Dunbar.pdf; accessed July 2008.

37. ISUS, a community trade-school program, helps students to earn a high school diploma and credit toward an associate's degree, as well as to gain industry-recognized construction certifications. Many of the students are African American.

38. Anonymous personal communications with the author.

39. Quoted in Jason Roberson, "Wright-Dunbar a Model for Success," *Dayton Daily News*, February 22, 2004.

40. Quoted in Jason Roberson, "Wright-Dunbar a Model for Success," *Dayton Daily News*, February 22, 2004.

41. *Dayton Business Journal*, November 8, 2002.

42. Quoted in Shannon Joyce Neal and Jim Bebbington, "Phoenix Project Gets $10M," *Dayton Daily News*, November 13, 2003.

43. "City Approves Housing Funds," *Dayton Business Journal*, January 17, 2008.

44. Jason Roberson, "Affordability Key to Housing Market," *Dayton Daily News*, January 22, 2003.

45. Quoted in Joanne Huist Smith, "Plan Set to Raze Run-Down Buildings," *Dayton Daily News*, December 16, 2004.

46. Jacob Dirr, "Dayton to Use Federal Money for Demolition of Blighted Properties," *Dayton Business Journal*, October 24, 2008.

47. The addresses and number of demolitions could not be made available from the city's community planning and neighborhood development department. The statement here is based on interviews with city leaders.

48. Jacob Dirr, "Dayton to Use Federal Money for Demolition of Blighted Properties," *Dayton Business Journal*, October 24, 2008.

49. Quoted in Joanne Huist Smith, "City Targets Junky Yards," *Dayton Daily News*, April 7, 2005.

50. In a related action in 2006 McLin voted in favor of a city commission disclosure ordinance to ensure that code violations were resolved before residential properties changed hands. This ordinance potentially helps to force property owners to keep their property up to code, and it also may prevent court proceedings. The ordinance may also have aesthetic benefits for neighborhoods. For more information on the ordinance, see City of Dayton, Ordinance 30565-06, Introduced by Commissioner J. Williams, June 7, 2006. Retrieved from http://www

.cityofdayton.org/departments/bs/Documents/disclosureordinance
_only.pdf; accessed July 2008.

51. Calem et al., "The Neighborhood Distribution of Subprime Mortgage
Lending."

52. *Dayton Daily News*, November 2, 2005.

53. *Dayton Daily News*, March 27, 2008.

54. National Housing Trust Fund, "President Signs Housing Trust Fund
into Law on July 30, 2008." Error! Hyperlink reference not valid.

55. Quoted in *Dayton Daily News*, May 20, 2007.

56. *Dayton Daily News*, August 8, 2002.

57. *Dayton Daily News*, January 2, 2003.

58. Popkin et al., "A Decade of HOPE VI."

59. U.S. Department of Housing and Urban Development (HUD), "Home
and Communities."

60. Dayton Metropolitan Housing Authority, "What Is DMHA's Public
Housing?" Attempts to determine the number of public housing units
within Dayton were unsuccessful. A representative from the DMHA
indicated that there were some units within the city that were not
managed by the DMHA.

61. "Old Dayton View Neighborhood Planning District."

62. *Dayton Daily News*, September 13, 2002.

63. Quoted in *Dayton Business Journal*, September 6, 2002.

64. Attempts to learn the outcome of the suit were unsuccessful. It appears the suit was dismissed.

65. Testimony of Greg Johnson, executive director of DMHA, to the city
commission on September 5, 2007.

66. Transcript, Dayton City Commission meeting, September 5, 2007.

67. The demolition of outdated public housing structures in favor of the
construction of community-centered units with more green space
was part of a larger trend nationwide to make public housing units
aesthetically more appealing.

68. City of Dayton, Department of Planning and Community Development, Citizen Participation, "The ORION Solution."

69. *Dayton Daily News*, November 17, 2005.

70. *Dayton Update*, Fall 2007.

71. For more information, visit http://www.omegabaptist.org/site/MS_7.
html.

72. Author's interview with Rashad Young, July 16, 2008.

73. Author's interview with Rashad Young, July 16, 2008.

74. Author's interview with Rashad Young, July 16, 2008.

75. Quoted in *Dayton Daily News*, November 23, 2007.

76. Quoted in *Dayton Daily News*, November 20, 2007.

77. Author's interview with Rashad Young, July 16, 2008.

78. Author's interview with Rashad Young, July 16, 2008.

79. Author's interview with Rhine McLin, June 26, 2008.

80. Author's interviews with Alvin Freeman, August 7, 2008, and B. Cato Mayberry, August 8, 2008.

81. Author's interview with Don Black, July 23, 2008.

82. Author's interview with Annie Bonaparte, August 5, 2008.

83. Author's interview with Claude Bell Sr., August 5, 2008.

### 7. Trickle-Up Public Opinion

1. Kleppner, *Chicago Divided*, 155.

2. Lane, "Black Political Power and Its Limits," 61.

3. Harold Washington increased the contracts awarded to minority firms in Chicago from nine to sixty in a three-year period. However, we have no idea to what extent this figure meets a city ordinance or good-faith goal that requires a certain percentage of minority participation in the contracting process. Without that clear understanding, the stated increase during those three years could be substantively meaningful or simply symbolic. It could be significant, for example, if minority contractors received the average of the total dollar amount relative to their proportion within the city's population. See Mier and Kari, "Decentralized Development."

4. See Brown, "Race and Politics Matter," 26.

5. Given the structure of government, it is expected that Toledo would generate more interviews, as Mayor Ford had a larger direct impact on more individuals due to Toledo's strong-mayor format of representation.

6. For dates of the city council and city commission minutes and agendas, see appendix 2. Included is a sample content analysis rubric for the reader to better understand how the content analysis was performed and then applied to the data.

7. C. Bullock and MacManus, "Policy Responsiveness to the Black Electorate."

8. Cingranelli, "Race, Politics and Elites."

9. The other interview questions were largely helpful in covering the more recent racial and political context identified in chapters 3 and 5, as well as in helping to determine the role of ideology and partisanship locally (e.g., in respect to the variables at play when public officials considered the mayor's policy and program proposals within the city council or city commission). Moreover, the remaining questions

asked the interviewees their perspectives on the role of the business community in the administration, the business climate in the city, and the relationship between the mayor and civic leaders. Respondents were asked a series of closed and open-ended questions. For closed questions the interviewer marked the appropriate reply. For the sole open-ended question being analyzed, the interviewer created dummy variables of Yes, No, and N/A.

10. The N/A category had a large number of respondents who were ignored because they were public officials in office at the time. I did not want to create a conflict of interests given the nature of the question, so I did not ask this question of public officials.

11. See Svara, *Facilitative Leadership in Local Government*, and Pressman, "Preconditions of Mayoral Leadership."

12. See Stone, *Regime Politics*.

13. While the findings do not tell us whether it was this variable that determined Ford's greater pursuit of black interests, the fact of a larger white middle-class population in a city where the mayor is found to have more actively pursued black interests is notable.

14. See C. Jones, "The Impact of Local Election Systems on Black Political Representation," and Karnig and Welch, *Black Representation and Urban Policy*.

15. See Browning, Marshall, and Tabb, *Protest Is Not Enough*.

16. CareNet is discussed in chapter 3 above.

17. The quoted materials are from specific interviews. Here, author's interview with Bill Brennan, August 4, 2008.

18. Author's interview with Bill Brennan, August 4, 2008.

19. Author's interview with Robert C. Savage, July 2, 2008.

20. Author's interview with James M. Murray, July 2, 2008.

21. Author's interview with Thomas S. Crothers, June 18, 2008.

22. Author's interview with Bill Brennan, August 4, 2008.

23. Author's interview with Jack Ford, June 24, 2008.

24. Author's interview with Thomas S. Crothers, June 18, 2008.

25. During the 2005 reelection campaign the city's main newspaper, the *Toledo Blade*, regularly referred to Ford and Finkbeiner as different stylistically. A September 15, 2005, editorial titled "A Study in Contrasts" highlights this pervasive comparison.

26. Based on author's interview with Bill Brennan, August 4, 2008. Brennan is an example of a business leader whose voting preferences may have changed between 2001 and 2005.

27. Author's interview with business leader who chose to remain anonymous, August 7, 2008.

28. Author's interview with Ken Sulfridge, August 5, 2008.
29. Author's interview with Rhine McLin, June 26, 2008.
30. Author's telephone interview with Phil Parker, president and CEO of Dayton Area Chamber of Commerce.
31. Author's interview with business leader who chose to remain anonymous, August 7, 2008.
32. "Kest for Mayor," *Toledo Blade*, November 4, 2001.
33. Jack Ford, State of the City address, February 2005.
34. *Toledo Blade*, November 6, 2005.
35. Author's interview with Jack Ford, June 24, 2008.
36. Author's interviews with a former politician and lawyer who chose to remain anonymous; interviews with Francis Szollosi, June 25, 2008; Paula Ross, June 23, 2008; and James Ruvolo, June 19, 2008.
37. Author's interview with Jack Ford, June 24, 2008.
38. Author's interview with Rashad Young, July 16, 2008.
39. Author's interview with Rhine McLin, June 26, 2008.
40. Author's interview with Rhine McLin, June 26, 2008.
41. Author's interview with Rhine McLin, June 26, 2008.
42. Much of the analysis on McLin confirms earlier research on black weak mayors' limited substantive impact in black communities. See Piliawsky, "The Impact of Black Mayors on the Black Community."
43. See Svara, *Facilitative Leadership in Local Government*, and Pressman, "Preconditions of Mayoral Leadership."
44. Author's interview with Alan Bannister, June 28, 2008. Ford's executive order near the end of his administration to enforce the city's minority good-faith goals in contracting is another example of his use of the strong-mayor form of government to advocate for black interests. See "Ford Reaffirms City Goal for Minority Contractors," *Toledo Blade*, March 25, 2004.
45. The director of water and director of public works positions are filled by the city manager. However, the author's interview with Carole Grimes (a former member of the Dayton Metropolitan Housing Authority Board), August 5, 2008, suggested McLin had significant influence over those appointments.
46. Gay Rights Ordinance, No. 30698-07, Dayton City Commission. Passed November 21, 2007. Amended sections 32.02–32.06, 35.14, and 35.16.
47. See "For McLin, Stand on Gay Rights Worth the Political Cost," *Dayton Daily News*, November 5, 2009.
48. The "street level" reference is borrowed from the author's interview with McLin.

49. See Browning, Marshall, and Tabb, *Protest Is Not Enough*, and C. Jones, "The Impact of Local Election Systems on Black Political Representation."
50. Swain, *Black Faces, Black Interests*.
51. Tate, *Black Faces in the Mirror*.
52. For more information, see "The Future of Local Government Administration," and Svara, "Effective Mayoral Leadership in Council-Manager Cities." The statement regarding the numbers of black mayors in weak-mayor systems is based on November 2008 data from the National Conference of Black Mayors website, which has figures for the number of black mayors of cities with populations over fifty thousand.
53. Stone, *Regime Politics*.
54. Svara, *Facilitative Leadership in Local Government*.
55. Tate, *Black Faces in the Mirror*.
56. Gamble, "Black Political Representation."

*8. Racial Populism*

1. A. Lewis, "Between Generations," and R. Perry, "Deval Patrick and the Representation of Massachusetts' Black Interests."
2. Nelson, "Black Mayoral Leadership in the Twenty-First Century."
3. McCormick and Jones, "The Conceptualization of Deracialization."
4. Jerit, "How Predictive Appeals Affect Policy Opinions."
5. Sorell, "Hobbes's UnAristotelian Political Rhetoric."
6. Foss, "Abandonment of Genus," 367.
7. Foss, "Abandonment of Genus," 377.
8. Craig and Hurley, "Political Rhetoric and the Structure of Political Opinion."
9. Koch, "Political Rhetoric and Political Persuasion," 211.
10. Gamson and Modigliani, "Media Discourse and Public Opinion on Nuclear Power."
11. See Gamson, *Talking Politics*; Gitlin, *The Whole World Is Watching*; Kinder and Sanders, *Divided by Color*; and Pan and Kosicki, "Framing Analysis."
12. Koch, "Political Rhetoric and Political Persuasion."
13. Glaude, *Exodus*, and Foner, *The Voice of Black America*.
14. Nelson and Meranto, *Electing Black Mayors*, 340.
15. Rich, *Coleman Young and Detroit Politics*, 212.
16. Metz and Tate, "The Color of Urban Campaigns," 264.
17. Quoted in Kleppner, *Chicago Divided*, 210 and 155.
18. Metz and Tate, "The Color of Urban Campaigns," 264.
19. Thompson, *Double Trouble*, 58.

20. Colburn, "Running for Office," 33.
21. Colburn, "Running for Office," 33.
22. Colburn, "Running for Office," 37.
23. As noted, the question of how best to address black interests has been debated in terms of the universal or targeted impact of initiatives and has received much scholarly attention. While the universalism/targeted universalism debate is not framed in the context of rhetoric, the dichotomy explored in chapter 1 best explains how the framework functions. The framework also matters as a politician in support of a policy often first rhetorically introduces (in a speech) policies that are later implemented. The rhetoric used to support the policy often correlates with how the policy is implemented as either targeted and universal or traditionally universal.
24. Author's interviews with Alan Bannister, June 28, 2008; Bob Bell, July 2008; and Bob Savage, July 2, 2008.
25. Ford, State of the City address, February 21, 2002.
26. West, *Race Matters*, 12. West notes how a focus on infrastructure can be an example of a politician's commitment to common humanity.
27. Ford, State of the City address, February 21, 2002.
28. Ford, State of the City address, February 21, 2002.
29. CareNet, "Making a Real Difference in the Lives of the Uninsured."
30. Ford, State of the City address, February 21, 2002.
31. Ford, inaugural address, January 2, 2002.
32. Ford, State of the City address, January 16, 2003.
33. Ford, State of the City address, January 16, 2003.
34. Ford, State of the City address, January 25, 2005.
35. U.S. Department of Housing and Urban Development, Community Planning and Development, "Instructions for Urban County Qualification."
36. U.S. Department of Housing and Urban Development, Community Planning and Development, "Instructions for Urban County Qualification."
37. Ford's efforts, however, did not decline. As a March 25, 2004, *Toledo Blade* article suggests, late in his term Ford wrote a five-page executive order reaffirming that "city contractors must make good faith efforts to include minority and women-owner businesses as subcontractors."
38. McLin, State of the City address, February 24, 2004.
39. McLin, State of the City address, February 15, 2006.
40. McLin, State of the City address, February 14, 2007. While McLin did not publicly recognize the significance of Young serving as the city's

first black male city manager, she did in her interview with me (June 26, 2008) comment on his youth and racial identity. Moreover, she noted she had an interest in running for reelection in part to ensure that Young had a stable base to remain in the position.

41. Author's interview with Rhine McLin, June 26, 2008.

42. For a roster and detailed explanation of additional select activities not included within the case study chapters, see appendix 2. For a yearly examination of Ford and McLin's policy actions and program development to improve black quality of life, see appendix 2.

43. Foss, "Abandonment of Genus."

44. See, for example, Rev. Dr. Martin Luther King Jr.'s April 1963 "Letter from a Birmingham Jail."

45. Perry, Huey L. "Deracialization as an Analytical Construct."

46. Gamble, "Black Political Representation," 421. See also Clay, *Just Permanent Interests*, and Guinier, *Tyranny of the Majority*, 47.

47. Fenno, *Going Home*, 7.

48. M. Williams, *Voice, Trust, and Democracy*, 192.

49. See Dawson, *Behind the Mule*, and Tate, *From Protest to Politics*, 21–29.

50. Gillespie, "Meet the New Class."

51. Gillespie, "Meet the New Class."

52. Orey and Ricks, "A Systematic Analysis of the Deracialization Concept," 326, and Hamilton, "Deracialization."

*9. Target Practice*

Cunnigen, "Black Leadership in the Twenty-First Century."

1. Author's telephone interview with Jack Ford, January 14, 2009.

2. For an example of how the deracialization approach was and is used by scholars to explain the political behavior of black elected officials, see McCormick and Jones, "The Conceptualization of Deracialization"; for a more recent examination, see Persons, "From Insurgency to Deracialization."

3. Ford, State of the City address, February 17, 2004.

4. McLin, State of the City address, February 14, 2005.

5. M. L. King, "Letter from a Birmingham Jail." Error! Hyperlink reference not valid.

6. M. L. King, "Letter from a Birmingham Jail."

7. Take, for example the issue of gay rights. Scholars and media pundits have suggested why gay rights should be viewed as a civil rights issue. See Icard, "Black Gay Men and Conflicting Social Identities"; Cohen, *The Boundaries of Blackness*; and Lee-St. John, "Viewpoint." However, others share a different view. See Wadsworth, "Reconciliation Poli-

tics," and Solomon, "Nothing Special." A more recent example is the tension noted within the membership of the NAACP, as a few leaders, such as Julian Bond and Coretta Scott King, have noted that gay rights are in line with the organization's mission. In May 2012 the National Board of the NAACP voted to support marriage equality. Thus proponents of gay rights have long framed the issue as a human, rights-based issue with ties to the civil rights movement. However, others view their concerns as distinctly different from the context of rights, human or civil. For more information, see G. Lewis, "Black-White Differences in Attitudes toward Homosexuality and Gay Rights," and Bond, "Is Gay Rights Really an Issue?"

8. For more information concerning how appealing to citizenship may effectively protect minority interests, see Kymlicka, *Multicultural Citizenship*.

9. Swain, "Race and Representation."

10. Cruse, "New Black Leadership Required."

11. See Sjoquist, *The Economic Status of Black Atlantans*; Stone, *Regime Politics*; and M. Jones, "Black Mayoral Leadership in Atlanta."

12. McCormick and Jones, "The Conceptualization of Deracialization," 78.

13. Browning, Marshall, and Tabb, *Protest Is Not Enough*, 220.

14. Kinder and Sanders, *Divided by Color*; Feldman and Huddy, "Racial Resentment and White Opposition to Race-Conscious Programs."

15. Steele, *White Guilt*; Harvey and Oswald, "Collective Guilt and Shame."

16. Feldman and Huddy, "Racial Resentment and White Opposition to Race-Conscious Programs," 178.

17. Feldman and Huddy, "Racial Resentment and White Opposition to Race-Conscious Programs," 180.

18. Feldman and Huddy, "Racial Resentment and White Opposition to Race-Conscious Programs," 181. Given that memberships to conservative political organizations like the Republican Party are largely white, the usage of "conservative" can reasonably be understood to refer to whites.

19. Inversely the racialization approach allows for the denial of race-specific disparities that may exist in service delivery in municipal and other jurisdictions, while an approach that universalizes the interests of blacks as important to everyone can improve the political and social climate. Because the approach emphasizes a common-humanity, human-relations theme, it likely has a larger impact on disadvantaged blacks than deracialization and perhaps even racialization.

20. West, *Race Matters*, 6.
21. West, *Race Matters*, 8.
22. West, *Race Matters*, 11–12.
23. Bowers and Rich, *Governing Middle-Sized Cities*, 223.
24. See Stone, "Political Leadership in Urban Politics"; Chatterjee, *Local Leadership in Black Communities*; Smith, *We Have No Leaders*; Marable, *Black Leadership*; and West, *Race Matters*; Walters and Smith, "Black Leadership"; Davis, *Perspectives in Black Politics and Black Leadership*; and Persons, "From Insurgency to Deracialization."
25. Hopkins and McCabe, "After It's Too Late."
26. Stone, "Political Leadership in Urban Politics."
27. Bowers and Rich, *Governing Middle-Sized Cities*, 218. See also Ammons and Newell, *City Executives*, and Banfield, *Big City Politics*.
28. Bowers and Rich, *Governing Middle-Sized Cities*, 218.
29. Hunter, *Community Power Structure*.
30. See Gottfried, *Boss Cermak of Chicago*; A. Bullock, *Hitler*; George and George, *Woodrow Wilson and Colonel House*; Maddi, *Personality Theories*; C. Hall and Lindzey, *Theories of Personality*; and Kotter and Lawrence, *Mayors in Action*.
31. Rich, *Coleman Young and Detroit Politics*, 218. Ford may be an example of James Cunningham's public entrepreneur model, with the exception that reform appears not to be an explicit recognizable component of the model. For Cunningham, "Nearly any bold thrust of a mayor—initiating an urban renewal project, promoting jobs for blacks, intervening with the Board of Education for curriculum reform, setting up an elite tactical police unit—risks the loss of the votes of certain groups whose interests may be harmed, while it chances the gain of the votes of many whose interests may be advanced" (*Urban Leadership in the Sixties*, 15). While Cunningham's model is comprehensive in its risk-taking approach, it does not explicitly emphasize reform.
32. Rich, *Coleman Young and Detroit Politics*, 36.
33. Author's interview with Jack Ford, June 24, 2008.
34. McLin may be an example of Leonard Ruchleman's multihat model, with the exception that she herself admits poor performance and little interest in ceremonial functions. However, her active role in the Montgomery County Democratic Party and her legislative experience in the Ohio Statehouse make her a strong candidate for this model. See Ruchleman, *Big City Mayors*. For more information on the multihat model, see Kotter and Lawrence, *Mayors in Action*, 29.
35. Kotter and Lawrence, *Mayors in Action*, 21. For more information on the public entrepreneur model, see Schumpeter: *Capitalism, Social-*

*ism, and Democracy*, and "Economic Theory and Entrepreneurial History"; and Cunningham, *Urban Leadership in the Sixties*.

36. Stone, "Political Leadership in Urban Politics," 107.
37. Author's interview with Jack Ford, June 24, 2008.
38. Ford's health care network, CareNet is still in operation. For more information on CareNet, see appendix 2.
39. Hunter, *Community Power Structure*.
40. Stone, "Political Leadership in Urban Politics."

### Epilogue

1. Baldwin, *No Name in the Street*, 185.
2. Baldwin, *No Name in the Street*, 189.

### Appendix B

1. Page, *Who Deliberates*, 112.
2. A similar newspaper coverage methodology was utilized in R. Perry, "First Impressions."
3. For Ford: 108 minutes/agendas for the entirety of his term in Toledo, 2002–2005; for McLin: 386 minutes/agendas from the beginning of her term in 2002 through August 1, 2008.
4. The listing of names may be incomplete and is based on information from a telephone interview with Alan Bannister, a former campaign official and administration appointee of Ford.

## REFERENCES

Abney, F. Glenn, and John D. Hutcheson. "Race, Representation and Trust: Changes in Attitudes after the Election of a Black Mayor." *Public Opinions Quarterly* 45 (Spring 1981): 91–101.

Ammons, D. N., and Charldean Newell. *City Executives*. Albany: State University of New York Press, 1989.

Anttonen, Anneli. "Universalism and Social Policy: A Nordic-Feminist Revaluation." *Nordic Journal of Feminist and Gender Research* 10 (October 2002): 71–80.

Associated General Contractors of Northwest Ohio, Inc., v. Sandra A. Drabik, Director, Department of Administrative Services; Reginald Wilkinson, Director of Rehabilitation and Correction. N.d. Retrieved from http://vlex.com/vid/36185309. Accessed August 1, 2012.

Baker, Samuel A., and David H. Feldman. "Revealed Preferences for Car Tax Cuts: An Empirical Study of Perceived Fiscal Incidence." College of William and Mary, Department of Economics, Working Paper #8, November 2004.

Banfield, E. C. *Big City Politics*. New York: Random House.

Barnett, W. Steven, Kirsty Brown, and Rima Shore. 2004. "The Universal vs. Targeted Debate: Should the United States Have Preschool for All?" *Preschool Policy Matters* 6 (April 1965): 1–15.

Bayor, Ronald H. "African-American Mayors and Governance in Atlanta." In Colburn and Adler, *African-American Mayors*.

Belsky, Eric S., and Nicolas P. Retsinas. "New Paths to Building Assets for the Poor." In *Building Assets, Building Credit: Creating Wealth in Low-Income Communities*, ed. N. P. Retsinas and E. S. Belsky, 1–9. Washington DC: Brookings Institution Press/Joint Center for Housing Studies, Harvard University, 2005.

Biles, Roger. "Mayor David Dinkins and the Politics of Race in New York City." In Colburn and Adler, *African-American Mayors*.

Bobo, Lawrence, and Franklin D. Gilliam, Jr. "Race, Sociopolitical Participation, and Black Empowerment." *American Political Science Review* 84 (June 1990): 377–93.

Boger, John Charles. "The Eclipse of Anti-Racist Public Policy." In *Race and Ethnicity in the United States*, ed. Stephen Steinberg. New York: Wiley-Blackwell, 2000.

Bond, Julian. "Is Gay Rights Really an Issue?" *Ebony* 59, no. 9 (July 2004): 142–46.

Bowers, James R., and Paul C. Baker. "William A. Johnson Jr. and Education Politics in Rochester, New York." In Bowers and Rich, *Governing Middle-Sized Cities*, 81–102.

Bostitis, David A. *2008 National Opinion Poll*. Washington DC: Joint Center for Political and Economic Studies.

Bowers, James R., and Wilbur C. Rich, eds. *Governing Middle-Sized Cities*. Boulder: Lynne Rienner Publishers, 2000.

Briand, Michael K. *Practical Politics*. Urbana: University of Illinois Press, 1999.

Brown, Robert A. "Race and Politics Matter: Black Urban Representation and Social Spending during the Urban Crisis." *National Political Science Review* 11 (2007).

Browning, R. P., D. R. Marshall, and D. H. Tabb. *Protest Is Not Enough: The Struggle of Blacks and Hispanics for Equality in Urban Politics*. Berkeley: University of California Press, 1984.

Bullock, Alan. *Hitler: A Study in Tyranny*. New York: Harper and Row, 1962.

Bullock, Charles S., III, and Susan A. MacManus. "Policy Responsiveness to the Black Electorate: Programmatic versus Symbolic Representation." *American Politics Research* 9, no. 3 (1981): 357–68.

Burns, Peter F. *Electoral Politics Is Not Enough: Racial and Ethnic Minorities and Urban Politics*. New York: State University of New York Press, 2006.

Burnside, Randolph, and Antonio Rodriquez. "Like Father, Like Son? Jesse Jackson, Jr.'s Tenure as a U.S. Congressman." In Gillespie, *Whose Black Politics?*

Button, James W. *Blacks and Social Change: Impact of the Civil Rights Movement in Southern Communities*. Princeton NJ: Princeton University Press, 1989.

Calem, Paul S., et al. "The Neighborhood Distribution of Subprime Mortgage Lending." *Journal of Real Estate Finance and Economics* 29 (2004): 393–410.

CareNet. "Making a Real Difference in the Lives of the Uninsured." Toledo/Lucas County Annual Report. Toledo OH: Gauthier Marketing, 2007.

Cayton, Andrew R. L. *Ohio: The History of a People*. Columbus: Ohio State University Press, 2002.

"Census 2000 Matters: Racial Changes in the Nation's Largest Cities: Evidence from the 2000 Census." Washington DC: Brookings Institution, April 2001.

Chatterjee, Pranab. *Local Leadership in Black Communities*. Cleveland: Case Western Reserve University, School of Applied Social Sciences, 1975.

Chung, Chanjin, et al. "Racial Differences in Transportation Access to Employment in Chicago and Los Angeles, 1980 and 1990." *American Economic Review* 91, no. 2 (2001).

Churchill, Ward. "To Disrupt, Discredit, and Destroy: The FBI's Secret War against the Black Panther Party." Retrieved from http://propagandhi.com/wp-content/empires/Ward_Churchill.pdf. Accessed July 3, 2012.

Cingranelli, David L. "Race, Politics and Elites: Testing Alternative Models of Municipal Service Distribution." *American Journal of Political Science* 25, no. 4 (November 1981): 664-92.

"CitiPlan Dayton: The 20/20 Vision Plan Report." 1999. Http://www.cityofdayton.org/departments/pcd/Documents/CitiPlan2020PDF.pdf.

"City Approves Housing Funds." *Dayton Business Journal*, January 17, 2008.

City of Dayton. *City of Dayton, Ohio Community Involvement Strategy*. April 15, 1995.

City of Dayton, Department of Planning and Community Development, Citizen Participation. "The ORION Solution." Retrieved from http://www.cityofdayton.org/departments/pcd/cp/Pages/TheORIONSolution.aspx. Accessed February 12, 2009.

City of Dayton City Charter. Retrieved from http://www.cityofdayton.org/cco/Documents/City_Charter.pdf. Accessed February 12, 2009.

"City of Dayton 2008 Action Plan." Retrieved from http://www.cityofdayton.org/departments/pcd/. Accessed February 16, 2009.

Clavel, Pierre. "Rochester: Two Faces of Regionalism." In *Economic Development in American Cities: The Pursuit of an Equity Agenda*, ed. M. I. J. Bennett and R. P. Giloth. Albany: State University of New York Press, 2007.

Clavel, Pierre, and Wim Wiewel. *Harold Washington and the Neighborhoods: Progressive City Government in Chicago 1983-1987*. New Brunswick NJ: Rutgers University Press, 1991.

Clay, William L. *Just Permanent Interests: Black Americans in Congress, 1870-1991*. New York: Amistad, 1992.

Cohen, Cathy J. *The Boundaries of Blackness: AIDS and the Breakdown of Black Politics*. Chicago: University of Chicago Press, 1999.

Colburn, David R. "Running for Office: African American Mayors from 1967 to 1996." In Colburn and Adler, *African-American Mayors*.

Colburn, David R., and Jeffrey S. Adler, eds. *African-American Mayors*. Urbana: University of Illinois Press, 2001.

Cose, Ellis. "Revisiting 'The Rage of a Privileged Class.'" *Newsweek*, February 2, 2009.

Craig, Stephen C., and Thomas L. Hurley. "Political Rhetoric and the Structure of Political Opinion: Some Experimental Findings." *Western Political Quarterly* 37, no. 4 (December 1984): 632–40.

Cruse, Harold. "New Black Leadership Required." *New Politics* 2, no. 4 (1990): 43–47.

Cunnigen, Donald. "Black Leadership in the Twenty-first Century." *Society* 43, no. 5 (July 2006): 25–29.

Cunningham, James V. *Urban Leadership in the Sixties*. Cambridge MA: Schenkman Publishing, 1970.

Cunningham, Kiran, Phyllis Furdell, and Hannah McKinney. *Tapping the Power of City Hall to Build Equitable Communities: 10 City Profiles*. Washington DC: National League of Cities, 2007.

Curvin, Robert. "Black Power in City Hall." *Society* 9 (September/October 1972).

Dahl, Robert A. *Who Governs? Democracy and Power in an American City*. New Haven: Yale University Press, 1961.

Davis, John, ed. *Perspectives in Black Politics and Black Leadership*. Lanham MD: University Press of America, 2007.

Dawson, Michael C. *Behind the Mule: Race and Class in African American Politics*. Princeton NJ: Princeton University Press, 1994.

Dayton Metropolitan Housing Authority. "What Is DMHA's Public Housing?" Retrieved from http://www.dmha.org/public.htm. Accessed February 16, 2009.

DeLeon, Richard E. "Research Methods in Urban Politics and Policy." In *Handbook of Research on Urban Politics and Policy in the United States*, ed. Ronald K. Vogel. Westport CT: Greenwood Press, 1997.

Dirr, Jacob. "Dayton to Use Federal Money for Demolition of Blighted Properties." *Dayton Business Journal*, October 24, 2008.

Dresser, Norine. *Multicultural Manners*, rev. ed. Hoboken NJ: John Wiley and Sons, 2005.

Drury, A. W. *History of the City of Dayton and Montgomery County, OH*. Vol. 1. Dayton OH: S. J. Clarke Publishing, 1909.

Dynarski, Susan. "The Consequences of Merit Aid." Cambridge MA: John F. Kennedy School of Government, Harvard University Faculty Research Working Paper Series, November 2002.

Eisinger, Peter K. "Black Employment in Municipal Jobs: The Impact of Black Political Power." *American Political Science Review* 76 (1982).

———. "Black Mayors and the Politics of Racial Economic Advancement." In *Readings in Urban Politics: Past, Present, and Future*, ed. Harlan Hahn and Charles Levine. New York: Longman, 1984.

Elazar, Daniel. *American Federalism: A View from the States*, 2nd ed. Boston: Thomas Y. Crowell, 1972.

Englehart, Laura. "MVHO Buys Former Urban League Building." *Dayton Business Journal*, July 26, 2012.

Engstrom, Richard L., and Michael D. McDonald. "The Effect of At-Large Versus District Elections on Racial Representation in U.S. Municipalities." In *Electoral Laws and Their Political Consequences*, ed. Bernard Grofman and Arend Lijphart, 203–25. New York: Agathon Press, 1986.

Faber, Don *The Toledo War: The First Michigan-Ohio Rivalry*. Ann Arbor: University of Michigan Press, 2008.

Fagan, Deborah, and Susan E. Howell. "Race and Trust in Government: Testing the Political Reality Model." *Public Opinion Quarterly* 52, no. 3 (Autumn 1998): 343–50.

Feldman, Stanley, and Leonie Huddy. "Racial Resentment and White Opposition to Race-Conscious Programs: Principles or Prejudice?" *American Journal of Political Science* 49 (January 2005): 168–83.

Fenno, Richard F., Jr. *Going Home: Black Representatives and Their Constituents*. Chicago: University of Chicago Press, 2003.

Ferman, Barbara. *Governing the Ungovernable City: Political Skill, Leadership, and the Modern Mayor*. Philadelphia: Temple University Press, 1985.

Flinn, Thomas A. "Continuity and Change in Ohio Politics." *Journal of Politics* 24 (1962): 521–44.

Foeman, Gerald H., II. "An Interracial Comparative Analysis of the Impact of Central-City Mayors during the Urban Transition of the 1980s: Social, Political, and Economic Indicators of Effect." PhD dissertation, Temple University, 1992.

Foner, Eric. *The Voice of Black America: Major Speeches by Negroes in the United States, 1797–1971*. New York: Simon and Schuster, 1972.

Foss, Sonja K. "Abandonment of Genus: The Evolution of Political Rhetoric." *Central States Speech Journal* 33 (1982): 367–78.

Franklin, Sekou. "Situational Deracialization, Harold Ford, and the 2006 Senate Race in Tennessee." In Gillespie, *Whose Black Politics?*

Frasure, Lorrie A. "Beyond the Myth of the White Middle Class: Immigrant and Ethnic Minority Settlement in Suburban America." *National Political Science Review* 11 (2007): 65–86.

Frey, William H. "America's Diverse Future: Initial Glimpses at the U.S. Child Population from the 2010 Census." Washington DC: Brookings Institution, 2011.

——. "Diversity Spreads Out: Metropolitan Shifts in Hispanic, Asian, and Black Populations since 2000." Washington DC: Brookings Institution, March 2006.

——. "Melting Pot Cities and Suburbs: Racial and Ethnic Change in Metro America in the 2000s." Washington DC: Brookings Institution, 2011.

——. "A Pivotal Decade for America's White and Minority Populations." Washington DC: Brookings Institution, 2011.

——. "America's Young Adults: A Generation on the Move." Washington DC: Brookings Institution, November 20, 2012. Retrieved from http://www.brookings.edu/research/expert-qa/2012/11/20-frey-qa; accessed April 1, 2013.

Friesema, H. P. "Black Control of Central Cities: The Hollow Prize." *Journal of the American Institute of Planners* 35 (March 1969).

"The Future of Local Government Administration: The Hansell Symposium." Washington DC: International City and County Management Association, 2002.

Gamble, Katrina L. "Black Political Representation: An Examination of Legislative Activity within U.S. House Committees." *Legislative Studies Quarterly* 32 (2007): 421–47.

Gamson, William A. *Talking Politics*. New York: Cambridge University Press, 1992.

Gamson, William A., and Andre Modigliani. "Media Discourse and Public Opinion on Nuclear Power: A Constructionist Approach." *American Journal of Sociology* 95 (1989): 1–37.

George, Alexander L., and Juliette L. George *Woodrow Wilson and Colonel House: A Personality Study*. New York: Dover, 1964.

Gilbert, Neil, ed. *Targeting Social Benefits*. New Brunswick NJ: Transaction Publishers, 2001.

Gilen, Martin. *Why Americans Hate Welfare: Race, Media, and the Politics of Antipoverty Policy*. Chicago: University of Chicago Press, 1999.

*Gillespie, Andra. "Meet the New Class: Theorizing Young Black Leadership in a 'Postracial' Era." In Gillespie, Whose Black Politics?*

——. *The New Black Politician: Cory Booker, Newark, and Post-Racial America*. New York: New York University Press, 2012.

——, ed. *Whose Black Politics? Cases in Post-Racial Black Leadership*. New York: Routledge, 2010.

Gitlin, Todd. *The Whole World Is Watching: Mass Media in the Making and Unmaking of the New Left.* Berkeley and Los Angeles: University of California Press, 1980.

Glaude, Eddie S. *Exodus: Religion, Race and Nation in Early Nineteenth Century Black America.* Chicago: University of Chicago Press, 2000.

Goering, John M., and Edward M. Kalachek. "Public Transportation and Black Unemployment." *Society* 10 (July 1973): 39–42.

Gold, David M. *Democracy in Session: A History of the Ohio General Assembly.* Athens: Ohio University Press, 2009.

Gordon, P., A. Kumar, and H. W. Richardson. "The Spatial Mismatch Hypothesis: Some New Evidence." *Urban Studies* 26 (1989): 315–26.

Gottfried, Alex. *Boss Cermak of Chicago.* Seattle: University of Washington Press, 1962.

Greenstein, Robert. "Universal and Targeted Approaches to Relieving Poverty: An Alternative View." In Jencks and Peterson, *The Urban Underclass.*

Grenell, Keenan D., and Gerald T. Gabris. "Charles Box and Regime Politics." In Bowers and Rich, *Governing Middle-Sized Cities,* 181–96.

Grogan, Colleen M., and Eric M. Patashnik. "Universalism within Targeting: Nursing Home Care, the Middle Class, and the Politics of the Medicaid Program." *Social Service Review,* March (2003): 51–71.

Guinier, Lani. *Tyranny of the Majority: Fundamental Fairness in Direct Democracy.* New York: Free Press, 1994.

Hajnal, Zoltan. *Changing White Attitudes toward Black Political Leadership.* New York: Cambridge University Press, 2007.

Hall, Calvin, and Gardner Lindzey. *Theories of Personality.* New York: Wiley, 1970.

Hall, Richard L. *Participation in Congress.* New Haven: Yale University Press, 1996.

Hamilton, Charles V. "Deracialization: Examination of a Political Strategy. *First World* 1 (1997): 3–5.

Hamilton, Dona Cooper, and Charles V. Hamilton. *The Dual Agenda.* New York: Columbia University Press, 1998.

Harvey, Richard D., and Debra L. Oswald. "Collective Guilt and Shame as Motivation for White Support of Black Programs." *Journal of Applied Social Psychology* 30 (2000): 1790–1811.

Hasenfeld, Yeheskel. *We the Poor People: Work, Poverty, and Welfare.* New Haven: Yale University Press, 1997.

Haynie, Kerry L. *African American Legislators in the American States.* New York: Columbia University Press, 2001.

Hero, Rodney. *Faces of Inequality*. New York: Oxford University Press, 1998.

Hinehart, John. "The Negro in a Congested Toledo Area." Master's thesis, Bowling Green State University, 1940.

"History." Warren AME Church. Retrieved from http://www.warren-ame .org/core/history.html. Accessed August 3, 2012.

Holzer, H. J. "The Spatial Mismatch Hypothesis: What Has the Evidence Shown?" *Urban Studies* 28 (1991): 105–22.

Hopkins, Daniel J., and Katherine T. McCabe. "After It's Too Late: Estimating the Policy Impacts of Black Mayoralities in U.S. Cities." *American Politics Research* 40, no. 4 (2012): 665–700.

Horton, D. "Race and Wealth: A Demographic Analysis of Black Home-ownership." *Sociological Inquiry* 62 (1992): 480–89.

Hunter, Floyd. *Community Power Structure*. Chapel Hill: University of North Carolina Press, 1950.

Icard, Larry. "Black Gay Men and Conflicting Social Identities: Sexual Orientation versus Racial Identity." *Social Work Practice in Sexual Problems* 49, nos. 1/2 (1986): 83–93.

Ifill, Gwen. *The Breakthrough: Politics and Race in the Age of Obama*. New York: Doubleday, 2009.

Jaynes, Gerald, and Frederick McKinney. "Do Blacks Lose When Diversity Replaces Affirmative Action?" *Review of Black Political Economy* 31 (September 2003): 111–24.

Jencks, Christopher, and Paul E. Peterson, eds. *The Urban Underclass*. Washington DC: Brookings Institution, 1991.

Jerit, J. "How Predictive Appeals Affect Policy Opinions." *American Journal of Political Science* 53 (2009): 411–26.

Johnson, Everett. "A Study of Negro Families in the Pinewood Avenue District of Toledo, Ohio." Master's thesis, University of Toledo, 1929.

Johnston-Anumonwo, I. "Race, Gender, and Constrained Work Trips in Buffalo NY, 1990." *Professional Geographer* 49 (1997): 306–17.

———. "Commuting Constraints of African American Women: Evidence from Detroit, Michigan." *Great Lakes Geographer* 7 (2000): 66–75.

———. "Persistent Racial Differences in the Commutes of Kansas City Workers." *Journal of Black Studies* 31 (May 2001): 651–70.

Jones, Bryan D., and Lynn Bachelor. *The Sustaining Hand*, 2nd ed. Lawrence: University Press of Kansas, 1993.

Jones, Clinton B. "The Impact of Local Election Systems on Black Political Representation." *Urban Affairs Quarterly* 11, no. 3 (March 1976): 345–56.

Jones, Mack H. "Black Mayoral Leadership in Atlanta: A Comment." In *Black Electoral Politics*, ed. Lucius Jefferson Barker. National Conference of Black Political Scientists. Piscataway NJ: Transaction Publishers, 1990.

———. "Black Political Empowerment in Atlanta: Myth and Reality." *Annals of the American Academy of Political and Social Science* 439 (September 1978).

Judd, Dennis R., and Todd Swanstrom. *City Politics: Private Power and Public Policy*. New York: Harper Collins, 1994.

Kain, J. F. "Housing Segregation, Negro Employment and Metropolitan Decentralization." *Quarterly Journal of Economics* 82 (1968): 175-97.

Kaptur, Marcy. Rep. Floor Statement, U.S. Congress, House of Representatives, February 27, 1990.

Karnig, Albert K. "Black Representation on City Councils." *Urban Affairs Review* 12 (1976): 223-42.

Karnig, Albert K., and Susan Welch. *Black Representation and Urban Policy*. Chicago: University of Chicago Press, 1980.

Kasarda, John. "Urban Change and Minority Opportunity." In *The New Urban Reality*, ed. Paul Peterson. Washington DC: Brookings Institution, 1985.

Keller, Edmond J. "The Impact of Black Mayors on Urban Policy." *Annals of the American Academy of Political and Social Science* 439 (September 1978): 40-52.

Key, V. O. *Southern Politics*. Knoxville: University of Tennessee Press, 1949.

Kinder, Donald R., and Lynn M. Sanders. *Divided by Color*. Chicago: University of Chicago Press, 1996.

King, Athena, Todd Shaw, and Lester Spence. "Hype, Hip-Hop, and Heartbreak: The Rise and Fall of Kwame Kilpatrick. In Gillespie, *Whose Black Politics?*

King, Gary, Robert O. Keohane, and Sidney Verba. *Designing Social Inquiry: Scientific Inference in Qualitative Research*. Princeton NJ: Princeton University Press, 2001.

King, Martin Luther, Jr. "Letter from a Birmingham Jail," April 16, 1963. University of Pennsylvania, African Studies Center. Retrieved from http://www.africa.upenn.edu/Articles_Gen/Letter_Birmingham.html. Accessed August 1, 2012.

Kleppner, Paul. *Chicago Divided: The Making of a Black Mayor*. DeKalb: Northern Illinois University Press, 1985.

Koch, Jeffrey W. "Political Rhetoric and Political Persuasion: The Changing Structure of Citizens' Preferences on Health Insurance during Policy Debate." *Public Opinion Quarterly* 62, no. 2 (Summer 1998).

Kotter, John P., and Paul R. Lawrence. *Mayors in Action*. New York: John Wiley and Sons, 1974.

Kraus, Neil. "The Significance of Race in Urban Politics: The Limitations of Regime Theory." *Race and Society* 7 (2004): 95-111.

Kraus, Neil, and Todd Swanstrom. "The Continuing Significance of Race: African-American and Hispanic Mayors, 1968-2003." *National Political Science Review* 10, no. 1 (March 2005): 54-70.

———. "Minority Mayors and the Hollow Prize Problem." *PS: Political Science and Politics* 34, no. 1 (March 2001).

Kymlicka, Will. *Multicultural Citizenship*. New York: Oxford University Press, 1995.

Lane, James B. "Black Political Power and Its Limits: Gary Mayor Richard G. Hatcher's Administration, 1968-87." In Colburn and Adler, *African-American Mayors*.

Latimer, Margaret K. "Black Political Representation in Southern Cities." *Urban Affairs Review* 15 (1979): 65-86.

Lee-St. John, Jeninne. "Viewpoint: Civil Rights and Gay Rights." *Time*, October 25, 2005.

Levine, Bertram. *Resolving Racial Conflict*. Columbia: University of Missouri Press, 2005.

Levstik, Frank R. "The Toledo Riot of 1962: A Study of Midwest Negrophobia." *Northwest Ohio Quarterly* 44 (Fall 1972).

Lewis, Angela K. "Between Generations: Deval Patrick as Massachusetts' First Black Governor." In Gillespie, *Whose Black Politics?*, 177-94.

Lewis, Gregory B. "Black-White Differences in Attitudes toward Homosexuality and Gay Rights." *Public Opinion Quarterly* 67, no. 1 (2003): 59-78.

Lieberman, Robert C. *Shifting the Color Line*. Cambridge MA: Harvard University Press, 2001.

Loyacano, Marjorie E. *A History of Race Relations in the Miami Valley*. Dayton OH: Carillon Historical Park, 2002.

Maddi, Salvatore R. *Personality Theories*. Homewood IL: Dorsey, 1968.

Madison, James. *Federalist*, no. 10, 1787.

Manza, Jeffrey. "Race and the Underdevelopment of the American Welfare State." *Theory and Society* 29 (December 2000): 819-32.

Marable, Manning. *Beyond Black and White*. New York: Verso, 1995.

———. *Black Leadership*. New York: Columbia University Press, 1998.

Marschall, Melissa J., and Anirudh V. S. Ruhil. "Substantive Symbols: The Attitudinal Dimension of Black Political Incorporation in Local Government." *American Journal of Political Science* 51 (January 2007): 17-33.

Massey, Douglas S., and Nancy A. Denton. *American Apartheid*. Cambridge MA: Harvard University Press, 1994.

―――. "The Dimensions of Residential Segregation." *Social Forces* 67 (1988): 281–315.

―――. "Hypersegregation in U.S. Metropolitan Areas: Black and Hispanic Segregation along Five Dimensions." *Demography* 26 (1989): 373–93.

Massey, Douglas S., and Mitchell L. Eggers. "The Ecology of Inequality: Minorities and the Concentration of Poverty, 1970–1980." *American Journal of Sociology* 95 (1990).

McCormick, Joseph P., II, and Charles E. Jones. "The Conceptualization of Deracialization." In *Dilemmas of Black Politics*, ed. Georgia Persons. New York: Harper Collins, 1993.

McLafferty, S., and V. Preston. "Gender, Race and Determinants of Commuting: New York in 1990." *Urban Geography* 18 (1997): 192–212.

―――. "Spatial Mismatch and Employment in a Decade of Restructuring." *Professional Geographer* 48 (1996): 420–31.

McLin, C. J., with Lillie P. Howard and Sarah Byrn Rickman. *Dad, I Served: The Autobiography of C. J. McLin, Jr.* Dayton OH: Wright State University Press, 1997.

Metz, David Haywood, and Katherine Tate. "The Color of Urban Campaigns." In *Classifying by Race*, ed. Paul E. Peterson. Princeton NJ: Princeton University Press, 1995.

Midgley, James, Martin Tracy, and Michelle Livermore. *The Handbook of Social Policy*. New York: Sage, 2000.

Mier, Robert, and Kari J. Moe. "Decentralized Development: From Theory to Practice." In Clavel and Wiewel, *Harold Washington and the Neighborhoods*.

Mkandawire, Thandika. "Targeting and Universalism in Poverty Reduction." Geneva: United Nations Research Institute for Social Development. Social Policy and Development Program Paper, no. 23, 2005.

Moore, Leonard N. *Carl B. Stokes and the Rise of Black Political Power*. Urbana: University of Illinois Press, 2002.

Morgan, Kathleen O'Leary, and Scott Morgan, eds. *City Crime Rankings: Crime in Metropolitan America*, 14th ed. Washington DC, November 2007.

Myers, Phineas Barton. *Ninety-Five Years after Lincoln*. New York: Exposition Press, 1959.

Myrdal, Gunnar. *An American Dilemma*. New York: Harper and Bros., 1944.

National Housing Trust Fund. "President Signs Housing Trust Fund into Law on July 30, 2008." Retrieved from http://www.nlihc.org/doc/NHTF-word-doc.pdf. Accessed February 16, 2009.

Nelson, William E. *Black Atlantic Politics*. Albany: State University of New York Press, 2000.

———. "Black Mayoral Leadership: A Twenty Year Perspective." In *Enduring Tensions in Urban Politics*, ed. Dennis Judd and Paul Kantor. New York: Macmillan, 1992.

———. "Black Mayoral Leadership in the Twenty-first Century: Challenges and Opportunities." In *Black and Latino/Latina Politics: Issues in Political Development in the United States*, ed. William E. Nelson, Jr., and Jessica Perez-Monforti. Miami: Barnhard and Ashe Publishers, 2006.

———. "Black Mayors as Urban Managers." *Annals of the American Academy of Political and Social Science* 439 (September 1978).

———. "Cleveland: The Rise and Fall of the New Black Politics." In *The New Black Politics*, ed. Michael B. Preston, Lenneal J. Henderson, Jr., and Paul Puryear. New York: Longman, 1982.

Nelson, William E., Jr., and Philip Meranto. *Electing Black Mayors: Political Action in the Black Community*. Columbus: Ohio State University Press, 1977.

Nye, John V. C., Ilia Rainer, and Thomas Stratmann. "Do Black Mayors Improve Black Employment Outcomes? Evidence from Large U.S. Cities." Unpublished paper, 2010.

Ohio History Central Encyclopedia Archive. Retrieved from http://www .ohiohistorycentral.org/entry.php?rec=562. Accessed August 20, 2012.

"Old Dayton View Neighborhood Planning District." Northern Ohio Data and Information Service 2000 Census of Population and Housing, Maxine Goodman Levin College of Urban Affairs, Summary File 3, Cleveland State University. Retrieved from http://www.cityofdayton .org/departments/pcd/Documents/2000%20CensusPDFs/Northwest/SF3old%20dayton%20view.PDF. Accessed February 18, 2009.

Orey, Byron D. "Deracialization or Racialization: The Making of a Black Mayor in Jackson, Mississippi." *Politics and Policy* 34, no. 4 (2006): 814–836.

Orey, Byron D'Andra, and Boris Ricks. "A Systematic Analysis of the Deracialization Concept." *National Political Science Review*, January 2007.

Orr, Marion. *Black Social Capital*. Lawrence: University Press of Kansas, 1999.

———. "The Struggle for Black Empowerment in Baltimore: Electoral Control and Governing Coalitions." In *Racial Politics in American Cities Revisited*, 2nd ed., ed. Rufus Browning, Dale Marshall, and David Tabb, 201–19. New York: Longman, 1997.

———, ed. *Transforming the City*. Lawrence: University Press of Kansas, 2007.

Page, Benjamin. 1996. *Who Deliberates*. Chicago: University of Chicago Press, 1996.

Pan, Zhongdang, and Gerald M. Kosicki. "Framing Analysis: An Approach to News Discourse." *Political Communication* 10 (1993): 55-75.

Perry, Huey L. "Deracialization as an Analytical Construct in American Urban Politics," *Urban Affairs Quarterly* 27, no. 2 (1991): 181-91.

———. *Race, Politics and Governance in the United States*. Gainesville: University Press of Florida, 1996.

———. "Richard Arrington Jr. and Police-Community Relations in Birmingham, Alabama." In Bowers and Rich, *Governing Middle-Sized Cities*, 103-20.

Perry, Ravi K. "Black Mayors in Non-Majority Black (Medium-Sized) Cities: Universalizing the Interests of Blacks." *Ethnic Studies Review* 32, no. 1 (Summer 2009): 89-130.

———. "Deval Patrick and the Representation of Massachusetts' Black Interests." *Trotter Review* 20, no. 1 (April 2012): 9-41.

———. "First Impressions, 'America's Paper' and Pre-Primary Black Presidential Candidates: *The New York Times* Coverage of Rev. Jesse Jackson (1983), Rev. Al Sharpton (2003), and Sen. Barack Obama (2007) Campaign Announcements and Initial Days." *Ethnic Studies Review,* Fall 2012.

———. "Introduction." In R. Perry, *21st Century Urban Race Politics*.

———. "Kindred Political Rhetoric: Black Mayors, President Obama and the Universalizing of Black Interests." *Journal of Urban Affairs* 33, no. 5 (December): 567-90.

———, ed. *21st Century Urban Race Politics: Representing Minorities as Universal Interests*. Bingley UK: Emerald Group Publishing, 2013.

Persons, Georgia. "From Insurgency to Deracialization: The Evolution of Black Mayoralties." In Davis, *Perspectives in Black Politics and Black Leadership*, 92-94.

Peters, Margaret E. *Dayton's African American Heritage: A Pictorial History*. Virginia Beach VA: Donning, 1995.

Peterson, Paul E. *City Limits*. Chicago: University of Chicago Press, 1981.

Phillips, Anne. *The Politics of Presence*. Oxford: Clarendon Press, 1995.

Piliawsky, Monte. "The Impact of Black Mayors on the Black Community: The Case of New Orleans' Ernest Morial." *Review of Black Political Economy* 13 (March 1985): 5-23.

Pitkin, Hanna Fenichel. *The Concept of Representation*. Los Angeles: University of California Press, 1967.

Policy Matters Ohio. "Foreclosure Growth in Ohio 2009." March 2009.

Popkin, Susan J, Bruce Katz, Mary K. Cunningham, Karen D. Brown, Jeremy Gustafson, and Margery A. Turner. *A Decade of HOPE VI: Research Findings and Policy Challenges*. A Roof over Their Heads: Changes and

Challenges for Public Housing Residents Research Initiative. Washington DC: Urban Institute, 2004.

Porter, George H. "Ohio Politics during the Civil War Period." Doctoral dissertation, Columbia University, 1911.

Porter, Tana M. *Toledo Profile: A Sesquicentennial History*. Toledo OH: Toledo Sesquicentennial Commission, 1987.

Powell, John A. "Obama's Universal Approach Leaves Many Excluded." Retrieved from HuffingtonPost.com., December 2009. Accessed January 22, 2010.

——. "Post-Racialism or Targeted Universalism?" *Denver University Law Review* 86 (2009): 785–806.

——. *"Post-Racialism or Targeted Universalism?"* In Powell, *Racing to Justice.*

——. "Race, Place, and Opportunity." *American Prospect*, September 21, 2008. Retrieved from http://prospect.org/article/race-place-and-opportunity; retrieved March 3, 2009.

——, ed. *Racing to Justice: Transforming Our Conceptions of Self and Other to Build an Inclusive Society*. Bloomington: Indiana University Press, 2012.

Powell, John A., and Stephen Menendian. "Race vis-a-vis Class in the U.S.?" *Poverty and Race*, November/December 2006. Retrieved from http://www.prrac.org/full_text.php?text_id=1099&item_id=10192&newsletter_id=90&header=Symposium:%20Structural%20Racism; accessed October 13, 2008.

Pressman, Jeffrey L. "Preconditions of Mayoral Leadership." *American Political Science Review* 66 (1972): 511–24.

Preston, Michael B. "Big City Black Mayors: An Overview." *National Political Science Review* 2 (1990).

——. "Limitations on Black Urban Power: The Case of Black Mayors." In *The New Urban Politics*, ed. Robert Lineberry and Louis Masotti. Boston: Ballinger, 1976.

Pulera, Dominic. *Sharing the Dream: White Males in Multicultural America*. New York: Continuum International Publishing Group, 2004.

Putnam, Robert D. *Bowling Alone*. New York: Simon and Schuster, 2000.

Reed, Adolph. "The Black Urban Regime: Structural Origins and Constraints." In *Stirrings in the Jug*, ed. Adolph Reed, 79–115. Minneapolis: University of Minnesota Press, 1999.

——. *Class Notes: Posing as Politics and Other Thoughts on the American Scene*. New York: New Press, 2000.

Rich, Wilbur. *Coleman Young and Detroit Politics: From Social Activist to Power Broker*. Detroit: Wayne State University Press, 1999.

——. "Foreword." In Perry, *21st Century Urban Race Politics*.

Roberts, Dorothy E. "Welfare and the Problem of Black Citizenship." *Yale Law Journal* 105 (April 1996): 1563–1602.

Roediger, David R. *How Race Survived U.S. History: From Settlement and Slavery to the Obama Phenomenon*. New York: Verso, 2008.

Rogers, Reuel R. "Black Like Who? Afro-Caribbean Immigrants, African Americans, and the Politics of Group Identity." In *Afro-Caribbean Immigrants and the Politics of Incorporation*, ed. Reuel R. Rogers. New York: Cambridge University Press, 2006.

Rosanvallon, Pierre, and Barbara Harshav. *The New Social Question: Rethinking the Welfare State*. Princeton NJ: Princeton University Press, 2000.

Rothstein, David, and Sapna Mehta. "Foreclosure Growth in Ohio 2009." *Policy Matters Ohio*, 2009.

Ruchleman, Leonard, ed. *Big City Mayors*. Bloomington: Indiana University Press, 1969.

Runciman, David. "The Paradox of Political Representation." *Journal of Political Philosophy* 15 (2007): 93–114.

Saad, Lydia. "Economy Reigns Supreme for Voters: More Than Half Rate It 'Extremely Important' to Their Vote for President." Princeton NJ: Gallup Poll, October 29, 2008.

Saltzstein, Grace Hall. "Black Mayors and Police Policies." *Journal of Politics* 51, no. 3 (August 1989).

Sawhill, Isabel V. "Comments on 'Targeting within Universalism: Politically Viable Policies to Combat Poverty in the U.S.' by Theda Skocpol." Unpublished paper, 1989.

Schumpeter, Joseph A. *Capitalism, Socialism, and Democracy*. New York: Harper and Row, 1947.

———. "Economic Theory and Entrepreneurial History." In *Explorations in Enterprise*, ed. G. J. Aitken. Cambridge MA: Harvard University Press, 1965.

Sjoquist, David. *The Economic Status of Black Atlantans*. Atlanta: Atlanta Urban League, 1988.

Skocpol, Theda. *Social Policy in the United States*. Princeton NJ: Princeton University Press, 1995.

———. "Sustainable Social Policy: Fighting Poverty without Poverty Programs." *American Prospect*, June 23, 1990.

———. "Targeting within Universalism: Politically Viable Policies to Combat Poverty in the United States." In Jencks and Peterson, *The Urban Underclass*.

Smith, Robert C. *We Have No Leaders*. Albany: State University of New York Press, 1996.

Solomon, Alisa. "Nothing Special: The Specious Attack on Civil Rights." In *Dangerous Liaisons: Blacks, Gays, and the Struggle for Equality*, ed. Eric Brandt, 59–69. New York: New Press, 1999.

Sonenshein, R. J. *Politics in Black and White: Race and Power in Los Angeles*. Princeton NJ: Princeton University Press, 1993.

Sorell, Tom. "Hobbes's UnAristotelian Political Rhetoric." *Philosophy and Rhetoric* 23, no. 2 (1990): 96–108.

State of the Cities Data Systems Census. Retrieved from http://socds .huduser.org/census/totalemploy.odb. Accessed October 17, 2008.

Steele, S. *White Guilt: The Content of Our Character*. New York: Harper Perennial, 1990.

Stokes, Carl B. *Promises of Power: A Political Biography*. New York: Simon and Schuster, 1973.

Stone, Clarence. "Political Leadership in Urban Politics." In *Theories of Urban Politics*, ed. D. Judge, G. Stoker, and H. Wolman, 96–116. Thousand Oaks CA: Sage, 1995.

——. *Regime Politics*. Lawrence: University Press of Kansas, 1989.

Svara, James H. "Effective Mayoral Leadership in Council-Manager Cities: Reassessing the Facilitative Model." *National Civic Review* 92, no. 2 (July 2003): 157–72.

——. *Facilitative Leadership in Local Government: Lessons from Successful Mayors and Chairpersons*. San Francisco: Jossey-Bass Publishers, 1994.

——. "Mayoral Leadership in Council-Manager Cities: Preconditions versus Preconceptions." *Journal of Politics* 49 (1987): 207–27.

——. *Official Leadership in the City: Patterns of Conflict and Cooperation*. New York: Oxford University Press, 1990.

Swain, Carol M. *Black Faces, Black Interests: The Representation of African Americans in Congress*. Cambridge MA: Harvard University Press, 1996.

——. "Race and Representation." *American Prospect*, May 17, 2004.

Tate, Katherine. *Black Faces in the Mirror: African Americans and Their Representatives in the U.S. Congress*. Princeton NJ: Princeton University Press, 2003.

——. *From Protest to Politics: The New Black Voters in American Elections*. Cambridge MA: Harvard University Press, 1993.

Thompson, J. Philip. *Double Trouble*. Cambridge: Oxford University Press, 2006.

Toledo Chapter of the NAACP. "Containment of Minority Groups through Housing." Unpublished pamphlet, Local History Room, Toledo-Lucas County Public Library.

"Toledo City Planning Commission: City Planning Community History." Toledo OH: Center for Archival Collections. Retrieved from http://

www.bgsu.edu/colleges/library/cac/lr/page40928.html. Bowling
Green State University. Accessed July 12, 2012.

"Toledo War." Ohio History Central, July 1, 2005. Retrieved from http://
www.ohiohistorycentral.org/entry.php?rec=562. Accessed August 10,
2012.

United Nations. *World Urbanization Prospects: The 2005 Revision*. Department of Economic and Social Affairs/Population Division, October
2006.

U.S. Census Bureau. *American Community Survey 2006 Summary File:
Technical Documentation*.

——. *County and City Data Book: 2000*. Washington DC.

——. *Population of the 100 Largest Cities and Other Urban Places in the
United States: 1970 to 1990*. Washington DC, June 1998. Working Paper
No. 27.

——. *2005-2007 American Community Survey 3-Year Summary File: Technical Documentation*. Http://www2.census.gov/acs2007_3yr/summary
file/.

U.S. Census Bureau. *2009 Population Estimates*. Retrieved from http://
www.census.gov/popest/cities/tables/SUB-EST2009-01.csv. Accessed
June 22, 2010

——. "2010 Census Interactive Population Search." Retrieved from http://
www.census.gov/2010census/popmap/ipmtext.php?fl=39:3977000.

U.S. Commission on Civil Rights. *Employment Opportunities for Minorities
in Montgomery County, Ohio*. Columbus: Ohio State Advisory Committee, 1989.

——. "Race Relations in Toledo: A Summary Report of a Community Forum." Columbus: Ohio State Advisory Committee, 1989.

U.S. Department of Housing and Urban Development (HUD). "Home and
Communities: Public and Indian Housing—HOPE VI." Washington DC,
2007. Retrieved from http://www.hud.gov/offices/pih/programs/ph/
hope6/. Accessed October 17, 2008.

——, Community Planning and Development. "Instructions for Urban
County Qualification for Participation in the Community Development
Block Grant (CDBG) Program for Fiscal Years (FY) 2001-2003." May 22,
2000. Retrieved from http://www.hud.gov/offices/cpd/lawsregs/
notices/2000/00-7.pdf. Accessed August 10, 2012.

U.S. Department of Justice, Office of Public Affairs. "Justice Department
Settles Lawsuit against the City of Dayton, Ohio, Alleging Discrimination against African Americans in the Hiring of Police Officers and
Firefighters." February 26, 2009. Retrieved from http://www.justice
.gov/opa/pr/2009/February/09-crt-172.html. Accessed August 1, 2012.

U.S. Federal Bureau of Investigation. *Crime in the United States, by State.* Washington DC: FBI, 2003, 2004, 2005, 2006, 2007.

U.S. Supreme Court. Dayton Board of Education v. Brinkman, 433 U.S. 406. 1977.

Van Alstyne, William W. "Civil Rights: A New Public Accommodations Law for Ohio." *Ohio State Law Review* 22 (1961):683–90.

Vey, Jennifer S., and Benjamin Forman. "Demographic Change in Medium-Sized Cities: Evidence from the 2000 Census." Washington DC: Brookings Institution, July 2002.

Wadsworth, Nancy D. "Reconciliation Politics: Conservative Evangelicals and the New Race Discourse." *Politics and Society* 25, no. 3 (1997): 341–76.

Walters, Ronald, and Robert Smith. "Black Leadership: Toward a Twenty-First Century Praxis." In Davis, *Perspectives in Black Politics and Black Leadership.*

Watras, Joseph. *Politics, Race and Schools: Racial Integration, 1954–1994.* New York: Garland Publishing, 1997.

Welsh-Huggins, Andrew. *No Winners Here Tonight: Race, Politics and Geography in One of the Country's Busiest Death Penalty States.* Athens: Ohio University Press, 2009.

West, Cornel. *Race Matters.* New York: Vintage Books, 1993.

"What Is DMHA's Public Housing?" Dayton Metropolitan Housing Authority. Retrieved from http://www.dmha.org/public.htm. Accessed February 16, 2009.

Wheaton, Emmett L. "The Social Status of the Negro in Toledo, Ohio." Master's thesis, University of Toledo, 1927.

Williams, B. F. "Interracial Activities in Toledo." *Southern Workman* 54 (April 1925): 162–65.

Williams, Lee. "Newcomers to the City: A Study of Black Population Growth in Toledo, Ohio, 1910–1930." *Ohio History* 80 (1980).

Williams, Melissa S. *Voice, Trust, and Democracy: Marginalized Groups in the Failings of Liberal Representation.* Princeton NJ: Princeton University Press, 1998.

Wilson, James Q. *Negro Politics: The Search for Leadership.* New York: Octagon Books, 1980.

Wilson, William Julius. "Public Policy Research and the Truly Disadvantaged." In Jencks and Peterson, *The Urban Underclass.*

———. "Race-Neutral Policies and the Democratic Coalition." *American Prospect*, March 21, 1990. Retrieved from http://prospect.org/article/race-neutral-policies-and-democratic-coalition; accessed March 3, 2009.

———. *The Truly Disadvantaged.* Chicago: University of Chicago Press, 1987.

———. *When Work Disappears.* New York: Vintage Books, 1996.

Woody, Bette. *Managing Crisis Cities: The New Black Leadership and the Politics of Resource Allocation*. Westport CT: Greenwood, 1982.

Word, Fletcher. "Mayor Jack Ford: Focusing on Fiscal Responsibility and Helping People." *Sojourner's Truth*, September 7, 2005.

Wright, Sharon D. *Race, Power, and Political Emergence in Memphis*. New York: Routledge, 1999.

Young, Iris Marion *Inclusion and Democracy*. New York: Oxford University Press, 2000.

———. *Justice and the Politics of Difference*. Princeton NJ: Princeton University Press, 1990.

# INDEX

abandonment. *See* property

Abney, David, 146

Act to Regulate Black and Mulatto
Persons (1804), 77–78

affirmative action, 2, 16, 38, 48, 59,
66, 116–24, 183

African American Legacy Project, 36

African Methodist Episcopal (AME)
Church, 23, 44

AIDS, 50–51

Aid to Families with Dependent
Children, 12, 17–18

Allen, Dixie, 85

Appalachian whites, 77, 271n5

Arrington, Richard, Jr., 32

Art Tatum African American Resource Center, 35–36

Art Tatum Jazz Festival, 189

Ashford, Michael, 70–72, 113

Associated General Contractors of
America (AGC), 109, 110

Atlanta GA, xxviii, 6–7, 25–26, 183, 203

Baker, Paul C., 31

Baldwin, James: *No Name in the
Street*, 213–14

Barbee, 82

Bebley, Thomas, 114

Bell, Claude, Sr., 151

Bell, Michael P., 36, 65

Black, Don, 151

Black, Jay, 73

"black America," representing, xxx,
196

black constituents: access and empowerment of, xxvii, 3, 7, 11, 156–
57; as majority, 25; mobilization of,
182; need for support from, 72–73;
participation of, 3, 6, 45–49, 50, 79,
96–97; wealth creation by, 113, 114

black interests, xxii, xxiii, xxix, xxv,
27, 29, 31–32, 155–58, 159–64,
258n54, 284n13, 287n23; "active
pursuit" of, 256n20; as American
interests, xxxiv–xxxv, 206; congressional representatives and,
xxix, xxx, 8, 9–10; definition of,
255n4; indirect advocacy of, 152–
53; and municipal employment,
67–69, 88, 89, 99, 117, 122, 150,
156–57, 169, 172, 187, 192; partisanship and, 9–10, 173–74, 175,
260n49; priority boards and, 87;
socioeconomics and, 64; symbolic, 208; universalized, 17, 18–19,
107, 123–24, 152–53, 155, 195–96,
198, 200, 202, 206, 212, 213; as
white interests, xxxiii–xxxiv. *See
also* targeted universalism

black jeremiad, 182

black male establishment, 171

Dayton OH (*continued*)
polarization in, 75–76, 80, 100–101, 190, 192, 193, 272n25; retaining retailers in West Side, 148–50; service delivery in, 99, 101, 129, 147, 159; unemployment in, 127, 132, 279n19; West Side, 141, 142–43, 146, 148–50

Dayton 2003 Celebration of Flight, 137

Dayton Dialogue on Race Relations (CCRR), 104

*Dayton Forum*, 79

Dayton Metropolitan Housing Authority (DMHA), 145–47, 152, 282n60

Dayton Urban League, 38–39, 265n33

Democratic Voters League, 271n1

Democrats and Democratic Party, 170, 210, 214; divisions among, 64, 74, 174, 269n78

demographics, shifts in, xxi, xxviii–xxix, 1, 24–27, 53, 81, 105, 127, 258n55

deracialization, xxiii, xxiv, 18, 180, 196, 202, 203, 204, 212; definition of, xxiv–xxv

descriptive representation, 9–10, 260n45. *See also* substantive representation

Dinkins, David, xxvii, 29

DiSalle, Michael, 35

diversity, 186, 187–88, 197; among ethnic groups, 13; in black community, xxix, xxx, 255n4; commitment to, 59

Dixon, Richard Clay, 38, 88

Dobson, Ken, 110, 112

Douthitt, Weldon, 110

Dresser, Norine, 57–58

drugs, 46, 50, 52

Drury, A. W., 78

DuBois, W. E. B., 34

Dunbar, Paul Lawrence, 136, 137

economic issues, xxviii, xxxiii, xxxv, 2, 4, 6, 12, 14, 28, 29, 34, 45, 59, 69, 70, 71, 74, 90–91, 100, 101–2, 105, 107, 126–27, 129, 148–50, 151, 165, 166, 169, 183, 206, 255n4; race relations and, 74, 211

education, 2, 64, 73, 94, 132, 185, 186–87; black-white achievement gap in, 127, 131; desegregation of, 82–85

Eggers, Mitchell L., 13

Eisinger, Peter K., 2

Elazar, Daniel, 42–43, 76, 266n8

Ellis, Crystal, 36

employment, black, xxvii, xxviii, 2, 24, 44, 67, 69, 73, 74, 80, 91, 115, 120; and competition with whites, 70; and salary disparity with whites, 67

Engelhart, Laura, 265n33

equity agenda, 128–29

ethics, 195–96, 199, 200–202

ethnic succession, 24–25

Feldman, Stanley, 205

Fenno, Richard F., xxx, 196

Ferman, Barbara, 11

Finkbeiner, Carleton, 53, 54–55, 57, 64, 65, 66, 67, 69, 71–72, 74, 122–23, 169, 170, 178, 208, 214, 270nn84–85, 284n25

Fit for Kids, 186

Ford, Jack, xxix, 19, 24, 32, 34, 36, 46, 47–48, 155, 159, 164, 165–67, 169–70, 172, 174, 175, 177, 178, 179, 199, 200, 207, 210, 211, 269n68, 284n13, 291n38; mayoral campaigns of, 58–61, 64, 65–66; mayoral election of, 61–62; mayorship of, 62–66, 67–74; municipal contracts and, 107–24, 276n30, 285n44,

287n37; perceived weaknesses of, 165–67; post-mayoral career of, 214–15; publicity and, 51–52, 60–62, 71; and responsiveness to black community, 52, 67, 69–74, 115, 162–63, 165, 167, 170, 177, 199; rhetoric of, 185–90, 193, 194, 195, 197; as social worker, 46, 49; as state representative, 54, 58; style and personality of, 166–67, 169–70, 176, 208–9, 284n25, 290n31; on Toledo City Council, 47–48, 49–54; transition team, 116–17

Ford Plan 2002, 116–17
foreclosures, 130–31, 278n15
Foss, Sonja K., 181, 195
framing, definition of, 181–82
Franklin, Shirley, 25
Frederick Douglass Community Association, 44
Freeman, Alvin, 151
"friendship lunches," 125
Friesema, H. Paul, 1, 107
Fuller, James, 75–76

Gabris, Gerald T., 32
Gamble, Katrina L., xxx
gay rights, 98, 105, 164, 173, 214; as civil rights, 288–89n7
gentrification, 137
Gibson, James Slater, 44
Gibson, Kenneth, xxvii
Gilliam, Franklin D., Jr., 3
Gilligan, John, 75
"good ol' boy" network, 120, 122, 124
Greater Dayton Premier Management, 145–47, 152, 282n60
Great Migration, 43
Great Society, 85
Greenstein, Robert, 13, 15, 262n63, 262n67
Grenell, Keenan D., 32
Grimes, Carole, 285n45

Grogan, Colleen M., 263n77
Hajnal, Zoltan, xxxii, xxxvi
Hall, Dave, 76
Hamilton, Charles, 18
Hamilton, Dona, 18
Harvey, Richard D., 205
Hatcher, Richard, xxvii
Hayes, Rutherford B., 23
Hayes-Tilden Compromise, 23
Haynie, Kerry L., xxii
health care, 2, 70, 157, 186, 270n89, 291n38
Henry, Robert C., 22
Hero, Rodney, 266n8
hiring, discrimination in, 48, 265n33
historically black universities (HBUs), 23, 39
HIV/AIDS, 50–51
"hollow prize," 1, 3, 5, 19, 107
homeownership: black access to, 132–33; as financial safety net, 132; racial disparity in, 134–35
HOPE VI (Housing Opportunities for People Everywhere), 145–47
housing, 2, 7, 35, 51, 52, 82, 87, 129–48, 152, 168–69, 185, 189, 265n33, 278n13, 278n15, 279n25, 282n60; "affordable" vs. "low-income," 134, 279n25; assistance, 189; government-subsidized, 134; public, 145–47, 282n60, 282n67; race relations and, 144; segregation, 133, 144
Housing and Economic Recovery Act (2008), 144, 278n15
Housing and Neighborhood Strategies Task Force (Dayton), 143
Housing and Urban Development (HUD), 47, 131, 134, 145–46, 189, 278n15, 279n25
Huddy, Leonie, 205
humanity. See common humanity, rhetoric of; targeted universalism

mayoral style. *See* Ford, Jack; leader-
ship; McLin, Rhine
Mayor's Time, 186
McCarty-Harris, Yulanda, 73, 122,
123, 124
McClellan, John, 45
McCormick, Joseph P., xxiv–xxv, 17,
203, 204
McCormick, Stan, 114
McCorry, Jerome, 149–50
McGee, James H., 36, 39, 75
McIntyre, Milton, 114–15
McLin, C. J., Jr., 36, 38, 75, 81, 151,
168, 169, 171
McLin, C. J., Sr. ("Mac"), 38, 80,
271n1
McLin, Rhine, xxix, 19, 24, 32, 37, 125,
126, 129–53, 155, 159, 164, 165,
167–69, 172–73, 174, 175, 176, 179,
199–201, 207, 211, 278n13; appointments of, 126, 150, 172,
277n3, 285n45, 287n40; behind-
the-scenes approach of, 148–49,
171; black perceptions of, 151–53;
bridging racial divide, 93, 94, 125,
144, 192; election of, 94, 96–98,
125, 274n71; mayoral campaigns
of, 89–94, 101–2, 105; and neighborhood redevelopment, 129–53,
281n50; post-mayoral career of,
214, 215; and responsiveness to
black community, 134, 148–52,
162–63, 169, 171; rhetoric of, 189–
94, 195, 197; as state senator, 85,
88, 91; style and personality of,
92–93, 168, 169, 170–71, 173, 175,
209, 210
media coverage of campaigns, 61, 97
media portrayals of African Americans, 71
Menendian, Stephen, 263n83
Meranto, Philip, xxviii
Metz, David, 182

Miami Valley Housing Opportuni-
ties (MVHO), 265n33
Mier, Robert, 6
minority business enterprises (MBEs),
120, 275n6; definition of, 108-9;
participation rates of, 122-23
Minority Business Enterprise Act,
108, 109; lawsuit challenging, 109
Minority Contractors and Business
Assistance Program (MCBAP), 108,
109, 110, 275n6
minority groups, competition
among, 203
*Minority Monitor*, 53
Miscannon, William, 45
Mitchell, Lester, 76
Model Cities, 85–86
Moe, Kari J., 6
Montgomery County, 127, 130
Moore, Lee, 111–12
Moore, Leonard, xxvii
moralistic political culture, 43
multihat model of leadership,
290n34
municipal employment of minori-
ties, 67–69, 88, 89, 99, 117, 122,
150, 156–57, 169, 172, 187, 192,
270nn84–85, 270n87
Myers, Phineas, 76–77, 271n5
Myrdal, Gunnar, 262n74

National Association for the Ad-
vancement of Colored People
(NAACP), 35, 38, 201, 266n13,
289n7; Toledo chapter, 44
National Association of Minority
Contractors, 146
National Conference for Communi-
ty and Justice (NCCJ), 102-3
National Conference of Concerned
Citizens, 34
National Housing Trust Fund Cam-
paign, 144

CPSIA information can be obtained at www.ICGtesting.com
Printed in the USA
BVOW07s0318071113

335622BV00003B/3/P